Conversations With My Grandchildren

MARION MOSTNY

CONVERSATIONS WITH MY GRANDCHILDREN

A JOURNEY THROUGH THREE CONTINENTS

2007

Conversations With My Grandchildren

CONTENTS

ACKNOWLEDGEMENTS

I wish to thank my teacher, Dr. Roberta Reynolds, of the College of San Mateo, for her guidance and advice, and for believing in me when I was not sure that this book was worth writing. It was her enthusiasm and support that made it possible.

To my children, I owe a debt of gratitude for putting up with my questions and doubts, and for giving me the strength to finish this work. Thank you for the gift of the new computer. It has been an enormous help.

To all my grandchildren, who inspired me to tell the story of my life:

You are the reason for writing this book. I wanted you to know where you came from and how our experiences influenced your own lives.

My special thanks to my daughter, Yvonne, who spent countless hours editing the manuscript and preparing it for publication. Without her, it would have never materialized.

Special thanks to my husband, Kurt, for patiently listening to my constant doubts and questions regarding these stories, for believing that this was a worthwhile effort, and for being my best friend and confidant for sixty happy years.

INTRODUCTION

This book is dedicated to my grandchildren, Jenny & Tom Kriskey, Steven & Rachel Hejtmanek, Jeroen & Elke Van der Steen, Julian, Renee and Jordan Nouri, and Jacqueline Mostny, and to my great-grandchildren Abbie and Zoe Kriskey. They are the love of my heart.

These "Conversations" are not supposed to be a chronological account of my life, but rather a glimpse into my personality and the events that shaped my life. They will explain to you my idiosyncrasies and behavior in different situations, and the unconventional decisions that I have been known to make.

You will be able to see that, in spite of the troubles and anxieties that befell my family, my life turned out to be successful and happy. I have always been a positive thinker, and have learned that the pain that was inflicted on us at certain times, could be endured by the belief that endurance and hope would allow me to emerge with a healthy mind and a confident outlook.

I hope that you will have a better understanding of who we, your Omi and Opi, are and how our experiences have molded your parents' lives and, in a certain way, your own upbringing.

I apologize for perhaps repeating certain expressions and situations more than once. My mind has been traveling through sixty years of memories, and, in certain moments, speech patterns and/or occurrences may have been mentioned several times. Please bear with me. Writing this book has been a heart-wrenching experience. My love and devotion for all of you enabled me to finish it.

Your Omi/Mimi Marion

MY GRANDPARENTS' HOUSE

It is April of 1990 and I am in Berlin, the city where I was born. I am standing in front of what was, long ago, my Grandparents' house. There is a small plaque on the left side of the entrance door that wasn't there when I was a child. It reads:

> "In this house, as in many houses
> on this street, lived a Jewish family.
> They were forcibly removed in 1942
> And have not been heard of since then.
> We, their neighbors, remember them."

I remember them, too. Oh, how I remember them! I look up to the window that used to be their living room, and (no need to close my eyes) see the apartment, the furniture, my Grandmother Gertrud, whom we called Omi, my Grandfather Max (Opa) and my Great-Grandmother (Oma Feldblum—which was her last name, to distinguish her from Omi), who was my grandmother's mother, widowed, and lived with them.

***

"FIRE! FIRE!" I yell, as I ring the doorbell. My Omi knows. I'm coming home from school and need to <u>run</u> to the bathroom. Of course, there are toilets in the school, but one doesn't use them unless it is <u>absolutely</u> necessary. "One never knows who uses the bathrooms and how clean they are" is the established rule. My brother is better off. Boys don't have to <u>sit</u> where dirty people sat before. He never yells "FIRE!" when he rings the bell.

Anyway, after rushing to the bathroom and almost not making it on time...I feel a lot better. I now take my RANZEN off my shoulder. A Ranzen is a leather backpack in which we carry our books to school. We are not allowed to use a briefcase or carry anything in our hands. Rules of the school: "Health and Safety Regulations concerned with bent backs, stooped shoulders and bringing forbidden things to school." Ranzen are inspected very often. Only on Tuesdays, for Gymnastics, do we bring our uniform and tennis shoes in a linen bag with our initials on it, and this bag we are permitted to hang on one arm, besides the Ranzen on our back.

Our schools have all kind of rules, but now I am at Omi's house. Not many rules here! My brother Gert and I come to my grandparents' house every day after school. We used to go home to our own place, two blocks away, but ever since my father lost his job because his boss, a Jewish man, had to close his business, my mother had to go to work (secretly) and there isn't anybody in our house to watch us.

My father goes out every day looking for work, but Jewish men are not wanted anywhere, so we spent most of our time at my grandparents. We love it, although Omi makes us do our homework, and we have to help a little with the housework since Jews are not allowed to have outside help anymore. Omi and Opa are not as strict as our parents. But then, I explained to my brother, they are much older and not supposed to get excited. Omi's birthday was not long ago. She is <u>FIFTY-FIVE</u>. I pretend not to know how ancient they really are. It makes them happier. Somehow, older people always worry about their age. I wonder why? Perhaps they think they will die soon? I am careful not to ask.

My grandfather sits in his leather chair by the window, reading, always reading. As a Jew, he cannot work anymore either. He is very serious and seldom smiles, but I don't mind. He tells me every day how much he loves me and how he knows I am going to be somebody important one day. I have overheard Omi and Opa talking and know that they are afraid and constantly worried about the situation of the Jews in Germany.

"Everybody is our enemy," he repeats over and over again. "You can't trust the neighbors, or even your non-Jewish friends." I want to say something important that will make him feel better, but all I do is tell him, over and over, how much I love him and that not EVERYBODY is his enemy.

I just had my ninth birthday. We didn't have a large party, again because we are Jewish. In our school, which is run by Jewish teachers, they tell us not to make too much noise in our houses, not to have huge parties, and especially never to show off.

I really admire my grandfather. He must be the most intelligent man in all of Germany. He and I have a secret. Every day after school, before I do my homework, I sit with him in his leather chair, he puts his book aside, and picks up his encyclopedia. He opens it on any page and we pick four words, four every day, and he explains them to me. I am sure he wants me to be as intelligent as he is and I wait for our WISDOM FOOD, as he calls it, every day.

My brother and I do our homework in different rooms. This way, my brother, who is a year and a half younger than I, cannot disturb me. He, of course, is too young to get WISDOM FOOD from Opa. He knows nothing! (I'm not supposed to say that. My mother always tells me, "Just because you are older and taller doesn't mean you are smarter," but I know I am. Ask Opa!)

Because I am nine (almost!) and know how to behave, I get to sit in the living room. What a beautiful room! It has high ceilings and huge windows that are oval shaped on the top. The curtains are sheer silk with patterns of flowers and butterflies, which you can only see if you get real close to the window. You are not supposed to touch the curtains, even if your hands are clean. They wrinkle, I guess. Or maybe they cannot be replaced if something happens to them. Who knows, there are so many things forbidden these days and we are not to ask questions all the time. So I try to be grown up and UNDERSTANDING.

The walls in the room are paneled. Brown mahogany panels. (I know, because I asked.) On one side, the entire wall is covered by a buffet. It is gorgeous. There are drawers on the bottom and the top is divided in three parts: A carved door on each side, and the entire middle is one large mirror. If I stand at a certain angle or on a stool (forbidden!) I can see myself in the mirror. Sometimes, when nobody is looking, I get one of Omi's hats, put it on and try on faces in the mirror. It is such a pity that we cannot go to the movies anymore (again, because we are Jews.) The women in the movies wore such lovely hats. Watching them was almost as nice as watching the film.

I don't really know what the problem with the paintings is. I think they are lovely, and I have seen the same ones in the art books that Opa has shown me.

"Maybe we should sell them," I have heard Omi say, "before they take them."

Who would take them? I don't understand and I don't want to ask. I do notice that everybody is upset. They all talk in whispers and turn the radio off as soon as I appear. Good thing our teachers are more open. They tell us how dangerous it is for us Jews to stay in Germany, and sometimes they leave a newspaper on their desk and we try to read what it is that is so dangerous. There are always Hitler's speeches, pages and pages of them, but we don't have time to read all of it. A lot of our friends are leaving for other countries, but what does that have to do with the paintings in my Omi's house? It is all so difficult!

My grandparents' house also has a <u>Gentlemen's Room</u>. I will never understand why they call it a Gentlemen's Room when ladies sit in it also. My grandparents have a piano in there, on which my mother and grandmother play (or used to play when they were not so sad and worried all the time.)

Sometimes, in the evening, friends come over to play Bridge. Then they all sit in the Gentlemen's Room, ladies and men. But anyway, for whatever reason the room got its name, there is a whole wall of books, books and more books. It feels like being in the library. Only better, because these books are ours. You can take as much time as you want to read them. Of course, Opa has shown me where the books are that Gert and I are allowed to read, but once in a while, we sneak another one and look through it to see why "they are not for children." Mostly it is stuff that you learn in school anyway: history, biographies of famous people, German and Jewish poets, some "Krimis" (Mystery novels) that my great-grandmother loves. My brother and I love to lie on the thick carpet and read and read. My brother only takes thin books. They are faster to finish. (His patience is only seven-and-a half-years old.)

My favorite room in that house is my grandparents' bedroom. What a paradise. The huge four-poster bed with the enormous down covers and pillows. What a place to hide in!

The best part of the bed is that one can slide under it and hide in the middle where nobody can reach. Whenever Gert and I do something nasty, like eat marmalade out of the jar in the kitchen, and then by mistake drop the jar and make a mess on the just-scrubbed kitchen floor, (before my grandmother comes running and we hear, "What was that noise and who is where he is not supposed to be?") we race into the bedroom under the bed, right in the middle and then we wait. Omi can never reach us there and we won't come out until she promises not to be mad or punish us.

Once, Omi got so mad that she took a broomstick and tried to sweep us from under the bed, but we stayed and didn't move until she left. It was then that my little brother said to me, "You know, a mother is always a mother. Not even the best grandmother can replace her." I thought that was pretty clever.

Of course, the house has a bathroom. Enormous room. It has a marble floor, black and white, a huge bathtub which stands on four oval shaped feet, like a German Dachshund; two sinks with beautiful gold faucet, a toilet and a bidet. Bidets are <u>shameful</u> according to Oma Feldblum. I don't see why. My brother pees in it when the toilet is occupied and one can also use it to wash your feet while sitting on the toilet. Rather convenient, I think. But here we have rules, "Going to the toilet is a private matter," Omi always says. "It is not a place to visit or read, or G-d forbid <u>EAT</u>. One does one's business and leaves." So why is there a bidet and a toilet, a combination made for visiting? Maybe the architect who designed the house did not believe so strongly in privacy?

Oma Feldblum has a room for herself. Or almost for herself. It used to be hers alone until recently, when my grandmother and her sister, Tante Paula, started a home business. Both my grandfather and my Uncle Walter (Paula's husband) were no longer allowed to work and "we cannot live off the savings alone," Omi says. My grandfather had an import business and brought curtains, drapes, tassels and decorative fabrics from Switzerland. His line is called <u>POSAMENTERIE</u>. I love that name. It sounds so elegant and refined. He still has a lot of samples that we are allowed to play with. Omi has made some beautiful doll dresses with these samples. Uncle Walter used to be the manager of a business selling industrial goods. (Since INDUSTRIAL GOODS doesn't sound elegant or interesting, I never asked what it was that he sold.)

So Omi and Tante Paula opened a workshop. They put two electrical sewing machines in Oma Feldblum's room and are making ties. Hundreds and hundreds of ties. Every day, a gentleman brings rolls of silk. My mother told me, in secret, that this man had been an employee of Opa's, not Jewish, and had promised to help when they closed the business. Omi spreads the material out on a large table, cuts the ties from paper patterns, and Tante Paula then puts a piece of lining in them and sews them together into ties. She sews them one attached to the other until there is a long string of ties, and I am allowed to help and separate one from the other. Tante Paula says this is a very important job, because if you cut the thread between the ties too short, the whole tie unravels and is lost. So I am very careful and glad that they give me such an important task.

Oma Feldblum, who is pretty old, (I think she is seventy-five) is not allowed to use the scissors any more. She used to help also, but one day she "tried to cut her wrist" I heard my mother say. I don't believe it. She just wasn't careful. Why would she want to cut her wrist? Because she is Jewish? Does everything have to do with being Jewish? I wish I were older.

Maybe they would tell me more. This way, I have to guess and imagine things. Tante Paula never explains anything either. I have tried to ask her, but they all say the same: "Don't worry about anything. As long as we are all together, you are fine." Guess they are right.

Oma Feldblum's room is very large and sunny and the two sewing machines really don't bother. She has a bed with a wooden headboard, but it is smaller than Omi's. It's an interesting bed. It has a needlepoint cover that she made when she was young and she has it covered with pillows. Embroidered pillows, knitted pillows, silk pillows, hand painted pillows. I love to look at them and touch them and she has a story to go with every one them. She tells me of her "young years." Heavens, that must have been in prehistoric times. But I never question anything. Her stories are so fascinating. We think our parents are strict, but compared to Oma Feldblum's mother and father, ours are angels. Maybe she exaggerates a little or maybe being so old, she forgot...

Oma Feldblum's room is blue. Light blue flowered wallpaper, a blue and gray Persian rug "that my husband, may he rest in peace, bought me for one of our last anniversaries," and a pale blue tulle curtain that flutters in the wind when the window is open. It is a peaceful room. Pity that the sewing machines make so much noise. You can't really dream and imagine things.

The piece of furniture I love best is her armoire. It is light brown wood, with mirrors on both doors, and each handle has a tassel hanging from it. Sometimes, Oma Feldblum lets us open it. What marvels she has! Hats with feathers and little nets in the front to hide your face, skirts with ruffles, crinoline underskirts to make you look wide on the bottom and small on top, lace blouses with embroidered cuffs. I adore her clothes.

Even my brother thinks they are fun to look at. Oma Feldblum wears boots with high heels and buttons in front and sometimes she gives us pennies when we help her button them with a button hook.

Oma Feldblum has a secret that only Gert and I know. She is a NASHER. She likes sweets. My Omi adores her and gives her anything she wants, but it seems she is not supposed to have sugar, but she wants to. So, sometimes in the afternoon, when Omi and Tante Paula are busy with their ties, Oma Feldblum gives us fifteen pennies and sends us to the KONDITOREI (Coffee House) across the street to buy her a bowl of whipped cream. We love it. The whipped cream costs about ten pennies and for the other five pennies we buy a bag of cake crumbs. They are so good! They taste of chocolate, streusel, cheesecake, rumcake, all mixed up. The way you eat them is to make a hole on the bottom of the paper bag and pour the crumbs into your mouth. On the way home, we usually stick a finger in the whipped cream and lick it. Delicious! Sometimes you can tell because the pattern on top of the whipped cream gets messed up. What we do then is drop the entire bowl on the floor, in the paper bag, of course, and then Oma Feldblum thinks we are just clumsy and doesn't notice the finger traces on the cream. You really get inventive when you want something really bad!

My second favorite place in the entire house is the kitchen. Most of what I know I learned from Omi in the kitchen. While she stirs and whips and cuts and kneads, she loves to visit and I can ask her all those many, many questions that I have. We have the best conversations in the kitchen. The stove is black iron. It works with gas. Next to it is the oven with one door on the top, and one on the bottom. She can make two cakes at the same time and often does. In a corner are the icebox and the KOCHKISTE, which is a small sort of trunk lined with cork. You put the hot pots in there to keep them warm. Omi uses it mostly to keep rice and potatoes hot while she cooks the meat and vegetables on the stove. I have also seen her wrap the hot pots in newspaper and place them in the Kochkiste. That keeps them even hotter, she says.

The floor of the kitchen is shiny like a mirror. It is made of linoleum, a new material that my grandfather had installed not long ago. The kitchen used to have a hardwood floor that needed to be waxed and polished every day. This linoleum is a wonderful invention. It makes cleaning so much easier. All you do is scrub it with hot, soapy water, dry it and then go over it with a woolen rag to polish it. It doesn't take more than half an hour to clean the entire floor. Now that Jewish people are no longer allowed to have German ladies as household help, it is important to make the cleaning jobs easier.

The kitchen window looks out onto a small garden in the next building. You can see trees and hear birds singing, which is not very common in the middle of the city, but Omi says the kitchen was one of the main attractions of this house when they moved in, fifteen years ago, before I was even born.

I love all the gadgets in the kitchen. Here is the meat grinder, always on the same spot on the kitchen table. The big screw that fastens the machine made a big hole on the bottom of the tabletop; that's why it is never moved. It would just make another hole on another spot. On a shelf, on the wall by the window, Omi keeps the coffee mill, and sometimes I get to grind the coffee. The best way to do it is to sit on a chair or stool, open your legs, squeeze the coffee mill between your knees and turn the handle. I love the smell of fresh ground coffee. Sometimes, I get distracted or excited and I drop the coffee mill. All the beans and the ground coffee spill on the floor. If nobody were there, I would just sweep it up and put it back in the mill. The coffee gets boiled anyway, and the kitchen floor is so clean it really doesn't matter. But Omi won't allow it. She throws all the coffee out. "Haste makes waste," she says then, and makes me feel bad.

When Omi bakes a cake, which is very often, and especially for Friday night Shabbat dinner, I help. I stir and stir the dough and stick my fingers in it to lick. Raw dough tastes the best. Better than the baked cake. When Omi pours the dough into the mold, she always leaves some in the mixing bowl for me to scrape. Depending on what kind of cake it is, she leaves more or less in the bowl. Dough for cheese or chocolate cake is the best. Dough with yeast is no good.

Omi tells me about my mother when she was a little girl, about my uncle John, (my mother's brother) and how they fought when they were children, but how they became good friends when they grew up. She tells me about herself, when she was Oma Feldblum's "Rock and Strength." There are five children, all girls, and she is the oldest. I can't imagine Omi, Tante Paula and Jenny, and Else and Lene, who are twins, being children, but I guess at one time they were my age. Hard to believe. Omi cries when she tells me about her past and how carefree they were. I hate to see her upset and I tell her so. She then cleans her hands on her apron, hugs me and says, "Oh, Mulli (my pet name) what is to become of us?"

I don't know what is to become of us and it scares me to see her so upset. I love this house so much and I adore my grandparents. Why does everybody think that "something is to become of us?" I feel like crying also, but I try not to.

***

Somebody touches my shoulder. My Omi? No, no, this is April of 1990, fifty years later. The woman speaks to me in German, "Are you looking for somebody? You look like a foreigner. Does this house remind you of something?"

"I used to live here," I say. "Can't be," she replies, and shakes her head. "Only Jews lived in this house and they are all dead. Killed."

I turn away. They are not dead, not to me. They are very much alive, in my heart and in my memory, and in my conversations with my grandchildren.

SCHOOL

Berlin, March 1933

Today is my first day of school. You have to be six years old to get into first grade, and I will be six only on my next birthday in May, but they let me start a little earlier, because I already know all the letters of the alphabet and can read the signs on the streets. I guess I am now almost grown up, going to a real school. I wasn't even scared when Mami took me this morning. She said not to worry, but I don't think the school looks like it's for little kids. It is so big and gray, almost like the Post Office. No curtains on the windows, no grass or flowers; just a big old scary building.

Last night, my Omi and all my aunts came to the house to celebrate. They gave me my ZUCKERTUETE (a cone shaped cardboard container about two feet high, painted with flowers and hearts) full of candy and chocolate to take to school. I know that all the other children will have a Zuckertuete also. It's what you get on your first day of school "to sweeten the moment," as my Omi says, but I bet mine is the biggest. It's pink with flowers and a ribbon on the side, really pretty. I wonder if they let us eat candy in school. I guess we will have to share, but maybe we don't have to give any away, just exchange one kind of candy for another. Even if my brother, who is only four, didn't get a Zuckertuete, I was told to share with him.

It's not fair, by the time he gets his in two years, I will have forgotten how many candies I gave him!

I am wearing the new dress that Mami bought for me. It is a very pretty Scottish dress with a white collar, and I promised I wouldn't get it dirty. I'm wearing new brown boots, the ones with little buttons in front and, ugh, I have to wear my long woolen stockings because it is still very cold. I wanted to wear my new white socks, but my Mami wouldn't let me. I hope that the other mothers are as strict as mine, and all the girls are wearing their long woolen stockings. I sure don't want to be the only one! I have a new hat that I love. It matches my dress.

I am also carrying my new <u>RANZEN</u> on my back. It looks like a backpack, but it's made of leather and has my name on it in gold letters. Today, there is only my sandwich in it, but when we get homework and use pencils, books and copybooks, it will be a real important thing to carry.

My classroom is number 1-B, and I find it all by myself. Nobody helped me. It is a big room and there are rows and rows of little tables, each one with a chair behind it. The teacher sits on an armchair, behind a huge desk that stands on a platform she calls a <u>Podium</u>. I guess she needs to be high up so she can see everybody.

"Good morning, girls," she says, really strict. (It's a girls' school. There are no boys.)

"Line up by height over there. The short ones in front, taller ones at the end." I am a little taller than most of the girls, so I get to stand at the end of the line.

"Now go sit down in the same order," she says. I end up towards the back of the room. "Later, you will be sitting according to your grades," the teacher says. "The ones with bad grades will be in front, where I can watch them all the time." I hope that I stay in the back forever.

Why can't she smile, I wonder. We haven't done anything wrong yet. We just got here. I guess that's what my Opa meant last night when he said, "You will now taste the seriousness of life."

Mrs. Krug (that's the teacher's name) tells us what the rules are: no talking, no turning around to look at the other girls, no laughing, no eating in class, no fooling around. If you want to speak, lift your arm and point with your index finger into the air. She will see it and call on you. No yelling, "Miss, Miss" without being asked. "We are all sophisticated people. (I need to look up in the encyclopedia what "sophisticated" means.) It just sounds scary.

Mrs. Krug also tells us that at first, we will be writing with a pencil. Later, when we know all the letters and can write real words, we will be writing with ink. I can't wait to use my new penholder, with the shiny pen that you have to stick in the front of the holder. And Oma Feldblum made this little knitted bag for me to put the ink bottle in so that it cannot fall when it sits on the desk. I am excited about writing with ink. Pencils are for little children, like my brother. Ink is for real students, like me!

After a long, long time we are allowed to take a short break. Mrs. Krug explains that we will have a short pause of a few minutes, to go to the bathroom, and one long break for lunch.

"At lunchtime, you leave the classroom and go out to the schoolyard. The rooms need to be ventilated and you will only return when the bell rings. Understood?"

It isn't hard to understand, but why is she so unfriendly? I will have to ask if all the teachers in the school are like her. Perhaps she has terrible children herself and thinks we are all like them.

After the bathroom break, the teacher keeps explaining what real school is like. "It is not a playground," she says. "You better learn this on your first day. School forms character and prepares you for life." (I need to look up "character".) I think this is all a little bit boring. I learn more from my Opa's encyclopedia lessons. But I listen. Carefully. Maybe tomorrow Mrs. Krug will ask, "What exactly did I say yesterday?" and then I better know the answer.

I want to be a good student. I want to learn to read so that nobody needs to tell us stories or read them to us. It will be so exciting to read a book all by myself!

Oh, good, the bell is ringing. This is for the long break. Out we go in a perfect line, again by height. Now I am, of course, one of the last ones to get out…it isn't fair.

The schoolyard is ugly. It looks like the street, no lawn or sand, only stone (I think it's called "concrete".) If you fall on this, your knees won't look so good. But here is Mrs. Krug again, "No running, girls. You are to walk around the yard in groups of three. Nice and slow, like little ladies."

When are we going to play? Or is everything forbidden here? My cousin, Horst, who is already eight and in third grade, said school was fun. Was he joking? Or did he not have a Mrs. Krug for a teacher?

We have to sit on benches while we eat our lunch. No walking and eating at the same time. I need to find out if this is forever or only on the first day?

My second day and all the days after are the same. Mrs. Krug never smiles. She is nice but strict. Every morning, we have to stand in line and she checks our fingernails. Good thing mine are always clean. My mother watches that. Otherwise, she makes you stand in front of the whole class and tells everybody that you are an "<u>unhygienic</u>" person. And then she checks your neck and ears too. She says that if you don't keep your hands clean, you certainly don't believe in washing the rest of your body either. And she repeats over and over again, "A clean child grows up to be a clean adult with a clean mind." I don't exactly understand what she means. How can you wash your mind? But that's what she says.

I have been in school now for a year. Things are still the same, strict and lots of VERBOTEN. But I have learned to read and am already allowed, sometimes, to write with ink. I guess I am a big girl now. We learned to write the date in our copybook every day, and this is why I remember what day this is: the 20th of April 1934.

This morning, Mrs. Krug told us that today is Hitler's birthday. I wonder who Hitler is. Is he the man my parents talk about when they are worried? Why is his birthday important?

It is noontime, but the bell for the long break hasn't rung yet. What's going on?

"Nobody is allowed on the schoolyard today," Mrs. Krug announces. "We have to work on new seating arrangements in the classroom."

I am surprised. Why can't we sit where we always sit? But before I can lift my right arm and extend my index finger into the air, she says, "All Jewish children go sit in the back of the room."

I am confused. Aren't all children Jewish? And if not, what are they? Some of the girls go in the back. I am already there anyway.

"You, Levy, and you, Rappaport, didn't you hear me? I said in the back of the room." Mrs. Krug now sounds really mean. "Or don't you know that you are a Jew?"

Eight of us sit at the tables in the back. What are they going to do with us? I want to go home and be with my mother, but we are not allowed to leave the school until classes are over.

My Omi always picks me up from school and we walk home. Today, I cannot wait for her to come. I tell her what happened. She doesn't say anything. She just looks very sad and doesn't speak much on the way home.

In the evening, after dinner, my mother says to me very quietly, "Please be a good girl and go to bed. Do your washing quickly and you may read your new book in bed, but please stay in your room. We are having company."

Company? In the middle of the week? And I am allowed to read in bed with the light on? Something is really wrong. Mrs. Krug will be furious tomorrow if my neck isn't clean, and I sure don't want to stand in front of the class as an example of an unhygienic girl. Somebody please tell me what is happening.

I leave the door to my room open, but although I try hard, I can't hear what my parents are talking about in the living room. The Schlesingers are here, my Uncle Alfred, the Blumenfelds from across the street and the Meyers, who live on the second floor in our house. They are not playing bridge, as they often do. They are whispering. If I were only nine or ten, perhaps they would tell me, but at seven, they think you are just a baby and don't understand.

The next morning, Mami tells me that I don't have to go to school. I am not sick or anything but my mother says that from now on, I will go to a different school. "But why?" I ask. I like my school and by now I am used to stern Mrs. Krug. My mother looks at me with sad eyes and just sits there. I am scared.

"Are you sick, Mami? What is happening? And why did Papi not go to work today? Please tell me. Is it my fault?"

"I guess you should know," my mother says, "it's hard to explain, but I will try." I sit and wait.

"You must have heard about Hitler in school, haven't you?" Mami starts, "Hitler is a very bad man and he hates

Jewish people. Nobody knows why, but he does. We need to be very careful. Don't talk to anybody on the street and never, never repeat to anybody whatever you hear in this house. Do you understand this?"

"Sure, Mami, but what does that have to do with not going to school anymore?"

"Hitler does not want Jewish children to be together with German children. He wants people to believe that Jews are bad and sick and that being near them would make others sick. This is, of course, not true, but many people believe him. The teachers in your school believe him, and we must be careful. You will be going to a new school next week. It is a Jewish school where only Jewish children go. There will be boys and girls together."

A new school. Is that good or bad? Will the teachers be as mean as Mrs. Krug?

"Will the teachers also be Jewish?"

"Of course."

"Do Jewish teachers look different?"

"No, darling, they are people like everybody else. But you will learn different things: Hebrew, Jewish songs and stories that Mrs. Krug would never tell you. It will be fun. All your friends will be with you."

That sounds good. My friend Steffi and Irene and Ulla all in the same class. I am getting excited.

"There will be one little change in the school schedule," my mother says, "you will not go to school on Saturdays as you did before, but on Sunday instead."

I know why. Saturday is Shabbat and Jewish people don't work on Shabbat. But to go to school on Sundays...?

***

My new school is called: Adath Jisroel Schule. It is near where we live. I can walk to school. You cannot see the building from the street. A garden in front with large trees hides the house. My Omi tells me that it used to be the private home of some Jewish people who gave it to the Synagogue to be used as a school. The rooms are small and there are fewer children than in Mrs. Krug's class. Omi says that all the children are Jewish, and nobody will say nasty things to us or call us ugly names. I still don't understand it. All the Jewish children and the Jewish teachers look like regular people. How can Hitler tell who is Jewish and who is not? We all speak German and play the same games as the kids in Mrs. Krug's school. What is different about us?

***

Berlin, 1937

By now, I understand. I understand very well. I am now ten years old, and we have been told by our parents, our teachers and our Rabbis what it means to be a Jew in Germany.

Hitler has published a book called Mein Kampf (My Battle) in which he explains why he hates Jewish people and how he will rid the world of them. Although many of our relatives and friends believe that Hitler's threats are impossible to carry out, many others are making plans to leave Germany.

My parents and grandparents never speak in front of my brother and I, but I pick up enough of the adults' conversations to know what is going on. Our teachers, however, talk to us.

The school program has been changed and is now completely different from the German schools. Although we are no longer allowed to speak to the children of our German neighbors, who used to be our friends, we know exactly what they do in their schools because our teachers explain the difference to us.

At Adath Jisroel, we are learning English, geography, math and history of the world, not just Germany's. We also have classes in photography, sewing and cooking, besides Hebrew and Jewish religion classes.

"You must be prepared," the teachers tell us. "G-d only knows where we will all end up living and we better be ready."

They don't care much about gymnastics, which was the big thing in the German school. We don't have music or art classes anymore either.

"You may never be able to go to school again," my favorite teacher, Dr. Sinasohn, says. "We are trying to give you as much knowledge as we can about as many subjects as possible. You may even have to go to work in a foreign country and you must be prepared.

Go to work? I am only ten years old. I am not a baby, but go to work? Doing what? And where? How I wish my mother would tell me more about their plans. But I guess they are afraid I might talk to the wrong people. I certainly wouldn't. I know and understand more than she thinks, but when I see my parents' sad and scared faces, I don't want to ask.

***

My school days in Germany ended in April of 1939, when we left for Chile. I was almost twelve years old, but no longer a child. Life had taught all of us, parents and children, a lesson that was not included in any school curriculum.

***

MY BROTHER

I learned early in life that nothing is perfect forever. My brother was born on December 20, 1928. Although I don't remember this, being a year and a half myself, I was told that I was not exactly enchanted about the competition. All of a sudden, the attention that I had enjoyed on an exclusive basis was now "divided" by two. He was a cute baby, like a new doll, but they wouldn't let me play with him. His name was **GERT**, but everybody called him **BUBI** or **KLEINER (THE SMALL ONE)**.

My mother told me that the winter of 1928 was one of the coldest in the history of Germany, and my little brother could not be taken outside until he was two months old. That meant he was around all the time, and for the first time, I heard the word "DON'T." "Don't lean into his buggy, it can topple." Or, "Don't squeeze his little face." Or, "Don't try to lift him from his bed. You can hurt him." I surely did not want to hurt him, I just wanted to play with him.

One day, I was about two years old and starting to speak in sentences. I watched my mother changing the baby. What a surprise. He had a little thing down below that I didn't have. Quickly, I pulled my panties down to make sure I did not have a little snake down there.

"What is this? Why does he have this tail? I don't have one of those."

"Because he is a little boy and you are a girl. Boys and girls look different."

This was interesting. "Does he pee and poop through that little thing?" I wanted to know. "Can it come off?"

"Don't you touch him down there, Mami said, "you can hurt him."

I promised I wouldn't. Maybe one day, when nobody was looking, I could look at it a little longer and see how it was attached to his tummy. Maybe they could get one for me also.

I got used to Bubi and when the weather became nicer and he could go out, I enjoyed pushing his buggy and showing him to people in the park.

As we got a little older, I loved having him around. He was friendly and I played with him. I pretended he was one of my dolls and included him in my games.

When Bubi was four years old, he went to a Kindergarten in the morning. (In Germany, Kindergarten is for little kids before they go to school, which starts with Grade 1).

We played together and I made sure that I was always the Mother, or Maid, or Teacher, so that he had to obey my orders. But he was a patient, sweet little guy and never complained. He loved his "older" sister.

In 1934, when he was six years old, he started school at the Jewish Schule Klopstockstrasse. At that time, we were not allowed to go to German schools anymore, so his being a Jew was impressed on him from the first day. All the Jewish kids from our neighborhood went to the same school and he had many friends. He went to birthday parties without me. My friends were "older" and I had my own little circle.

Everybody loved him. He was sweet and more so, he was funny. He clowned around and invented new gymnastic tricks that he taught to his friends. He was daring and not afraid of anything. My Omi always worried about him.

Because he was little for his age and more delicate than me, he got to go on winter vacations to the mountains with my grandparents "because he needed the extra attention." I was stronger and taller and got to stay home.

He learned to ski and was soon called "the snow-clown." Although I never learned to ski, we were pretty good at ice skating. Gert would run onto the rink, fall down a dozen times, get up and keep going. I was much more cautious. He would get on a bicycle and fly down the street. Not me. It took me a long time to get on one of those "machines."

We got along very well. I was his "big sister" and always knew things that Bubi didn't. I figured out family secrets that he never noticed and when I felt he needed to know, I would tell him. A sort of "quality control" system managed by me. I "filtered" the news to him that I felt he could understand.

Bubi was a very bad eater. It took hours and lots of "one more bite" for him to finish a meal. He tested the patience of both my mother and grandmother, and while I was already playing or reading, he sat at the table and munched on each bite. They used to tell him that "he would never grow up to be a big man," but that didn't impress him.

After school, we always went to my grandparents' house and had a young lady come and do homework with us. With him! I did my own. I didn't need help! Her name was Hannchen. She was 17 years old.

I remember exactly where we sat in Omi's house. Her bedroom was enormous and there was a little table in front of a full-size mirror. Bubi always sat where he could look into the mirror, and while Hannchen tried to explain the multiplication tables to him, he would look in the mirror, fix his hair, make faces and not pay any attention. But even when she was frustrated, you couldn't really be mad at him. He was such a charmer. Only his grades in school were not that charming!

There were a lot of activities for us. Each Synagogue had special programs to keep us busy after school. Gert and I sang in the Children's Choir at our Temple, (Lewetzostrasse) especially on the High Holidays. To this day, I remember the beautiful melodies of the Hebrew prayers. Gert and I were sometimes chosen to sing a "Solo" and my parents and grandparents came to all our rehearsals and told us how proud they were of us.

Simchat Torah was celebrated in grand style. The main sanctuary was full of people, all of them armed with packages of candy. Each of us children brought containers made of paper or material, the Rabbi carried the Torah, and we paraded through the aisles so the grown-ups could put candy in our bags. Coming home, of course, the candy was counted and equally divided in two.

One of our favorite excursions was to visit Tante Ralchen. She was one of our great-grandmother's sisters and lived outside of Berlin in the country. We had to take a train to go there and usually went with Omi and Opa. The house was a beautiful old house with all kinds of toys and things around. We learned that they were not called "things," they were porcelain antiques and "memorabilia" from her younger years. We loved the word "memorabilia," although, of course, we were not allowed to play with any of them, but Tante Ralchen always gave us something to take home.

"You should start a collection of beautiful things early on," she would say. "It is a must for a cultural life."

We really didn't think that beautiful things that you cannot touch are part of "culture," but I guess all they wanted to do was raise us with a sense of elegance and refinement. We thought there was time enough to do this when we get older.

To get to the house, you had to cross a large garden with fruit trees and flowers. We were told that we could have any fruit we wanted but "it had to be washed." This took half the fun away. We passed the strawberry bushes, the blueberries, and the gooseberry plants and stuffed our mouths and pockets -without washing- before we even entered the house. Gooseberries have little thorns and it wasn't always easy to eat them quickly on the way to the entrance door.

Of course, Tante Ralchen had baked cookies and cake and made chocolate pudding with whipped cream. We loved going there.

Then came the emigration to Chile. Our entire life changed.

***

After getting halfway settled in Santiago, we were sent to school. Gert attended a boys' school and I went to a mixed High School.

We did not speak any Spanish, of course. His name was changed to **GERARDO** and the "BUBI" part of his life was finished. He was then ten years old. He was well-behaved and gave my parents little to worry about. It was all so strange for us, so very different from Berlin, and we had to learn a new language, new customs, new people, and try to make new friends. We were very busy and had little time for "tonteras" (stupid behavior). My parents did not worry. Had they only known...!

Gert was still daring and unafraid. Our schools were close together. We had to take a streetcar, but were supposed to walk. There was not enough money and "walking is healthy" we were told. "Need makes you creative" is a German saying. My brother proved this. He found out that you could wait until the streetcar started slowly and then jump on the back platform without paying. He did this without a second thought. I wasn't as quick as he, and sometimes, I ended up walking while he waved from the streetcar. My parents found out one day when one of his friends bragged about it, and they made him promise to stop. He tried, honestly, but the temptation was too great and the way to school too long...

Once he finished the Preparatorias (four years) it became evident that he was not college material, nor could my parents afford it. He was enrolled in an ORT School. ORT schools were maintained all over the world by Jewish institutions and donors and organized to teach professions rather than humanities classes. (ORT stands for ORGANIZATION FOR RETRAINING AND TECHNOLOGY and was founded 100 years ago in Poland to help immigrants in new countries to learn a trade.)

Gert studied Mechanics and graduated with very good grades. He found a job in a machine shop owned by Jewish people and started to work at sixteen. He had nice manners, was handy, friendly and punctual and his bosses liked him and took an interest in his future. They taught him not only the mechanics, but also the business side of the industry.

His first job lead to other, better ones, and eventually, he started his own business manufacturing tubing and pipes. He loved being his own boss, but with it came the worries about money, employees and the lack of private time. My parents could not help him and he did not want a partner. Too many of his friends had had bad experiences with such arrangements.

Fate intervened. Mr. Emil Kron, one of the people who had shared our first house in Santiago (the "Jewish house") had successfully opened a business buying and selling steel. He called Gert one day, "I'm desperate. I can't handle my business by myself any longer. Would you like to work for me? I offer you a partnership. I know you don't have capital to invest, but money I don't need. I need you!"

Gert became the manager of a very successful company and stayed there until for many years until we all decided to emigrate to the USA.

Over the years, my brother and I became very good friends. I loved him, trusted him and we shared many of the worries and joys that affected us during the difficult times in a new country. He was a perfect son. He lived with my parents, worried about them, helped them and they were very proud of him. He had many friends, and was very well- liked. He was funny, did not brag, and did favors for anybody who asked him. When we got married, Kurt considered him his brother and we had a wonderful, close relationship.

Gert had many girlfriends and dated and dated. He never really thought of getting married, not wanting to leave my parents alone; at least that was this reasoning. The fact was, he couldn't make up his mind. Eventually, though, his life changed, but that is material for another story.

SURVIVAL

My Father's Story

Berlin 1938

I better leave now," he said. His wife nodded a silent "Yes." The anguish in her eyes was unbearable. One last look at her and his children and he left, closing the door softly behind him. It was early in the morning and still dark outside. He walked down the two floors to the street, as usual. Do everything as usual, he said to himself, pain and fear almost paralyzing him. It is the only way…

It was November and bitter cold, but he did not lift the collar of his coat to protect his ears from the icy wind. No businessman wore his collar up. How ironic, he thought, when was the last time I was a businessman? For two years now, ever since they closed the Jewish company he worked for, he hadn't been a businessman or even a regular citizen. He was just a Jew. A persecuted Jew in danger of losing his freedom any minute. He willed himself not to dwell on the past. All that mattered now was the present, the immediate present, today, tomorrow and the next day. If he could make it through the next few days, perhaps he would have a chance. Ever since November 9, 1938, they had been nightly surprise visits by the German SA (Secret Police) and all men over 18 years were detained. For the last few days, the SA closed entire streets and picked up whoever looked Jewish to them. Nobody knew where they were sent or what happened to them.

A slender man, he had a delicate, elegant demeanor and a shy and reserved manner. With his dark blond hair, fine features and blue-gray eyes, he did not have the typical Jewish look, and he prayed that his appearance would help him survive.

He walked to the subway station. There was no question as to which train he would take. The first one to come in, no matter where it went. Preceded by a gust of wind and loud hooting, the number 30 pulled in. He boarded it. At this hour there were no seats available. Even better, he thought, seated people are always being observed and scrutinized. The standing public was trying to stay on their feet as the train lurched forward. He looked at the advertising posters on the train. No more TRINK 'NE MOLLE" (Drink a beer) or "KALT? ERHITZE DICH MIT DAUNEN" (Cold? Warm yourself up with down covers).

The signs now spewed out Nazi propaganda: Pictures of German girls in adoring poses smiling at Hitler. Signs forbidding German citizens to associate with Jews. Posters announcing that the Jewish world conspiracy was to blame for all of Germany's ills.

He forced himself to study the posters. Everybody else did, and he had to be like everybody else for the next few days.

He got off at HAUSVOGTAIPLATZ, the station that had been his "get-off" point for nearly twenty years to go to work. He walked the familiar streets to his old building and went in. People walked in and out, just as on any normal workday. Nobody paid attention to him. The elevator took him to the sixth floor. He got off, but did not stop at what had been his office. The door was now adorned with a swastika. Instead, he walked down the stair to the second floor, took another elevator to floor number five and, again, walked down, this time to the street. He checked his watch: Fifteen minutes spent. My G-d, how was he going to live through four days of this?

He repeated this game in four or five other buildings. He couldn't just walk the streets aimlessly. No German did that. You were busy and you had to look busy. There was no unemployment in Germany. Everybody was working. Hitler had seen to that. Only women with babies and a few Jews walked the streets on a weekday. They had nothing else to do.

He was out at the Platz again. Where to go now? He boarded a bus that pulled up at the curb in front of him. Once inside, he realized this was the bus that went to WEISSENSEE (the Jewish Cemetery). Heavens, no! That was the last place he could go to, although he would have liked to pray at his father's grave. Perhaps an answer to all this madness would come to him through his ancestors, who for generations had suffered persecution and hatred but had somehow been able to leave a legacy to future generations. Would his children be able to live to continue the chain? But no, the cemetery was out of the question. He rode on the bus for several stops and got off, only to take a streetcar going in the opposite direction.

He criss-crossed Berlin like this for several hours. At lunchtime, with people streaming out of buildings, it was easier to disappear in the crowd. He went to the public library, filled at that time with students during lunch break. They all wore the Hitler Youth's brown uniform. Little Nazis, trained in hatred early on. He decided not to take just any book. Instead, ostentatiously, he asked the librarian for the "HISTORY OF NATIONAL SOCIALISM" and sat down. Should he pretend to read or really look through the book, perhaps to find an answer to the many questions that nobody had been able to explain?

What motivated these Germans? Where did Hitler's hate for the Jews originate? Had they not fought Germany's wars, and had they not put Germany in the forefront of music, the arts, poetry, the sciences, medical discoveries, and had the world not recognized these talents and given credit to Germany for them? He couldn't read. His thoughts went back to his children. What would become of them? Could they be saved?

Where was one to go? He was only thirty-nine, but felt old, helpless and desolate. He hadn't confided his plans for these few days to any of his friends. The danger was not only to oneself, but knowledge of such plans would mean imprisonment and even death for any "conspirator" if something went wrong. He had to keep his secret to himself.

He returned the book, left the library and took yet another bus. This one went through the TIERGARTEN, the Park that divided Berlin in two sections. How many beautiful memories these paths held for him. He got off the bus. This is where he walked with his fiancée fourteen years ago, always accompanied, of course, by her brother or father.

In spite of the anguish of the moment, he had to smile. How old-fashioned his courtship had been and how short! He remembered the day he met her. New Year's Eve, 1923. They got engaged two months later, in February of 1924. He was living in Cologne at the time, and their engagement consisted of long love letters and short visits to Berlin, until they got married in January of 1925. How peaceful and happy life had been then. It was inconceivable that in such a few years their lives would be in danger, their businesses destroyed, their children attacked on the streets...why, why, why?

At the end of the park, the American Embassy loomed on the other side of the street. An omen? He walked over to the elegant gray building. Just as he turned the corner, he stopped. Hundreds of people were lined up in front of the Embassy, waiting to get in. Hundreds of Jews seeking refuge in America. He couldn't afford to join them. He had no papers, no appointment and, besides, he didn't have a relative in the United States who could extend an affidavit, a guarantee required to even apply for an entry visa. He continued walking. He envied those lucky hundred who had a chance to at least ask for asylum in America, even if only a few would be permitted to enter the United States.

In his mind, he reviewed every relative he had in the world. None came to mind. There was nobody in South Africa, nobody in Australia, nobody in Canada, nobody anywhere. He couldn't just go to an embassy or consulate and say: "I want to emigrate to your country." There were hundreds of thousands Jews desperately trying to get out of Germany, and most countries of the world were not prepared to let them in. Regulations, controls, capital investments, relatives with established businesses abroad, all kinds of demands he could not fulfill. And Palestine, the biblical land of the Jews, was off-limits, since the British, who had control over the country, would not allow any more Jews to settle there.

Until now, he and all his friends had been hoping that Hitler's threats were only that: threats. How could anybody fathom the destruction of hundreds of thousands of Jews as The Fuehrer had promised the German people? How could he destroy practically an entire people? It had to be only bravado and propaganda, and things would calm down.

Since Hitler's ascension in 1933, only five years had passed and now the persecution of the Jews was systematically carried out. Up to now, however, the victimizing had been mainly against Jewish property, not against Jewish lives. But the attacks of November 9th indicated that stronger measures were being taken to break down the Jewish spirit, and rid the country of this "dangerous enemy."

On November 9th, everybody was awakened after midnight by the howling of sirens, the deafening crash of broken glass and the smell of fire. Running out on the street, they saw their Synagogue burning, and so was every Jewish store and business in the neighborhood. Nobody dared to telephone a friend or relative in a different part of the city to find out if this was an isolated attack, or if the same had happened all over Berlin. If it had been a random assault, why scare the others? And if it was a planned, city-wide action, telephoning wouldn't help. The next morning it was clear. Every Synagogue in Berlin had been burned, Torah scrolls and prayer books torn, sprayed with blood and thrown on the streets, every window of every Synagogue and Jewish School smashed, furniture set on fire and demolished; hundred-year-old religious ornaments destroyed. It had been a systematic attack not only in Berlin but also in every city across Germany.

The Jewish communities were given no time to mourn their losses, clean up the destruction and re-group to make plans in the face of these vicious attacks. The next morning, November 10th, thousands of Jewish men were dragged from their homes and sent to concentration camps. It was now clear. Hitler meant what he said. All you could do was disappear for a while and try to make plans. That is what he was doing...

He found himself sitting on a bench in the Tiergarten near the American Embassy. Was he dreaming? How did he get here? And sitting down in the middle of the day! He got up quickly and continued walking. It was getting dark. He felt dizzy and tired and remembered that he had not eaten anything all day. Hunger was not his problem, but he couldn't afford to black out and be discovered. On an impulse, he took a streetcar to the train station, bought a ticket for Cologne (where he had lived before he got married), and boarded an overnight train. At least he could sit down. Sleeping was impossible anyway, but he had to spend the night somewhere. He would take another train back to Berlin in the morning.

He had survived one more day. He felt very fortunate. Fate had spared him until now, but it could not be for long. Mass detentions and transports to Concentration Camps were carried out every day. He saw masses of people at train stations, pushed into trains by SA Military Officers. Jewish men, mostly, but there were also women and small children. The scenes made him sick. He and his wife had decided that he should disappear for a few days, until their neighborhood had been "cleansed" of Jews, mainly the men. As long as he was alive and free, a miracle might happen and somewhere, somehow, they would find a way to leave Germany before the Nazis killed everybody. If he could just make it through the next few days…

He rode the train to Cologne, and back to Berlin in the morning. He needed a shave. He had, on purpose, not taken anything with him when he left the house. Just some money. He could hardly walk the streets of Berlin with a suitcase! He bought a razor, shaving cream and soap in the nearest drugstore, and had it packed in a small gift box.

Where to go to clean up? Right by the train station was the world-famous Hotel Adlon. It was the most elegant and expensive hotel in Berlin. In normal times, diplomats and wealthy foreigners made it their home. Now it was a nest for the Nazi Party. Should he dare go in? It might be the safest place. No Jew in his right mind would set foot in the Adlon Hotel. He silently thanked nature for making him blond, thin and unobtrusive. He could pass for an Aryan, Hitler's ideal of the perfect human being.

The lobby of the Adlon Hotel, lavishly decorated with paintings by old masters, velvet curtains and Louis XIV antique furniture, now resembled a military clubhouse. SS-Troops (the Storm Troopers, part of the Gestapo Secret Police) in their sinister black uniforms; brown-shirted SA-Soldiers (Hitler's Special Army) fully armed, filled every corner of the hotel's vestibule, sitting rooms, bar and dining room, their presence an insult to the refinement and elegance of the décor. They stood in every corner, watchful eyes towards doors and windows. They sat ramrod straight in otherwise comfortable chairs, ready to jump and attack at a second's notice.

His heart missed a few beats, but fright made him bold. He straightened up, looked forward, and with firm steps walked through the lobby to the Gentlemen's Room. Several soldiers were in there. He needed to relieve himself, but did not dare use the urinal for fear of being discovered. Jewish men are always circumcised; Germans never were. He lifted his right hand in the "HEIL HITLER" salute and entered a stall. When he came out, the soldiers were still there. Without hesitation, he opened his package and started to shave. Nobody bothered him. It was not uncommon that train passengers would use the bathroom facilities of a hotel after an all-night ride. He listened, heartsick, to the Nazi officers boasting of how many Jews they had arrested in the last two days, giving explicit details of how some of them had tried to resist, and by what means they had been "convinced." Laughter and backslapping followed every one of the stories.

"Forgive me, G-D," he prayed. "I have to laugh with them to avoid suspicion." And he laughed and applauded. He finished his shaving as quickly as he could, saluted again "HEIL HITLER," and left with determined steps, going back to the lobby and out to the street.

Tears of shame, anger and terror filled his eyes. He wanted to scream, to cry, to vomit, to castigate himself in some way. "What have I turned into? A monster, like the SS and the SA Officers? A traitor to my people, a man without pride and honor?" "No, no, no," he said to himself. "I am just a father and husband, trying to save my children and my wife. I need to survive a little longer to find a way out of this country, and I will do whatever it takes. If only I could dare contact somebody." But the telephones in every Jewish home had either been disconnected or tapped.

He went into a small restaurant nearby. In the back room was a public telephone. He looked around. The dining room was empty. He dialed his home number. It rang. At least it had not been disconnected, he thought, gratefully.

"Hello." His wife's voice. He started to cry but did not utter a word. She would know it was him, telling her he was still alive. He heard her breathing. He hung up, and bent in agony, collapsed on the floor of the room. "Please, dear G-D, he supplicated, "Don't let me faint here and be found. Give me the strength to get up and keep going. For the sake of our children, please..."

He slowly lifted himself, straightened out his clothes, and walked back into the dining room. The smell of food reminded him that he had not eaten anything since he left home the day before. He called the owner, who was in the kitchen. He needed to keep his strength. He ordered a soup and a beer. He ate the soup, but did not touch the beer. He never drank beer, but a beer bottle on the table looked "German", and he needed to think of every little detail if he wanted to survive.

The restaurant owner, a jovial, heavy German type, struck up a conversation with him while he was eating.

"You a visitor in Berlin, or out for an early lunch? Never seen you here before."

He hesitated only for a second. Safer not to chance a conversation. He cupped his ear, and leaning forward, asked, "Ha?"

"You a visitor?" The German raised his voice.

"Ha?"

"Oh hell, the only patron in here and he is deaf. My luck." He turned around and went back to his place at the cash register.

***

He spent the second and third day taking buses and streetcars from one end of the city to the other, and riding trains at night. Sleeping was impossible, but at last he could sit down and it was warm. During the day, he passed other consulates, of Venezuela, Bolivia, France, Italy. Everywhere, people stood in long lines, hoping against hope that their number would be called. All these countries had set quotas for the German Jews, and there were thousand of applicants for only a small number of entry visas. The panic was intensifying.

His desperation grew. Should he try to contact his brother or sister? Maybe they could think of a relative abroad. But if they knew of anybody, they surely needed to use such contacts for themselves. They also had children, his nieces and nephew, of the same age as his own daughter and son. No, calling them was not a solution.

He wandered through Berlin another four days and nights. Deaf in whatever restaurant he ate, "playing Nazi" when he needed a bathroom. Desperate, he longed to go home. He needed his wife. He needed his children. He had reached the point where he felt it was better to be dead together, rather than roaming the Nazi-filled streets like a nomad, in constant danger of being found.

He looked for another public phone and dialed his home number.

His wife answered immediately: "Hello…Yes."

He had not said a word, but understood that he could take the chance to return.

With German efficiency, the deportations had taken place street by street. Obviously, his street had already been "sterilized" of Jews, and the few that had been overlooked were safe, at least for the moment. He was one of the fortunate ones…

He took a final subway and went home. He cried when he saw his wife. Her face reflected the anguish of the past days. The pain in her eyes was unbearable. They embraced for a long time. No words were necessary. He was alive!

Together they decided not to speak of that week. The scars on his soul would be there forever. Perhaps later, some day, when they were safely out of Germany, they could tell their children, so that the miracle of his survival would not be forgotten.

***

ARE WE LEAVING?

December 1938

I can't believe how stupid boys are. I'm eleven, eleven and a half to be exact, and my brother is ten years old. He doesn't believe anything I say, although I know so much more than he does because I hear everything, or try to, that is being discussed between my mother and my father.

"I'm telling you, we are going to Shanghai. I heard them talk about it to Omi when they thought I wasn't listening."

"Shanghai?" My brother wonders, "What is Shanghai?"

"Dummy! Not <u>what</u> is Shanghai! It's <u>where</u> is Shanghai? "It is in China!"

I know so much because while I am learning the history and geography of the world, my poor brother is still memorizing the rivers and mountains of Germany. What good is that going to do him when we live in China?

"What are we going to do in China?" My brother still doesn't get it. But honestly, I should be nice and explain things to him. Nobody else will.

All our cousins and friends are having the same problem. Nobody tells them anything. I guess it is because our parents are afraid that we might say something to somebody, which might ruin their secret plans. Everybody mistrusts everybody else—even family members. We are not supposed to talk on the telephone because most telephones in Jewish houses are intercepted. (I love the word "intercepted," although it means something bad.) Mami and her mother, who talk several times a day on the phone, invented their own secret code. Of course, I have figured it out halfway, so I always know what they are talking about, at least the important parts.

"Shakespeare" means somebody is going to England. "We learned a new dance last week, the "Tango" indicates that entry quotas have been given out the week before for South America. "I'll wear my sheep coat," means Australia; and when I heard her say, "I bought three meters of crepe de chine silk for a New Year's dress," I know that they are talking about permits given for China by the end of the year.

You become pretty good at this after a while, and if everything else were not so sad and depressing, I could really have fun with these code-conversations.

"We are going to do in China what everyone else will do. Live there and become Chinese." While I am explaining this to my brother, I am wondering, how does one become Chinese? Can the food or the climate change a person?

"So why are we going to Shanghai?" I ask my mother, and after making me promise not to say a word to anybody, she tells me.

Somehow, my father's old boss found out that Shanghai offered to take 30,000 Jews without requiring visas or quotas. He got an entry permit through some Jewish organization, but had to sign a document stating that he would open a workshop there and manufacture women's clothing. Besides guaranteeing that he would employ a certain number of Chinese workers, he was allowed to provide work permits for three or four other Jews, and had offered one of these contracts to my father. A work permit assures a much faster processing of immigration formalities and by now, from what I hear through the CODE, every day counts.

I am a little afraid that we will have to learn to speak Chinese. We are taking English and French in school (and, of course, Hebrew, our school being Jewish Orthodox) but Chinese...? I console myself by thinking that yet another language won't hurt—and really, we don't have a choice!

I heard my mother say the other night, when she thought I was asleep and spoke in her normal voice, (not whispering) to my father, that she could work as a governess in Shanghai and teach rich Chinese children to speak German. It seems that my father won't be able to make much money there. Mr. Pilpel, his old boss, will not be able to pay much and he has already risked a lot by giving my father a work contract.

I have never given money much thought. We have all we need, less than some of the kids in my class who get new, expensive toys and clothes all the time and take trips to foreign countries, but certainly more than some of my friends whose parents, it seems, cannot afford any luxuries at all. I have been perfectly happy with my life and never worried about money until recently, when the word **"Money"** comes up in every conversation between my parents, the family and my parents' friends. I am only eleven years old. I should worry about money? What can I possibly do about it?

I can't sleep. I sit in my bed and think. Why are they doing this to us? As far as I know and learned in school, the Jews have done nothing bad to the Germans. So why, why do we have to go through all this? I don't want to ask too much. My parents are so worried all the time and I am sure they know why this is happening. I just wish they would trust me and share some of the secrets with me. Dr. Sinasohn, our school's principal, spoke to us the other morning and told us that we have to grow up really fast if we want to survive. And I know I have grown up. I want to survive! Maybe I should talk to Dr. Sinasohn. Perhaps he has some answers. But then, maybe if he finds out that we have a work permit and are leaving for Shanghai, he might tell other people, not on purpose, of course, and ruin it for us. G-d, how careful one has to be. Why, I wonder, why?

The work permit allows my father to start the <u>Leaving</u> procedures.

He went this morning to the Police to get the necessary **Permission to Leave.** From what I hear through the keyholes, this permit is only given if one can prove that there are no tax debts and no claims or lawsuits pending against the family, and that all real estate, jewelry, art collections and bank accounts have been delivered to the Nazi authorities. My parents are locked in their bedroom. I hear my mother crying, and although I know it is not nice to eavesdrop, <u>I just have to know</u>.

My father is saying very quietly: "Everything will be all right. As long as we get the children out alive, nothing else matters." I cannot go into the room. The door is closed and they would be angry. But I must find out what is making my mother so desperate. They don't want to believe it, but I <u>do</u> understand a lot more than they think!

My parents hardly sleep anymore. They are up all night, whispering.

I wish they would talk to me. I would never say a word to anybody. Stupid I am not! I tell my mother that Dr. Sinasohn spoke to us in school about children that are being sent on **Kinder-Transports** to England and Sweden, and that he was taking these boys and girls out of their regular classes. They will be getting **Not-Erziehung** (Special Emergency Education). Not-Erziehung is supposed to prepare them for life in a foreign country, where they will be without money and without their parents or family. This emergency education consists of classes in English, Math, Photography, Child-Care, Typing and Shorthand and other subjects that will help these kids to find jobs.

It sounds gruesome. <u>Jobs</u>? For kids my age? No more history or geography or even, sometimes as a treat, music class? Only the essentials to make a living?

Before I can ask the scary question, "Are Gert and I going on a Kinder-Transport?" my mother says, "You are not going anywhere by yourselves. Either we find a place where we can all go together or we all stay here. I will not allow the family to be broken up."

I am glad. I don't want to leave on a Kinder-Transport and live in another country, in strange people's houses without a soul who knows and loves you. Better to be in China with your family than being in England or Sweden all by yourself. Without Dr. Sinasohn, I wouldn't have known about the Kinder-Transports at all. How can I prove to everybody how grown up I really am?

"Our children are maturing at such speed and developing years at a time, not days at a time," Doctor Reich, our pediatrician, said when we went to get our shots last week. "It is dreadful, their youth is lost."

I don't see where my youth is lost yet. Looking in the mirror, my face has not changed at all, nor have I developed a bosom yet, but perhaps the doctor can tell that my insides have gotten old, especially what's in my head. Who knows?

Going to Dr. Reich has also become a problem. Being Jewish, he is no longer allowed to treat patients, and German doctors are forbidden to treat Jewish children. Before we go to Dr. Reich, my mother buys flowers and rings his doorbell, as if we were visitors. He now works in the basement of his house and we have to be <u>very</u>, <u>very</u> quiet. No screaming, not even crying when he stabs you with the needle. When something really hurts, you can only whisper, "Ouch," otherwise, neighbors might hear and denounce the doctor. He would immediately be deported to a concentration camp, and sometimes, they take the patients along with him.

If my mother and my Omi only knew how much I have already figured out, they would perhaps let me in on some of the plans that are being discussed. My brother is another story. He shouldn't be told. He is too young. Why scare him?

It upsets me that my mother keeps all this inside her.

She used to be such a fun person. She played the piano and sung the famous arias of the operas and operettas that she and Omi love so much. My father would joke:

"You couldn't make money on a stage as a diva." She would laugh and go on with her music. For a long time now she hasn't opened the piano, made jokes or played games with us. She just looks at us with those pained green eyes that used to twinkle not long ago. And my father (Papi) who used to tell us stories about his parents who had died before he got married, is so frantic trying to get papers, permits and documents, that he has no time for "tales of the past" as he calls them. I understand both of them. I know why they are so afraid. I just wish they would understand that I <u>do</u> <u>understand</u>.

After I tell my mother about Dr. Sinasohn and the Kinder-Transports, and remind her that I am eleven-and-a half and that she can trust me and share her worries with me, she shakes her head and says in a voice that doesn't sound like hers at all,

"Maybe you are right. I was thirty-seven a few months ago, and today, I feel like sixty. Perhaps you grew from eleven to eighteen overnight." Then she hugs me and holds me and

I think my ribs will break, but I love it. I just touch her anguished face.

"It will be all right, Mami, don't worry." I have no idea what I could do to make anything "all right," but I want my mother to know that I care and love her.

I see the papers on the table. Papers with swastikas and stamps and signatures and our name RAPHAEL printed in large, ominous (fabulous word!) looking letters with a Star of David. My mother no longer hides them. She shows them to me now. The title on the form reads: **JUDEN-SCHMUCK BESTIMMUNGEN** (Regulations for Jew-Jewelry.) It says that all Jews, whether they leave the country or not, must turn in every piece of jewelry, silverware, gold, art pieces, and antiques to the **Berliner Schmuck-Kammer** (The Berliner Mint). They allow each person to keep their wedding band, no other rings, no earrings, necklaces or anything else of value. We also have to turn over the silver candelabras that were given to my parents by my great-grandmother; all the silver trays, bowls, cutlery, coffee services, porcelain and paintings. Gifts and heirlooms that have been in the family for generations, everything has to be delivered to the Nazi Government.

"Do I have to give away my ring too?" I ask. I have this little gold ring with a dangling tiny heart that my great-grandmother gave me for my tenth birthday. That one also?"

"Yes, Goldkind (Child of Gold, another one of my nicknames) that one too. First of all, it is the law and besides, it could be too dangerous. We do want to leave..."

My father packs everything in boxes and goes. I want to look out the window to see if he finds a taxi, but my mother pulls me back.

"Let's forget we ever owned any of these treasures. If only this will save our lives."

My father does not come home that night, nor the next day, nor the next. My mother is frantic, and so are all our friends and relatives whose husbands have gone to "comply with the law." After standing in line for two days and two nights, my father comes home. He and thousand other Jews in Berlin have obediently delivered all their possessions and memories to the Nazi authorities.

"Look at the receipt they gave me," my father says, "as if they plan to ever return these things to us. I guess their brutal laws require a receipt even for memories and stolen treasures, and who would dare to question their laws?"

Our house looks empty now, as if we had been robbed. The walls empty of pictures. You can see where the wallpaper is darker where the pictures had hung. The cabinets are totally empty and gone are the beautiful plates with inscriptions like:

Engagement Party Hertha and Felix 25 February 1924
Or:
Piano Recital First Place Hertha Jacoby—1914
Or:
On the Birth of your First Child: May Sunshine Illuminate Her Life This one had a little sun engraved with my name)

Our fingers, arms and necks are now naked. No more rings, bracelets, necklaces or pendants.

My great-grandmother promised to buy me a new ring, not gold, of course, just so that I will remember her when we live in China.

I heard one of my teachers say that perhaps the Nazis had just given us a marvelous idea without knowing it. Fake jewelry made from cheap materials could become an industry that we could bring to the foreign lands that are taking us in.

***

I found out many years later that some Jews, less fearful and less "German-like" disciplined than my father, did not obey the Nazi demands. They turned over a few pieces of silver and gold, but kept the jewels and hid them on their way out of Germany, either by swallowing them or hiding them in "body holes," even ears and noses. It was not only for sentimental reasons that they refused to let the Nazis steal their possessions. They wanted to use them as "Monetary value" in whatever new country they would end up. Some of them successfully got their jewels out. Many others were caught by the German border guards and were immediately deported to Concentration Camps, if not shot on the spot.

My grandparents have no visa yet.

Mr. Pilpel did not send a work permit for Opa. I heard my father say, "Too much responsibility at his age." I don't think Opa's age is a problem. His sixtieth birthday is on March 11th, and that's not that old. But I guess Mr. Pilpel knows what he is doing. Perhaps the Chinese people don't like older men, or maybe Mr. Pilpel feels that my Opa can't work hard anymore. Perhaps my mother can get a work permit for her father once we get to China. I don't know how all this works, but I overhear my mother on the telephone with Omi, saying, "No matter what, I will not leave you behind in Germany." And then she gets off the phone and starts crying. I always like to know what the conversation is about and try to sneak around to hear, but I shiver when I see my mother cry every time she talks to her parents.

February 1939

We are not going to China. They say that Shanghai issued so many entry permits that there are not enough spaces on the vessels going there. My father and hundreds of our friends, neighbors and relatives have been gone for days, standing in line at the Steamship companies to get tickets. My father says the other night at dinner—and that was a surprise, since he never talks in front of Gert and me—that he sees very little chance of getting four tickets, and maybe they should contact Tante Jenny in Chile again.

Mother gives him a look that I already know and which means "the children are listening," and then they go into another room. "I hear my mother say something that sounds like "end it all" and my father, the sweetest, most patient person in the world, starts yelling at her. I never heard him yelling before. How complicated this all is. Why does Shanghai offer to let people in if they cannot supply steamer tickets? Wouldn't it be more practical if every entry permit came with a ticket attached? Of course, we would pay for them but at least there would be passages available. The grown-up world is so confusing right now, and every one of my uncles and aunts, who perhaps know the truth about all this, refuse to answer my questions.

"You are too young, let us worry about all this," is all I hear. My brother may be too young, but I am not, yet I can't put all the pieces together. If only I were fifteen or sixteen, it would be so much easier. They couldn't keep secrets from a sixteen-year-old woman, that's a fact.

I can't eat. My stomach is in a knot from worrying. What is going to happen now? Where are we going? Are we going anywhere? I guess at eleven you are not entitled to the real truth!

Many of my friends have already left. Steffi, my best girlfriend, is leaving for Shanghai in April. My father gave Sam Schlesinger his own work permit so that they could get authorization for entry to China. Steffi's father was in a Concentration Camp and they only let him go with the condition that he would leave Germany by April. Therefore, my father's work authorization was a lifesaver and my parents were happy to be able to help. Sam came back from the Camp a sick, devastated man. His hands were frozen and he looked like a skeleton. If anybody had to leave Germany, it was he. He would have died had they stayed.

My other friend, Irene Blumenfeld, went to America. I wonder why we cannot go to America. I heard it has something to do with quotas and affidavits. You learn a whole new vocabulary these days. I wonder if all this new wisdom will come in handy in the new country, if we ever make it to one.

My friend, Ulli Levy, went to Ecuador, in South America. They had to take Spanish lessons in a hurry. I am thinking: Chile is a neighbor country of Ecuador. Wouldn't it be wonderful if we ended up in Chile and I could visit Ulli in Ecuador? How far can it be, they look pretty close together on the map.

This is what I am mainly doing these days: Thinking, guessing and dreading.

What is to become of us?

ON THE WAY OUT

March 1939

It seems that we will be going to Chile, in South America, after all. Tante Jenny, my Omi's youngest sister, has lived in Chile for several years already. She has now been able to secure an entry visa for the four of us—my mother, my father, Gert and myself.

Oma Feldblum, my great-grandmother, loves to tell stories about her youngest daughter.

"She was seventeen when she eloped. Her father, G-d rest his soul, wanted to die or disown her, but did neither. We hoped it wouldn't last. When she divorced him, we were glad. Then she married Mr. Simke. The family felt like going into hiding. We were so ashamed! Divorced and re-married. How vulgar!"

Tante Jenny sounds like such an adventurous person. I wish I had known her when she was young. She seems to be quite different from the other aunts, who are all old-fashioned and proper.

"Tell me more," I say, "this is so fascinating."

"Well," Oma Feldblum continues, "the only clever thing she did was to leave Germany right after Hitler came to power. Mr. Simke wanted to go to Argentina. His dream was to become a landowner in the Pampa and grow sheep, which he, of course, never achieved. I tell you, Goldkind (child of gold) this man was neither respectable, desirable nor otherwise acceptable. Jenny left him in Argentina and went to Chile to join her son, Rodolfo, who had moved there in 1936. Tante Jenny's older son, Konrad, was in Johannesburg, South Africa, but she was closer emotionally and geographically to Rodolfo, and went to live with him."

And now, this same Tante Jenny, without an undesirable husband, was sending us a visa and saving our lives. She must be really someone special, a gypsy-type maybe? I can't wait to meet her.

Steamer passages to Chile are a little easier to find than tickets to other places. My behind-the-door-snooping has provided this valuable information. Not many people even knew where Chile was, let alone thought of emigrating to a place that had to be a jungle. Were Indians still living there?

My mother bought a book titled *THOUSAND WORDS OF SPANISH*. I looked through it and wondered, do they only have one thousand important words in Spanish, and who can pronounce those words? Hebrew, which I learn in school, seems easier than that.

But at least we have a visa and can buy ship tickets. On the radio, which we are not allowed to have, but which my father has hidden and listens to like everybody else, they constantly talk about **IMMINENT WAR.**

As if we didn't have enough worries already…Secretly, I think that if there were a war, perhaps the Nazis would be too busy to persecute the Jews and would leave us alone. Who can understand all this?

My parents have applied for the "**Jew-Action Inspection.**" The papers have just arrived. This is the official permission to leave the country. It comes with a list attached of what we are allowed to take: One table with four chairs, because we are four in the family, four beds, four sets of knives, spoons and forks. Four of everything; one for each of us. We may take all our old household goods, our clothing and our toys. No silver, jewelry, gold, art or anything valuable.

My mother has been sitting at her typewriter, (which hopefully, she may keep) for many nights, making lists of everything we will take. The "JEW LAW" demands that every single thing has to be listed: Dresses, shoes, socks, underpants, corsets, towels, napkins, handkerchiefs. Everything, everything has to be listed, even brassieres and cotton pads; how embarrassing! My mother's list is over ten pages long. It includes things such as:

- 2 woolen skirts, one long, one short
- 1 tablecloth, hand-stitched, Wedding gift from 1925
- 9 bandages for varicose veins, 5 new, 4 used
- One gray suit with vest, bought in 1937
- 3 wall plates, one chipped, Wedding gift from 1925
- 2 coffee pots, porcelain, gift, purchased 1934
- 1 pair of boys pants, brown, bought in 1938
- 6 pair of silk underpants, women's, purchased in 1938
- 6 pair of men's socks, some darned
- Darning yarn for socks, different colors, new
- 1.65 meter curtain material, unused, bought in 1937

As she types page after page, my mother whispers, "How cruel and barbaric this all is. Only a sadist would think of such a procedure."

I look up "SADIST" in the encyclopedia. It means "Brutal" and "Evil." What have we done to these people? While I am looking up these new words, I think of my Opa, who taught me to look up any new word to enrich my language. He always says, "You can learn more from me than in school." He is so right. I adore him.

Once these papers are filed, a German Officer will come to supervise the packing of the LIFT (a large wooden crate)and our suitcases. My mother says the day the man comes, she doesn't want me or my brother around. I am disappointed. I have my list of dolls with names, and books that I want to take, but I wish I could be there to make sure they pack my favorite doll, Horst, (named for my cousin) really carefully. He is almost the size of a two-year old boy. He'll get crunched on the way anyhow, but I don't want him to break. My Omi, who knows everything, says my mother is right. Children make people nervous and the Nazi inspector won't like Jewish children to begin with. While they are packing our stuff, we will stay in Omi's house. I hope it takes a few days to finish. I love to be at my Omi's.

The worst part of all, is that the visa is for only the four of us. There is no visa for my grandparents yet, and my mother is saying over and over, "I am not leaving without them."

I don't really know what they can do now, but somebody will have a solution to this, I am sure. Grown-ups always come up with a solution.

April 1939

We are ready to leave. What terrible weeks these last ones have been!

We have been staying at Omi's while our things were

being packed in the presence of the German Officer and with all the neighbors curiously watching.

How things have changed! Mrs. Koch, who lives in the apartment next to ours, and used to be friends with my mother, pretends she doesn't know we are leaving. I have seen her open her door, check to see if any of us, or any of the German Officers are nearby, and then hurriedly go down the stairs. Her twin sons, who are my age, are no longer allowed to speak to us. That is a known fact. They belong to the *HITLER-JUGEND (HITLER YOUTH)* and they will be punished if they have any contact with us.

I heard in school that the parents of the Hitler-Jugend are afraid of their children. There are special prizes for those who tell on their parents, and many do, and the parents then disappear suddenly, when they are not even Jewish! The Koch twins, I'm afraid, would rather win points with the Hitler-Jugend than protect their parents. To them, it is an honor to destroy "Enemies of the Reich." That is one of the first lessons they learn.

"Don't blame Mrs. Koch," my mother says, "it's not personal against us. She is just afraid."

It is really, really hard to understand how a mother can be afraid of her children (I can see the other way around), but then so many things are impossible to understand right now.

We are still going to school. What for, I don't know. Half of our class has left, or is about to leave. The teachers themselves are preparing to get out and yet "ORDNUNG MUSS SEIN" (There has to be order). And everybody pretends everything is as it should be.

We have gone to the dentist to get all our teeth fixed (even the ones "just-in-case.") I went to the hospital for a few days and had my tonsils removed. We got all kinds of shots. I am sure some are not necessary, but my parents have explained that we have to take care of everything while there are still Jewish doctors and money available.

I have read in the *Permission to Leave* papers that every Jew is allowed to take only ten Marks with him. That means forty Marks for our entire family. When I think that I get one Mark a week allowance now, what is ten Marks? What are we going to eat? Or is there somebody in Chile who will lend us money? How are we going to leave with only ten Marks each? Perhaps my parents have been able to send some money to Tante Jenny in Chile? The worst part is, I cannot ask anybody. Money matters are never discussed with us children, and even less now that everything is so secret and dangerous.

My mother is so sad and nervous, I don't want to add to her worries. My father, who is thin anyway, has almost disappeared. Not really, but he is so skinny and pale that I don't dare to hurt him with money questions. My Omi, whose visa has not yet arrived, and who will not be leaving with us, how can I ask her something so unimportant as money, when we all know that their lives are in danger? It would be nice and somewhat reassuring to know a little bit more about the money situation, but I guess for now, I am left to worry about that, too.

The other thing that really worries me is the remark about the DOCTORS. Are there no doctors in Chile? People don't get sick? Or do they just lie down and die? Somehow, it doesn't make sense. Tante Jenny and Rodolfo live there, and they must see a doctor now and then. But wouldn't that be a Spanish doctor whom one couldn't talk to? Better not get sick.

Anyway, I can't think about all this at the same time.

***

We leave on April 5, 1939. The day before, my father went

to the German Finance Ministry to turn over all his money, Bank accounts and Savings books. They gave him a receipt. He cried when he filed it with all the other papers. He had made copies of all his documents in case he needed them in Chile.

Only my grandparents come to the train station "ANHALTER BAHNHOF" in Berlin. The other relatives all have come to our house in the last few days to say goodbye. So many tears and hugs and tears again. It has been very, very sad. A few of the families are leaving soon also, to Shanghai, Cuba, Bolivia and other unknown places. The rest of them don't have a visa and cannot leave.

My mother promised them to try to get entry permits for them once we get to Chile.

"Once we are there, it shouldn't be so difficult," she says, "It will all work out. Don't worry."

I can see in my mother's eyes that she is not sure it will all work out, and the others know that, too. But they pretend to "keep their sanity" (words of my Omi).

And all the secrecy these last few weeks...

"Don't talk to anybody about leaving" we were told, "just say goodbye to your teachers, thank them for their unselfish help and wish them luck for the future. Don't discuss anything with anybody. You never know who is listening. G-d forbid, something goes wrong the last minute."

It is just terrible. Now you cannot even trust your best friends? I am almost twelve and so are my friends. We are definitely not babies and <u>know</u> whom to trust. But in these troubled days, we have learned not to question anything.

As long as I live, I will never forget my Omi and Opa's faces as they kissed us good-bye. (In later years, I wondered how they survived those last minutes; they knew in their hearts that they would never see any of us again.)

We are about to board the train. My mother says, so quietly that it scares us, "I am not setting foot on this train without my parents." My father cries, my grandparents beg, we are being pushed onto the train, one more hug, one more kiss, one more look—the train starts moving. We wave and wave and wave and then they are gone....

***

Our destination is Genova, Italy, where we will board the vessel *"VIRGILIO"* which will take us to the Chilean port of Valparaiso. From there, another train ride to Santiago, where the famous Tante Jenny is waiting for us. Although my brother and I are very sad about leaving our Omi and Opa, our cousins and friends, we are also excited and a little scared about the trip. An Italian Luxury Liner! We did not know then that my father had to "promise" the German Government that we would leave no later than April 8th. He had to sign a guarantee against his life in order to get all the necessary permits.

He therefore had to accept whatever tickets were available, and the only ones he could obtain happened to be on a Luxury Liner. Actually, there were only three tickets left, so my brother is traveling as hidden baggage. But instead of the normal capacity of 1750 passengers, the "Virgilio" had booked close to 4000 people for this trip, and my parents assume and hope that nobody will notice one extra, little ten-year old boy.

Of course, we don't show our excitement to my mother or father. They are so preoccupied, nervous and depressed that it doesn't seem right to have any other feelings right now.

"Let's not fight on the trip," Gert says to me. "We don't want to make them mad, O.K.?" It is O.K. with me. Although my brother can be a pain sometimes, I love him, and lately, he also has learned to stay out of the way and not bother anybody. I like him a lot better these days. Maybe by the time we get to Chile, I will like him even more, who knows? But he is a good brother and my friend.

The trip to Italy takes twenty-two hours. Long hours. There are a large number of other emigrants on the train, but there is no conversation or visiting. Everybody stays in their compartment. I guess it is again, the famous secrecy. Not to tell anybody where you are going. Will this ever end? Will I be able to have a loud, open conversation with somebody when I get to Chile? Or will the "eye-rolling" and "finger-on-the-lips: Silence" be our way of communicating in the future? I hope not.

We reach the border between Germany and Italy. A place in the Alps called "<u>Brenner-Pass</u>." My mother whispers to my father, "We are almost out, almost out." But my father shakes his head, "Not yet..not yet."

And just then, we suffer the first of many frightening experiences as emigrants. The train stops in the middle of the night. Nazi Officers come on board and yell orders:

"Everybody out of their seats. Cripples, children, blind or deaf, out of your seats. Present your documents and be ready for body inspection!"

Terrified, we all line up. My father presents our papers (thank heaven they are in order) and is then ordered to remove his clothing. Jacket, shirt, then the pants and underpants. And this in front of all the other passengers on the train. I do think, though, that nobody really cares. We are all too scared to worry about a naked behind. I hope they don't look at me really close. I have my secret, my little bosom. And if any of these Nazi men touches me, I will die on the spot.

There are about thirty officers, almost one for each passenger in our wagon. The one with my father touches him <u>everywhere</u>. I don't look. I am so embarrassed. My mother's face is white with fear and shame, but she just looks ahead as if she doesn't know us. Of course, the officer finds nothing on, or in my father. Now it's my mother's turn. She takes her blouse off and the officer puts his hand in her brassiere. I don't dare look at her. He then sticks his fingers in her ears and nose and says, "You Jew-Women discover holes everywhere when it comes to hiding things. Get dressed. I don't feel like putting my finger in your asshole. You aren't pretty enough!"

I can't believe they would say things like that in front of ladies and children, but I guess as an "emigrant" I will have to get used to many new, terrible ways.

Finally, four hours later, they are finished. They took some people off the train, and they haven't come back yet. Now the Italian Gendarmes come on the train. Although we don't understand their language, they are at least a little friendlier than the Germans. They check our passports, visas, exit and entry permits, and after another two hours of waiting, the train moves forward again.

We are now in Italy. The minute the Italian border officials leave the train, my mother collapses. The lady in front of us, now that Germany is behind us, comes over and brings mother a cup of tea and gives her some kind of pill.

"We are out now, Schatzi ("Treasure"—my parents' name for each other.) "We are out, out...no more Germany," my father says to my mother. And then he whispers (but I hear him), "Look at the children. They are frightened."

My mother now smiles that sad, half-crying smile that I

will see on her face until the day she dies, "Oh, ja, we are out, away from everything and everybody."

Then she tells us, "Try to go to sleep. We still have hours of travel before us."

But who can sleep? I am scared, sad and (secretly) excited.

***

CROSSING THE OCEAN

April 6, 1939

We have just arrived in Genoa, Italy, and will be boarding the ship "Virgilio" on the eighth of this month. My brother and I had fantasized about our Italian holiday, but it doesn't look as if this is going to be much fun. Hundreds of emigrants—young people, old people, families with children, grandparents and babies—are milling around at the dock looking at the ship, checking to see if their suitcases and other belongings are being taken aboard. Everybody is nervous, nobody speaks Italian. All we hear is German, although it is not the same accent we are used to. There are people from the south of Germany, from Austria, from Czechoslovakia, and although they speak German, it sounds different. The language is the same, but the inflections and accents are specific to certain areas.

We are staying in a penzione near the docks. Most of the other travelers are living there also, or in similar places nearby. It seems to me that all of them want to watch the ship, to make sure it doesn't disappear or leave without us. Besides, a penzione is cheaper than a hotel, and since we are only allowed to take ten Deutsche Mark per person out of Germany, (the equivalent of about fifteen/twenty dollars per person), everybody is counting pennies. We buy bread and cheese for lunch and dinner. It's O.K. Once we get on the ship, we will eat really good food, my mother says. Since only first-class tickets were available for this trip, we will travel in luxury. My father says that the <u>luxury</u> is the fact that we are on a ship leaving Germany, never mind the food or accommodations.

I am not sure if I will ever be able to travel to Italy again in my life, and wish we could have looked around a little and gotten to know some Italians. It is so amazing. Even the little kids speak Italian, and I wish I could, too. But we cannot communicate with them. I am very worried. How is this going to work in Chile, where everybody speaks Spanish? Who are we going to talk to, and how are we going to become part of a new society without knowing anything about it. Not the language, nor the background, nor the people?

The shame is that in the last few years in Jewish school, they had no time to teach us history of South American countries—or any other country for that matter. Our teachers were concerned with preparing us for the "hard future that awaits us." We learned English, French and Hebrew, in case we decided to go to Palestine; typing, shorthand, math, cooking, housekeeping, philosophy, geography and the history of the Jews. We were being readied for a life that demanded logical thinking, hard work and practicality. There was no time for frivolous subjects in our schools. And we are only eleven years old!

Of course, our parents and the parents of the other kids do not allow us to walk around Genoa alone. First of all, we can be spotted from far away as foreigners, with our new clothes, shoes and coats. They were bought two sizes too large for us so we could grow into them "when we won't have any money to buy new things." None of the Italian children in Genoa wear new clothes, shoes or hats. Perhaps on Sundays, they wear nice clothes to church, but not every day! Also, a lot of us are blond and blue-eyed, and really stick out among the dark-haired Italian kids.

The Jewish organizations in Berlin had warned our parents to try not to be noticed in the countries that we had to cross. I can't understand how hundreds and hundred of people, all in one area, all looking panicky and fearful, can remain unnoticed…Therefore, we stay close to our parents.

I like hanging around the grown-ups because I get to hear things. My brother, who is nine-and-a half, also wants to know what is happening, but doesn't have the patience to listen. He doesn't pay attention. I do. Even if my mother speaks in French to my father, so that we don't understand, I know enough French from school to get the idea. I feel very bad. I know eavesdropping is not nice, but a person under these circumstances must know what is going on. It is so unsettling otherwise and, perhaps by listening to other people's conversations, I can give my mother or father a new idea that they had not thought of in all this commotion. I stay without complaining and listen. Most of the conversations are about money (or the lack of it), about transfers of capital, which my grandfather talked about a lot before we left, about jobs in Chile, and how people were planning to go about finding them, and other information.

The three days in Genoa go by very fast, and on April 8th, we board the ship. Even with the nerves, the tears and the commotion, this is the most exciting, and yet fearful, event I have ever experienced. Only that it is an adventure whose end nobody knows. It is a voyage into our new world, a world without relatives, without friends, without money, without security. But, as my father keeps saying, "We are out, that's the only thing that matters, and we must be grateful for this chance to escape." My mother, having left her parents behind, doesn't feel that way. I know. I see her cry and hear her talk to the other women about her doubts:

"It is so terrible to be torn between your children and your parents," she says, "Why couldn't we get out together?"

On the train platform in Berlin, when we said good-by to my grandparents, my mother swore that as soon as we arrived in Chile, she would get the visas for them "before I put a morsel of food in my mouth." I know that she didn't mean this literally, but I pray that we see my Omi and Opa again soon. It is lonely and sad without them!

Our cabin is so small that two of us have to sit on the beds while the other two get dressed or undressed. All four of us cannot stand at the same time. There are three beds. A cabin for three was the last one my father could get. Gert is traveling as a *Stow Away*. He has to sleep on two chairs put together. But he is small and skinny, and will be fine on the chairs. I have a bed of my own, but I don't brag about it. I don't want to hurt my little brother's feelings!

There are seven hundred people in first class, fifteen hundred in second class, which is equipped for one thousand, and two thousand in third class, which normally holds twelve hundred passengers. There are people everywhere.

The "Virgilio" is an Italian vessel, and I thought that it was impressive that they accommodated that many people. From what I hear, though, the owners of the vessel have made a lot of extra money by taking advantage of the desperate situation of the Jews trying to leave Europe. With the rumors of a war starting, people have booked passage wherever they could.

Many diplomats are also on the ship, leaving Europe and heading back to South America. The Chilean Consul in Rome is traveling with us, and so is the Commercial Attaché of the Embassy of Argentina in Vienna. Both of these men have children our age, and my brother and I are trying to talk to them in Spanish. I wish they would teach us, but all they do is make fun of us. They try to trick us by sending us to the headwaiter to ask for something, supposedly in Spanish, which turns out to be a dirty word. I can tell by the looks they give each other, that they are trying to get us in trouble. So before we fall into their trap, we tell them that we will try the sentence on their fathers first to see if our pronunciation is right, and their panic confirms my suspicions. So much for learning Spanish. We will have to wait until we get to Chile and to school, to properly learn the language, swear words and all.

The dining room is magnificent. Crystal chandeliers, beautiful table linens and dishes, silverware, flower arrangements and decorations. The food is absolutely divine. The whole trip could be so beautiful, if it weren't because it is not really a trip. It is an *emigration* and we cannot forget it. I see it in the sad and worried faces of all the grownups, in the tense conversations among the men, the whispers among the women. I worry again: what is to become of us? Will anybody ever laugh again?

There is a lady in the cabin next to ours. She is a grown-up, but not really. She travels with her mother, but she has no husband or children. I bet she is at least twenty-five years old, which makes her more my age than my mother's. Mami is thirty-eight. Milly, that's her name, has become my best friend. I can ask her anything, and she tells me the truth. Since she isn't my mother or a relative, she can afford to be honest. Milly tells me to enjoy the trip as much as I can, and not to worry about what is going to happen.

"Worry or not," she says, "It's going to happen anyway." I believe her and try to make the best of the days on the ship.

The very best is dinnertime. Waiters in uniform with white gloves serve at the tables. They even treat us children as regular people.

"Signorina, (that's **me**!) what is your pleasure tonight?" Nobody has spoken to me this way before. My parents, grandparents, aunts and uncles call me by my nickname "Mulli"—and the teachers in school harshly pronounce your first name until you are fifteen, and then they call you "Miss" and your last name. Of course, I never made it to "Miss." I left school before reaching this elegant milestone.

I wish I could show my classmates this aristocrat of a waiter, and have them listen to him addressing me as "Signorina." But that's not to be, so I enjoy it by myself.

After dinner, and instead of dessert, which is served an hour later in a separate, beautifully furnished salon, they always bring a tray with the most delicious cheeses. All you do is point at one or two kinds, and then begins the ritual: The waiter nods with an elegant shift of his head to the side, which indicates that he knows your preference. He then uses a silver cheese cutter and slices a large piece, which he picks up with a filigree spoon. He serves the cheeses with crackers on a crystal plate. At home, we only ate cheese in a sandwich, a thin slice between large slices of black or brown bread, or pumpernickel. It wasn't that there was ever a shortage of food for us, but "frugality and good manners" (my grandmother's favorite words) didn't allow us to pile up cheese in a sandwich. For workers, who did physical labor and needed extra nourishment, it was acceptable, but "nice people don't stuff themselves."

The cheese I like the best is called Bel-Baiese. It is creamy and tastes of almonds. I tell my brother to eat as much as possible. Who knows when we will get such a treat again? Maybe they don't have cheese in Chile.

Most of the people sit on deck chairs, day in and day out, with their Spanish-German dictionaries and a book by a man named Sauer, called "One Thousand Indispensable Words of Spanish" and practice their new language. They form little groups and study together. I listen to some of them and cannot believe what I hear. The first lesson in the book is, "The sword is unsheathed." The next sentence is, "The lily is white." What on earth are we going to do with such phrasing? What kind of living will our parents be able to make with such knowledge? Who invented this method of teaching for "Emigrants with urgent need for the knowledge of Spanish," which is what the foreword of the book says? I decide to forget it. I will learn Spanish when we get to Chile. At this point, it just seems another reason to worry.

My brother and I, and the children of the Consuls, spend time together. We play cards, and try to learn some Spanish from them, but mostly they laugh at us. We walk around the ship, discover every corner, and since our new friends can talk to the officers, (some of whom speak German) we learn a lot about the workings of this "swimming hotel."

I also watch some of the babies to give the mothers some time to relax. I **love** babies!

Mainly, we stay close to our parents and talk about the family left behind, or make plans for our life in Chile without the faintest idea of what to expect.

We cross the Straits of Gibraltar, and are then out to sea for sixteen days, without seeing anything but water. The total crossing time from Genoa to Chile takes 28 days, a long, long time.

Since my Opa (grandfather) and I have studied five new words every day from his encyclopedia, ever since my seventh birthday, and up to the day we left Berlin, I have a "rich vocabulary for my age," which is what my teacher wrote on my last report card. For the trip, my Opa gave me my very own encyclopedia, and also a World Atlas, so that we can follow the route that we are taking to South America. He emphatically told me to make notes so that I can tell him all the details when we see each other again. I am keeping a diary of everything that happens (which is not that much), everything we eat (which is very much), and any important thoughts that cross my mind. This way, I am sharing the voyage with my grandparents without forgetting any details.

Although we have strict orders not to leave the first class deck, Milly takes me down to the third class. Only then do I realize how lucky we are. They are crowded down there like sardines. There are no individual cabins, only large dormitories with hundreds of cots in them. Their dining room looks like a barn, with picnic tables, and I am sure they do not get served Bel-Baiese cheese by waiters in uniform. Cramped or not, our cabin is a palace compared to these accommodations.

The people in third class are not officially allowed "upstairs." They are, like all others, educated and elegant, and only ended up in third class because those were the only tickets available. They come to visit us in first class and blend in perfectly. At least they can spend their days in decent surroundings, and friendships develop with promises to "get together" once we arrive in Chile.

One lady, Mrs. Moses, has a little baby boy nine months old. I bring him up from third class every day to watch him. I heard some of the women talk about how Mrs. Moses delivered her baby son by herself in her house, hidden away. In Berlin, since 1936, Jews have not been allowed to have babies, and no doctor would come and help. The Jewish doctors have been forbidden to practice, and the German doctors would rather kill the mother and the baby before assisting a Jewish woman in giving birth to another "Jew swine," which is what we were called.

After sixteen days, we reach the port of La Guaira, in Venezuela, but are not allowed to get off the ship. The place looks ugly and dirty anyway, and we are only here for a day to take supplies. A day or two later, we stop at Cartagena, in Colombia, which looks just as dirty and unpleasant. Nobody is allowed off the ship, but nobody minds. This is not exactly a tourist place to visit.

Two days later, we reach the Panama Canal, one of the technical wonders of the world. It connects the Atlantic and Pacific Oceans. Ships can only cross through locks.

Engines installed on the ground pull them up through four different water levels. The vessel is lifted and dropped hundreds of feet of water, to make up for the different levels of water between the Atlantic and Pacific Oceans. This is such an experience that all the passengers on the ship, including the children, are allowed to stay up all night to watch. Normally, bedtime is ten o'clock for the children, and midnight for the grown-ups.

Our next stop is Cristobal Colon, in Panama. We are allowed off the ship and are greeted by "Uncle" Herman Hirsch, a good friend of my parents who emigrated to Panama a few months earlier with his wife and two daughters. They are so happy to see us that I forget how hot and humid it is. The Hirschs live in a little house. "It is not Berlin," Aunt Hirsch says, "but it is OUT." "OUT" represents escape, freedom, apprehension and uncertainty. It is constantly used by all the grownups. Even Milly sometimes uses it to describe our new life.

The Hirschs take us around the city. Most people wear white. White shirts, pants, shoes and hats, Panama hats. Uncle Hirsch buys a Panama hat for my father, who does not want to accept it. Uncle Hirsch tells him he can "well afford it." My mother looks very sad. The Hirschs owned an elegant dress shop in the center of Berlin, and are now working in a clothing factory, he as a presser, she as a seamstress.

"Well afford it?" my mother says, shaking her head, "what did we do to deserve this?" But then she looks at me and says "Remember, there is no shame in decent work. Don't ever beg or demand or expect others to take care of you. Work diligently at any task that is given to you, and you will do all right." And then she smiles her sad little smile and says, "Don't forget, as long as your father and I are here, you and Gert will always be provided for." But I am glad. If I can share her pain by letting her talk to me like this, at least I am taking my place in these "new circumstances."

Rita, the Hirschs' older daughter, tells me that her mother also shares her worries with her. Not like in Berlin, where things were normal, and they would send us out of the room whenever something serious was being discussed. These are the benefits of getting older, I explain to my brother.

We say goodbye to the Hirschs in the evening and go back to our ship, sad and happy at the same time. My mother tells me that the Hirschs are trying to get into the United States and are looking at Colon as a temporary stay. Perhaps we will meet again sometime. It doesn't seem likely, since we are going to the south of the continent, while they are now in the middle, waiting to go north.

Our next stop, a few days later, is Buenaventura, Colombia. There, it really hits us. If this is South America, we will never survive.

We are allowed off the ship, but don't dare to go very far into the city, if this is what you can call it. The filth and foul smell are unbelievable. Dirty, naked children, covered with eczema run everywhere, begging and grabbing us by the sleeves or our skirts. They are dark-skinned, with beautiful black eyes and would be cute if they were cleaned up. But the grown-ups look the same. Most of them have no teeth, are barefoot, and what they wear are rags. They are all filthy, and some of them go to the bathroom in the middle of the street. They don't have any underwear on, so our parents hurry us out of the port area, hoping that in the center of the city, life is more civilized. But it isn't. Dirty laundry hangs out of windows on cords strung across the street from one house to another. Street vendors peddle food that not even an animal without sense of smell would touch. Everything is dirty. The streets are either not paved at all, or paved here and there with cobblestones. Dog and human shit is everywhere, and we have a hard time walking through this mess.

Back on the ship, the grownups huddle in circles to comfort each other. The first glance of South America is certainly not what they expected, but "for the children's sake..." I listen to the conversation and think to myself, "For the sake of the children...what?" Would they swim back to Europe if they didn't have us children to take to the new world? It is so hard to understand grownups. Sure, if Chile is anything like this Buenaventura, it's not going to be a place where I would like to live either, but in the meantime, we are on the ocean and can only go forward.

The son of the Chilean Consul is such a good-looking boy, and his parents are so elegant, I am sure their home in Chile is nothing like Buenaventura. Milly agrees with me. She has had time to study the South American countries before she got on the ship. Like all Jews, she had lost her job. She had been the assistant of one of the famous architects in Berlin, and had planned on continuing her studies. Because she is Jewish, however, no school would allow her to register, so she spent her time waiting for the Chilean visa by reading as many books as she could about South America. And she knows a lot. "Chile is not like Buenaventura," she explains to the other ladies. "It is more modern and quite civilized from what I have read."

Of course, many of the emigrants don't believe her. "She is just trying to make us feel better," or, "What does she know? She isn't even married." I personally don't know what being married has to do with knowing anything about Chile, but I already have a reputation for being a big-mouth, I better not give my opinion. Everybody is upset enough, why make it worse?

From Buenaventura, we go to Guayaquil, in Ecuador. It looks a tiny bit better than Buenaventura, but not much, and you can feel the anxiety among the travelers on the ship.

While we were on the water for sixteen days, some of the men even told jokes, but now there is an eerie silence most of the time, and if it weren't for the wonderful food and the elegant waiters, I would be <u>really</u> worried. But Milly and I discuss the situation, and have come to the conclusion that at this point, there is absolutely nothing anybody can do but wait and hope. I talk to my mother about this, and she shakes her head.

"The things you have to worry and talk about are not matters that a child of eleven should even know about. You are much too old for your age." That's another mystery. How can I be too old for eleven, when I am eleven? I will be twelve next month, but I don't feel too old for twelve either. Who can answer all this....?

Our next stop is the port of Callao, Peru. We are only there for a few hours, but everybody leaves the ship to check out yet another "new world port." Callao is a pleasant surprise. It is clean and looks more hospitable than the Central American ports. People are also mostly dark-skinned, Indian looking, but they are dressed, the children look well-nourished and there is none of the utter poverty that we saw in the Central American towns. Next day, we stop in Mollendo, also in Peru, where we only stay for half a day and do not venture far from the ship.

And then comes Chile. The most northern part is Arica, which borders with Peru, and where the ship does not stop. Instead, we land in Antofagasta the next day, one port further south, and the last one before Valparaiso, our final destination. We are not allowed to disembark in Antofagasta. Of course, I ask "why not?" They explain to us that because the Chilean entry visas were given for certain regions in the country, everybody has to disembark and "immigrate" to Chile through Valparaiso. From there, we all go to the cities that have been assigned to us. We are bound for Santiago, the capital. Best choice!

I am getting very anxious, and not even my conversations with Milly take the apprehension away. I have stopped eating Bel-Baiese cheese after lunch and dinner, and that is a sign of utmost worry.

SANTIAGO DE CHILE

May 8, 1939

The SS "Virgilio" that brought us over from Italy landed this morning at the Chilean port of Valparaiso, the entrance door to our new life.

Everybody is standing at the railing, children in first row, and wonder how the small tugboats that surround our ship can pull it to the dock.

Down below, hundreds of people are waiting for the ship to land.

I ask who they are, and am told that these are relatives of the passengers, representatives of Jewish organizations, and police. There is an enormous number of curious Chileans who normally don't see such a big ship spit out wave after wave of strangers onto the Valparaiso shores. It is taking several hours for the immigration officials to check our entry visas and match us up with our respective relatives or sponsors. Health authorities board the ship to check the X-rays that everyone had to hold in their hands. And all the while, we are supposed to stay together on the deck in lines, like in school. For us kids, this is nothing new, and our parents have just lived through the terrifying lessons in "lining up" during the last months in Berlin for identification by the Gestapo, to get passports, visas and exit permits. So standing in orderly lines is something we all know very well.

I am concerned. All the parents look anxious and preoccupied. But the only ones I care about are my father and mother. Everybody wished us a "safe trip" when we left Germany, and we did get here safely. But now what is going to happen? This is our new world, new and scary. I feel as if I swallowed a bunch of ants, everything is crawling inside me, but I don't say anything. I close my eyes and try to imagine my aunt Jenny, who is waiting down there, and whom we will finally meet in person. To me, she is our lifesaver.

My great grandmother, Oma Feldblum, had told me all about her but I can't wait to hear her story from herself. Having been called "the black sheep" and "meshugge" (nutty) after sending us the visa, she progressed to being a "clairvoyant," a "genius" and "the only member of the family with a vision" for leaving Germany in 1934. I have heard these stories about Tante Jenny and her sons, partly when they were told to me, and partly when I listened in on conversations at family gatherings.

I am also curious to meet Rodolfo. That he was able and willing to put up an affidavit for the four of us is almost a miracle. He must be an angel to assume such a responsibility. I am sure he does not have to support any of us; my parents for sure will find work, but he will have to put up with us in his house and help us settle. Since our parents were not allowed to take any money out of Germany, Rodolfo's action is nothing less than saving four lives. I just hope he turns out to be as nice as he seems to be good!

***

We have been waiting for almost five hours, but finally the lines are thinning, and we are now the first at the railing and look for our relatives. It is a little difficult to try to find a face in this sea of human bodies. We don't know exactly what Tante Jenny looks like. But once again, our Tante comes through. For generations, our family has had a "**family whistle.**" It was invented by one of our great-grandfathers, who was an opera fan, and constantly whistled opera tunes. One of the bars was adopted by the family as **our whistle,** and it proved very useful to identify members of the family in parks, theaters or other crowded places.

True to tradition, and from high above on the ships deck, my father now whistles <u>our</u> tune. Over and over again. Until all of a sudden there is a faint whistle from below, and arms wave in our direction. The little lady, jumping up and down, hat in hand, her arms opening and closing as if to embrace us from the distance—has to be Tante Jenny. The whistling has stopped. Both my father and mother are crying, "There she is…our family…look at her…our "Godsend!" We can see Tante Jenny wiping her face with a handkerchief.

"I wonder where Rodolfo is," whispers my mother, the perennial Jewish worrier. "I hope nothing happened to him."

"Of course nothing happened to him. He must be working. We have cost him enough already, and he needs to be careful with his job."

My dear father always, always tries to reassure my mother and us when something is out of order. He has his worries classified by importance. Perhaps Rodolfo's not being there is a number three on his worry-list.

"We will see him soon enough. Don't get upset." And he gives my mother a little kiss on the cheek.

Gert and I wave and wave. We can see Tante Jenny shaking her head, as if she can't believe it is really us. What a moment!

One family at a time, we are allowed to disembark. Our papers have been found in order and we are given a number to claim our luggage from the Customs area.

Meanwhile, Tante Jenny has made her way to the bottom of the ship's stairway, and as we reach the ground, she just stands there, incredulous, still as a statue. A small woman, in her mid-fiftieth, with curly grayish/white hair, a round, doll-like face, and the most amazing blue dancing eyes that now are filling with tears.

"Let me look at you...Oh G-d, it can't be...Come here, come here, let me touch you." Tante Jenny laughs and cries at the same time. I look at my mother. Her eyes say it all, happiness for being here, gratitude to Tante Jenny for her sacrifice, and pain, heart-breaking pain, for not being able to embrace her own mother instead of her aunt, and guilt for having left her parents behind.

The customs area is, as expected, a zoo. There are over two thousand of us waiting to pick up our belongings, visiting with relatives or being interviewed by Jewish organizations. They tried to keep all of us children together in one area, but that didn't work.

"Marion, Gert, Susi, Hanna, Thomas...stay with us. Don't move away from here. Watch your new coat. You don't speak Spanish, don't get lost. We will never find you...we didn't come all the way from Germany to lose you in South America!"

All the parents are worried that in the confusion, they might pick up the wrong child. And then what? Obediently, we don't go far, say good-bye to our passenger friends and try to stay out of trouble. My friend, Milly, gives me a big hug and promises to look us up once we are settled. I give her Tante Jenny's last name, so she can find us. I don't know if there are telephones in Santiago or if Rodolfo has one.

But I can't worry about that right now. There are much more important questions to think about now that we left the safety of the ship, the wonderful food and our German-speaking world. Just hearing Spanish all around us, and observing the gesturing and hand signs in a language totally foreign to us, is frightening. I keep thinking how anxious my parents must feel. Nothing is normal for us. We are among strangers, and our only support is this little sweet lady, Jenny, who speaks Spanish as if she were born to it. (Later, we find out that her language is her own personal version of Spanish-German that she invented, but that allows her to survive in this Spanish world.)

By now, it is late afternoon. In all the excitement we forgot that we have not had lunch today, but nobody is really hungry. It proves my Opa's axiom, "What the brain does not think, the body does not feel." No sense complaining to our parents, so I tell Gert to keep his brain somehow occupied, and hope that he understands what I mean. He wasn't included in the philosophical conversations between my grandfather and myself. He was too young, so I can't expect too much.

Hungry or not, we and our luggage are being packed—and I mean packed—into buses that will take us to the railroad station, and from there by train to Santiago, the capital and our final destination.

If the port was a zoo, the train station is a circus. There must be more than a hundred people on the platform, dressed in dirty clothes, most of them barefoot, kids hanging on to them, carrying packages with live animals and bundles wrapped in newspaper. We are told that those are the "campesinos" (farm workers) going to their jobs on the fields south of Santiago.

Vendors with pushcarts are selling what must be food, since people are buying the stuff and putting it in their mouths.

"Dulces Chilenos, ricos, baratos, senorita, solo un peso..."

I have learned that "dulce" is sweet, "Chileno" is national, "rico" is rich and "barato" is cheap. But even if the offer doesn't make sense to us, the look of the food and the filthy wagon is definitely not inviting. We just shake our heads "no." And all the while the buses keep unloading our people and luggage, and the station is getting too small for this avalanche.

"Sit on the suitcases and don't let anybody take you or the bags," we are told.

I guess by now, our poor parents don't realize what they are saying. But we obediently sit on the suitcases and avoid eye contact with any Chilean-looking person, so as not to be stolen. It is quite embarrassing the way we stick out, nicely dressed, with shoes, gloves and hats.

I spot my friend Milly in the crowd. What a relief!

"Milly, is this what all Chileans look like? Are they all this poor?"

Again, my worry-bug bites me. "How are we going to live among them, when we look like princesses and kings compared to them? Or is Santiago different? Are there other Europeans in this country?"

I can't ask questions quickly enough. Milly might disappear any minute, and then there won't be anybody who will tell me the truth. Milly studied "Life in South America," and if she doesn't know, nobody does. I can't ask Tante Jenny either. First of all, she is busy running around and talking Spanish about the tickets and seats; and then, why would I bother her with these doubts, when she and Rodolfo have been living in Santiago for a few years already. And if they have been able to manage, so will we. There must be a different sort of Chilean people somewhere else. I sure don't want to appear ungrateful or arrogant. If anything, our Jewish teachers "vaccinated" us with feelings of gratitude for being alive, with sayings such as, "Arrogance always comes to a fall" and, "The obligation of a Jew in these times is to be humble, modest and grateful." One day, when "these times" are gone, perhaps we will be allowed to be proud and arrogant like other people.

Milly says, "No, no, no, not all Chilean people are like this. These here are farm workers or country folks who go to the big city to sell their wares. In Santiago, people dress like we do. Just don't worry and wait. Everything will work out fine."

I hope so, I sure hope so.

Finally, the train arrives; everything gets loaded—parents, children and luggage—and we are on our way to Santiago.

It is dark now; we are tired and hungry, but too excited to sleep. Tante Jenny and my parents try to talk, but there is such a noise in the compartment that I can't hear very clearly. Tante Jenny is asking about my Omi, her other sisters, the situation in Germany, friends, money and other vital points. But I can hear only sprinkles of words: Nazis…concentration camp…visas… illegal transports over the border…black money…suicide, words that, even without sentences, mean so much. This is not good. These are the times when I need information the most! First thing I will have to do when we arrive in Santiago, is to work on sharpening my hearing. I promised my grandparents that I would keep them informed of everything. But how can I, if I only hear drops of conversations?

The train ride takes four long hours. We are hot and exhausted, but we are not complaining. Tante Jenny has already said to my mother something that sounded like "wonderful children," and I tell my brother not to ruin her good opinion. Once she gets to know us better, she will find out for herself that we are not <u>that</u> perfect.

"En diez minutes, Santiago—solo diez minutos mas." The voice comes from somewhere in the darkness, but who cares. "Diez minutos" is easy to understand. Ten more minutes to Santiago! We are here!

The HICEM (Jewish Organization of Assistance to Immigrants) has reserved rooms for us in a boarding house in the center of Santiago, where we will stay until we find a place to live. A taxi is now taking us to Calle Monjitas 790, our first address in the new life.

There is Rodolfo. He greets us with hugs and kisses, which I think is very nice, considering that he is not used to children, and that we represent an intrusion into his up-to-now regulated life. He speaks very fast, German mixed with Spanish—which I think is a little bit show-offy—and I keep remembering my mother's warning: BEHAVE, PLEASE BEHAVE. So I give him a big embrace and tell him how wonderful it is to meet him. Which is the truth!

They take us to our room. It is night and therefore dark, so we cannot see much, but what we can see is not exactly inviting. The house is a Colonial-Spanish building, with a rectangular center patio in the middle. The rooms are located on all four sides of the courtyard. They are interior rooms without windows. Once you close the door behind you, it's like being in a cellar. No air, no light. Fortunately, my loving Opa had taught me to keep a "positive outlook" so I remember that "nothing bad lasts forever."

But positive or not, my outlook is rapidly declining. This is not at all how I had envisioned Santiago. But, once again, my Omi's voice echoes through my mind. "You are now almost an adult and your parents are counting on you." I really don't want to be an adult at twelve, but this is not the time to rebel. I am supposed to set a good example for my brother, and I promised my Omi and Opa that I would.

The "chandelier" in the room consists of a single light bulb. There are four beds, a table and three chairs. One of us, (I am looking at my brother) will have to sit on the bed.

The landlady brings us tea and a plate with cookies. Tante Jenny and Rodolfo wait until we bring our suitcases in and then leave. They live in an apartment, not far away, and will come back in the morning. We are too tired to undress, and fall asleep on top of the beds. This turns out to be a blessing.

The next night, when opening the beds made with clean, nice sheets, we see little black animals hopping around, which are definitely of South American origin. We had never seen anything like it in Berlin. The landlady bursts into a roar of laughter at our disgusted faces. She calls a neighbor who speaks German. "These are fleas, innocent little fleas, they don't harm anybody. They just bite. Never seen a flea before?" We hadn't. And to call them "innocent" is also an exaggeration. We are covered with fleabites the next day, and the itching does nothing to make our stay more comfortable.

"You will learn how to squeeze them between your fingers," we are told, but the thought of even touching these pesty little things makes me sick. I check my encyclopedia and find that fleas can transmit typhus and other illnesses. That's all we need right now! I decide, however, to worry about fleas and typhus at some later date.

Tante Jenny and Rodolfo come the next day with food, and we have a family meeting. For the first time in my almost twelve years, my brother and I are allowed to stay in the room. Even Gert isn't sent to play outside. There is no outside!

They decide that Rodolfo will look for a small house away from downtown Santiago, and we will all move in together, until our container with household goods arrives and my parents can get organized and look for work. In the meantime, they have to get in touch with the HICEM and their offices are downtown. This way, we can all walk and save on streetcar fare.

We go out during the day, my parents deal with the HICEM, and then we look around downtown. Although we do not venture too far away from the residence, we get an idea of the city and the people. Milly was right. This city is modern and the people look the same as in Berlin, except they are "browner" than we, and gesture with their hands while they speak. They are medium-well dressed and smile a lot. The women are quite pretty.

Lunch and dinner are included in the rent price at the residence, and although we have been warned not to eat anything uncooked, we are not suffering from hunger. A lot of the food we don't eat because we don't know what it is, but Rodolfo eats with us most evenings and that helps. When they serve a fruit that looks like a pear cut in half filled with oil, we refuse.

"This is called "Palta" (Avocado) and is very good. You smash it with your fork,mix the oil in, and then spread it on bread."

Even Rodolfo's explanation does not help. We just cannot swallow this. "You will get used to it," he says. Perhaps?

On the third night, we are awakened by a strange noise. It sounds like water dripping. It is. It has started to rain and the water is coming down through the roof, right on top of my father's and Gert's beds. Fortunately, in our luggage we had packed umbrellas, which in Europe are used **outside**, and now sleep with open umbrellas for the rest of the time in the residence. Between the water and the fleas, our nights are quite entertaining!

My twelfth birthday is on May 22. We are still in the residence, but have found a house and will be moving in a day or so. With tears in her eyes, my mother hugs me and gives me my birthday present, <u>a bag of peanuts</u>.

I understand, and tell her that we got so many new things before we left Berlin and gifts from the family, that I never expected anything. But she shakes her head over and over and sobs, "This is your youth? You deserve so much more. What have we done to you children?"

My father kisses me and looks at Mami. He says in his sweet, quiet way, "What we have done to them is save their lives, that's what we have done. One day they will understand."

I understand very well, and save the peanuts for when we get into the house.

FINALLY SETTLED—SANTIAGO-NUNOA

Santiago, May 1939

We have been living in the Residence in downtown Santiago for two weeks now. It's a good thing that I am blessed with more curiosity than most people. I hear things I should not, according to my father, and this saves me from having to ask or guess. It is most important to find out exactly what is going on at all times!

By snooping around, I learn that the CISROCO (Jewish Aid Society) is lending a small amount of money to all immigrants who need it to get settled, which is mostly everyone, since we all came without money. My parents also have received help to find a place to live. They also got a loan of one hundred dollars for my mother to buy a used sewing machine, to start working by taking in alterations. Of course, these loans have to be repaid so that future immigrants can also profit from this assistance.

Tante Jenny and Rodolfo gave up their apartment in downtown Santiago. Until my parents can find work, we will all have to live together to economize on expenses. We found this house in the district of Nunoa, Calle San Gregorio, where the schools are better than in the city. It is not a big house but it can accommodate all six of us, Tante Jenny, Rodolfo, and the four of us.

It is built in the Spanish style, a bungalow with an open circular center patio, light and cheerful. The courtyard is surrounded by a glass-covered galleria, which leads into four rooms, two on each side. Three are bedrooms, one is a dining room. In one corner is a passage that leads into the kitchen. The bathroom is located in the opposite corner. It has no window and opens onto the galleria. Rodolfo and Tante Jenny each get a bedroom, my parents have the other one, and Gert and I get to sleep in an alcove next to the kitchen, which in better times was perhaps a pantry. We each have a cot and a box in between, which serves as a nightstand and armoire. There is no room for anything else, but Tante Jenny borrows some nice blankets from a friend to add a nice touch. Gert is small anyway, so for him, there is more than enough room on the cot. I better not get much bigger—I might fall off. But we have promised not to complain and we don't.

The kitchen is old and ugly, but I was told that since I wasn't expected to cook, I should keep my mouth shut. If only the stove weren't so disgustingly dirty and old. It is Gert's duty and mine to wash the dishes and clean the kitchen, and all the grease and grime makes us gag.

"Be grateful to Rodolfo and Tante Jenny for all they are doing for us," says my mother. "This is a very small sacrifice that is being asked from you." So "gratefully," Gert and I clean and hate it.

My mother keeps apologizing to Rodolfo for being such a burden on him and bringing such turmoil into his life, but Rodolfo assures her that he was glad he could help and asks would she not have done the same for somebody else in the family. Besides, he goes to work early in the morning and does not return until the evening, so he does not face the everyday presence of two children.

I know that my mother's mind is constantly on Berlin and her parents. I try not to fight with my brother and not to talk back to my parents, but it is hard to be good all the time. I am not exactly happy myself. I miss my friends, my relatives, our normal life. But I make an effort to be pleasant and obedient. Things have to get better!

We now need to find a school. Rodolfo doesn't know much about children and less about schools.

"He did enough by putting up the guarantee for our visa," I hear my father saying. "He should certainly not have to worry about school for our children. We can find out by ourselves."

I keep thinking that yes, somebody should worry about our school. We have already had an unintended six-week vacation. We need to learn Spanish and keep up with our arithmetic and other subjects. We certainly don't want to become illiterates! I just wish I could discuss all this with a friend, but there isn't anybody…

I like Tante Jenny a lot. She laughs a lot, is always running instead of walking, knows half the population of Santiago and everything that goes on. At least, it seems so. She chatters in Spanish, and we admire her for it. Rodolfo calls her language Span-German. He says that all she does is add an "a" or an "o" to the German words, mixes in a few Spanish expressions and thinks she is fluent in Spanish. We can't judge, but she sounds very efficient and gets around. Wherever we go, we meet a "friend" of hers. Most of her friends are immigrants, but since she and Rodolfo have been in Santiago for several years already, they are considered natives.

Gert and I are a little afraid of Rodolfo. We are supposed to be model children whenever he is around, and that can get difficult. Tante Jenny never criticizes us, at least not to our faces. She seems to feel sorry for us, which is good and makes life easier for my brother and myself. It is absolutely impossible to be perfect all the time!

All of Rodolfo's friends are bachelors, and they admire him for putting up with us. The nicest of his friends is Gerhard Langer, who visits often, and always takes time to talk to us, although he also shakes his head when we run through the house.

The next priority is to enroll us in school. We are, by now, eager to go back to a regular schedule and get out of the house. Going to school will keep us from "living like wild animals," in the opinion of my parents.

Asking around, they found the perfect place for us. They enroll us in the Liceo Experimental Manuel de Salas. It is called "Experimental" because it is affiliated with the University of Chile, and is experimenting with new teaching methods and progressive textbooks. It follows the most modern guidelines in education. Most importantly, it is the first co-ed school in Santiago. Besides, the regular public schools are Catholic-dominated and separated for girls and boys, while the Liceo Manuel de Salas does not place primary emphasis on religion. We are very excited to be able to go to this special school. Although it is experimental, it is still a public school, and there are no fees to be paid which is critical for my parents.

The first day—what a shock! My parents don't have enough money to give us for bus fare so we walk to school. It takes us twenty-five minutes. Later, we learn from other kids that you can get on a streetcar without paying if you jump on the back platform. As the collector is busy taking money in the front, he cannot check the back, but on those first days, we don't know any of this, and just walk block after block.

The school is in a large, old-fashioned mansion. I am sure in colonial times, it was somebody's private palace. There is a beautiful garden in front, with flowerbeds and a small lagoon and a large park in the back. The classrooms are regular rooms, each one a different size, with wallpaper and mirrors on the walls and beautifully decorated ceilings. The students sit on long benches, six to a bench, facing a narrow table. Everybody wears a uniform. I don't have one yet. You have to buy it in a special store, but my mother bought a pattern and will make mine at home. The girl's uniforms are dark blue skirts, a white blouse and a dark blue jacket with the school's emblem. The boys have a blue suit, white shirt and a blue tie. We have to wear brown shoes and white socks.

While we are in school, the girls have to wear a white duster on top of the uniform, with our name and classroom number embroidered in red on the left side. The dusters stay in school during the week, and every Friday, we take them home to be washed, ironed and starched. My mother will make two of them for me, so that I can have a clean one every Monday.

I belong in the eighth grade, but there is no room for new students, not even for regular, Spanish-speaking. Altogether, counting Gert and myself, there are thirteen new immigrant children, between nine and twelve years old, being enrolled at the school at the same time. Others have been there for some time already. Although, we belong in different grades, they place us all in Quinta Preparatoria (fifth grade) until we learn Spanish...

A Jewish boy, who has been in the school for several months already, tells us that the school ran a lottery to decide which teacher would get the new *gringos*, and the fifth grade teacher, Mrs. Carter, lost out and got all thirteen of us. I am really concerned. The teacher talks, but I don't understand a single word. She writes something on the blackboard. I don't know what it is, or what we are supposed to do with it. She does not allow us to speak German. We can only whisper to each other when she isn't around. I hope I learn Spanish fast. This is terrible and very embarrassing.

Math classes are fine. I can, of course, read the numbers, and we learned this material long ago in Berlin. Geography is O.K. too. I can identify countries on the map and, as long as she does not talk about the Chilean landscape, I am fine.

The Chilean students in Fifth Prep. are the envy of the other classes. Because we, the foreigners, are in their class, their lessons are much slower, and while the teacher spends time with the "new ones," the regular kids in the class talk or fool around. They love us! Some of them treat us as if we were from another planet. We look different, act different, we speak a language they never heard before. Most of the Chilean girls have long, dark, beautiful hair. Ribbons and bows are not allowed. Most of them wear their hair in braids or ponytails. I wish I could braid my hair too, but mine is short and curly. And I am blond! I hated to have my hair cut before we left Berlin. But, since everything is a matter of money, they convinced me that short hair lasts longer, always looks neat and saves on haircuts. I really hate short hair, but then, given all the other problems, short hair is not the worst!

And our shoes...Before we left Germany, our parents bought us all new clothes and shoes one or two sizes too big to "grow into." Now we are wearing shoes with cardboard in them, and one can tell they are much too big. Some of the kids laugh at our shoes. I am embarrassed, but I won't tell my mother. She has enough other worries. My feet will just have to grow a little faster. Hopefully, by then the shoes will still be good.

***

October 1939

We have been in school now for three months. We speak Spanish, not perfect, but quite well. They have placed us in the grades corresponding to our age. I have made friends with some Chilean students, especially with Chilean boys! They are so cute! Most of them are dark haired and handsome. And they love blond, blue-eyed girls. My grades are very good because much of the material that is being taught we already learned in Germany. I am always asked to help with somebody's homework in math or geography. This does not hurt my popularity! I am afraid I'm beginning to get conceited, but I am watching it.

***

From the day we settle in the house, my mother starts to work on getting a visa for my grandparents. Tante Jenny has been working with the same attorney who got the entry permit for us, and has promised to help with the visa for my mother's parents. It should not be too difficult, because not only are my grandparents my mother's parents, but my Omi is also the sister of Tante Jenny, therefore directly related on two sides. But visas cost money, a lot of money, and we don't have any. Rodolfo sure has exhausted his financial capacity. Why do I know this? Because by now, my parents are so anxious that most of the conversations are taking place, if not in front of us, at least not in whispers.

We are now allowed to stay in the room, when something is being discussed. They must have decided that Gert and I might as well know what is going on. The worst part is that Tante Jenny does not want my mother to go with her to the lawyer. She never explains why, but she insists on going by herself.

My mother's heart is breaking with every day that passes. She feels she could do a better job by explaining to the attorney the <u>real</u> danger facing my grandparents in Germany, but she doesn't want to hurt Tante Jenny's feelings by insinuating that perhaps she is not "pushing" enough.

My mother thinks that Tante Jenny has been away from Germany for so long, that she may not be fully aware of the danger the Jews are in. Tante Jenny insists that she is doing the best she can, that people have paid for visas that turned out to be fakes, that her attorney is the best in this business.

And the days go by without a visa, and the letters from Omi and Opa ask desperately for news. I could cry. My mother is only thirty-eight years old, but she looks a lot older. How long can she take this, I ask myself.

***

My parents are waiting for our "lift" (a container-like wooden crate) with the household goods we were allowed to take out of Germany. My parents brought some Persian rugs, crystal and porcelain which they were able to hide from the German inspector who had to be present when the crate was packed. He drank a lot of beer while he was watching, and then had to go to the bathroom several times. That's when some of the pieces were quickly loaded and hidden under the stuff that he had already checked. My mother can't wait to get her "treasures," sell them and pay for the visa for her parents.

The crate arrives, but it is too large to be brought into the house, and we have to open it on the street and quickly unpack it. No time to look and enjoy the familiar things that we had in our apartment in Berlin. Now our house is really full! My mother starts sorting the pieces, these to sell, those to keep. She gives Tante Jenny a beautiful antique set of dishes as a gift. It has been in the family for many years, and means a lot to my mother and Tante Jenny. The German inspector, full of beer, decided that it looked old and dirty and checked it off as "kitchenware."

The lot for sale is much larger than the one to keep.

"It breaks my heart to part with these things." My mother sighs.

"But I only care about my parents' safety." Nobody contradicts her.

Like all other immigrants, they place an ad in the newspaper offering European goods for sale. There are wealthy Chilean families who love things "European" and don't mind spending money for them. The bad thing is that too many immigrants are selling their furnishings at the same time and, Rodolfo says, "The market is over-saturated." But we get some customers.

I watch my mother carefully doing her accounting every night in a booklet, as if neatness counts under any circumstances. She even confides in me that the money available is not nearly enough for two visas. She insists again with Tante Jenny, but she tells me, in secret, that she feels very guilty. "It's my parents' lives I am dealing with." I wish I could cheer her up, but I realize that only the visas can make her happy.

A close Chilean friend of Rodolfo's, a politician, spoke with my mother about the visa problem. He feels that perhaps a clarification of the entire situation might help her to understand the pressures that are being placed on the attorneys who "deal in visas."

My mother asks me to listen to the conversation to be sure she fully understands. The gentleman speaks some German, which helps. He was kind enough to write down a whole history for my parents and left a leaflet with them to study.

This is what it says:

"It is estimated that between 9,000 and 12,000 immigrants arrived in Chile between 1934 and 1939, mostly from Germany, Austria and Czechoslovakia. In November of 1938, President Aguirre Cerda, elected by a Center-Left coalition sympathetic to the Jews in Germany, allowed between 300 to 500 people per month to immigrate to Chile. But an anti-Semitic Congressman, Jorge Von Maree, of German extraction, lobbied to stop the "dangerous flood" of Jewish immigrants. It is expected that by 1940, entry visas to Chile will be stopped, particularly from Germany."

Rodolfo's friend offered to help my parents, but did not have much hope, given the anti-Semitic attitude of certain politicians.

My mother does not know how to thank him enough for his thoughtfulness and for caring enough to explain the situation, even if the news are not good. He insists, "that he would do anything to help Rodolfo and his family."

I am afraid for my mother. Just to see her makes me cry.

***

MY MOTHER

August 1939

I t is August 1939. I am twelve years old. We have been in
Chile for three months, and I have become my mother's
best and, for now, only friend. There is something very sad
about my mother, and I know it is because we left everybody
behind in Berlin; her parents (my Omi and Opa) all my uncles,
aunts, cousins and other relatives and all our friends. I know
she misses them terribly. We also left our nice apartment and
almost all of our belongings in Germany, but that doesn't seem
to bother her so much.

"Material things can be replaced," she says, "people
cannot." I catch her crying lots of times and her eyes are always
sad. She used to be so much fun when my brother and I were
younger. Even when we could no longer go to the Zoo or to
the movies, (being Jewish we were not allowed to visit certain
public places in Berlin) my mother invented games for us that
could be played anywhere, and we did not need permission
from anybody for it.

Our favorite was "Guess What They DO."

This game consisted of sitting on a bench in a little park
near our house, where we were still allowed to sit at certain
times a day, watching people and guessing who they were and
what they did. A man with a box would be a Jewish musician
who had to conceal his violin on his way to a clandestine concert;

the woman with three children was German and free to go wherever she wanted. They were on their way to a museum. My mother would then make a story about what exhibits they would look at and what they would see, and she would make it so real, that we didn't feel any need to personally go to the museum, which of, course, was off-limits to Jews.

Other times, we would invent names for the people we saw going by and pretend we knew them. We would then hold imaginary conversations with them, invite them to our parties and tell them about our exciting lives. Most of the time, we were foreign millionaires who just happened to be passing some time in Berlin on our way to other places. Depending on our geography class that week, we would pretend to be from Greece, or Italy, or even Gibraltar, and describe these places to our new "friends."

I understand why my mother is so unhappy now, but I miss the good times we used to have.

"Don't forget, don't ever forget," my mother says to me, over and over again. "All the people we left behind are your family. It might take some time before we see them again, but I want you to remember everything about them."

I wonder, how could I forget any of these people who have been part of my life for twelve years? When we left Germany, my Omi promised that it wouldn't be long before we would all be together again—and my grandmother always keeps her promises!

And how will I ever be smarter than the other kids, when my Opa is no longer here to teach me words from the encyclopedia? I want to believe that they will come very soon. Our lives are just not the same without them. It isn't fair; we only have one set of grandparents, while other lucky children have two pairs.

In the meantime, the months go by, and my mother has not been able to obtain the entry visas for her parents. All she lives for are the few letters that we get from our grandparents. The mail is censored by the Germans. The envelopes look scary with the swastika stamp on them; they are opened and red-stamped: "Opened and censored by the German Military Authorities." Sometimes, part of the letters are cut out. At times, we only get one or two pages that end in the middle of a word. My Omi numbers her letters and also the individual pages, so we can tell that something is missing.

Although they don't say much, what is written in code words that had been agreed upon before we left, shows how scared they are getting and how, one by one, close relatives and friends are disappearing without a trace. The saddest part is that every letter is signed, "Hope to see you very soon."

My mother cries. There is nothing we can say. Although my Omi tries to sound cheerful and tells us about their daily life, mostly the news are about family members who "have gone away." My mother doesn't even try to hide much from me anymore, and tells me that she and her mother agreed on a code for certain type of news. The code "have gone away" means they just disappeared; "on vacation" means that these people were lucky enough to be able to emigrate somewhere. When she writes, "we haven't seen so-and so," she is saying that she doesn't know where these relatives or friends are.

My father explained to me that some people get a visa for a certain country and leave without telling anybody. They are afraid that too many others, knowing of this chance, would also apply for permits and the quotas would be filled before they themselves can get out. It seems to me that this is outright selfish, but my father says he can understand why some people act in such a manner. "SURVIVAL" is the expression he uses.

"Everybody tries to get out. See how lucky we are. We are already out. If the war starts soon, as is expected, nobody will be able to leave Germany, so we have to forgive people who only think of themselves at a time like this.

It seems to me that everything we do is "at a time like this." Will there ever be another time?

I'm only twelve—what do I know?

My mother's days are filled with work, raising us children, and taking care of my father. Her nights, sleepless hours of guilt and pain.

"I should have never left without them," she whispers. "But then, what would have become of you two?" I wish I could think of an answer, but what can I say? I miss my Omi and Opa terribly. We talk about them constantly, a memory, a joke, some expressions they use. It almost seems that they are with us every night before we go to sleep.

"You know how much we love you," Mami says to my brother and me. "For you, we did the right thing. But perhaps we should have all waited together and not leave Omi and Opa alone in Berlin." She feels so guilty, and there is nothing we can say to her that will change her mood. I am trying to think like a grown-up to understand my mother, her suffering, her guilt and her anxiety. My father, the sweetest man I know, adores my mother, but is not a big help. If she is sad, he is sad. When she cries, he says, "Don't cry. We have the children and you have me." He fully understands her pain, but is not strong enough to lift up her spirit.

September 26, 1939

Today is my Omi's birthday. A very bad day for my mother. I don't know how to console her, and decided that I would make a "special celebration." It would be different from the way you usually celebrate birthdays, (which we have not done since we left Berlin), but a "memory birthday." We will spend the day remembering the exciting times with the entire family; the gifts, the wonderful cakes, all the aunts and uncles in the house. It was beautiful, and I miss it very much. I adore my grandmother. She has a special name for me. She calls me "meine Mulli" (my Mulli, an endearment.)

Since we now have no money, I stole some flowers from the neighbor's garden and brought them to my mother. We baked a simple "bread-cake" for the occasion, just to pretend… I told my mother to talk to us about her parents and make believe that they are with us. I don't know why, but my mother accepted the idea, and for once, told us the entire story and the reason why she was so sad and felt so guilty about leaving without them.

When my parents tried to escape Germany, they contacted everybody in the world who could send them a visa, which is what you needed to be allowed to leave Berlin.

My grandmother had three living sisters, Tante Else, who had emigrated to Palestine in 1933; Tante Paula got a visa from her son Henry, who had left for the United States in 1937, and was in the American Army. The youngest, the one they called "the gypsy," Tante Jenny, had left for Argentina in 1936, with her husband. Once there, she divorced him, and went to Chile with her younger son, Rodolfo. Her older son, Konrad, decided that Chile was not for him, and joined the British Army. He ended up in Johannesburg, South Africa, where he had a friend who offered him a job.

So, Tante Jenny, "the black sheep of the family," (this was always mumbled when I was around) was contacted with a plea for a visa for Chile. Rodolfo was then 24 years old, had a good job and supported his mother, who lived with him. He made the enormous effort to put up the guarantees and obtain a visa. He got permission for four people, meaning my parents, my brother and myself. There was no way he could have gotten visas for more people. He suggested that we leave first and, once in Chile, my mother could then apply for a visa for her parents. This sounded logical, but my mother was firm in her decision not to leave without her parents.

The problem was that my great-grandmother (my Omi's mother) lived with them. She was almost eighty years old and Chile did not give visas for old people, and my grandmother, in turn, was not leaving her mother behind. It was suggested that they place her in the Jewish old-age home. Omi wouldn't hear of it.

The entire family, including my grandparents, pressured my mother that my family had to leave because of us children. We had a right to live, they said, and my mother was committing a sin by endangering her children's' lives in refusing to go when she had the opportunity. Heartbroken, my mother finally accepted this.

The war started on September 1, 1939. The situation in Europe was getting more and more dangerous, and hundreds of thousands of Jewish people applied for visas everywhere. Chile and other South American countries had to close their borders. They could not absorb such a number of immigrants.

I am frantic. If my brother and I are the reason why my grandparents are still in Germany, part of my mother's pain and guilt is now **mine**! I need to grow up quickly to be able to help my parents. That's the least I can do.

Our birthday celebration did not turn out to be a very happy day. It made me sadder than I already am and now the

GUILT has been passed on to me. I explain all this to Gert and he says he understands.

My great-grandmother died on the first of July 1939, and there was no longer a reason for my Omi to stay in Germany. Tragically, it was too late. In 1941, we stopped receiving letters from my grandparents. We all knew what this meant.

We never heard from my grandparents again. After the war was over, the Red Cross International helped people in foreign countries to search for their relatives. By the end of 1946, we received a letter from the Red Cross in Switzerland, telling us that both my grandparents were deported in 1941 to the Concentration Camp Theresienstadt, in Czechoslovakia, where they died in 1943. My grandfather was used as a "horse" in front of a garbage truck, and my grandmother had to work in a plant sorting clothes and shoes that had been taken from the people that were burned in the ovens of the Extermination Camps at Auschwitz and Bergen-Belsen.

The date of their death was given as August 3, 1943.

***

1943

We have just moved out of the Jewish House on Washington Street to a modern apartment closer to the center of Santiago. We have three bedrooms, which makes life a lot easier. I have left school and am now working in an office located downtown. My bosses are Jewish immigrants.

My parents have installed their business in one of the bedrooms. My father is now only making women's coats and suits for different manufacturers, and my mother makes dresses for private customers. Mostly wedding and party dresses. Both of them still work much too hard and their health is deteriorating. My father has been suffering from stomach ulcers for a long time and they have gotten worse over the years. My mother suffers from high blood pressure and her migraines are still with her. It started in Berlin, when the trouble began, and she regularly gets excruciating attacks. But both of them ignore their problems.

"We should see Dr. Goepfert again," my mother says. "I can tell your stomach pains are getting worse. You moaned all night."

"I will see Dr. Goepfert when you make an appointment with Dr. Schuler," my father counters. "I am in better shape than you."

They look at each other, shake their heads and go back to work. Neither of them makes an appointment with the doctor.

Through all this, my parents are still *"Schatzi"* to each other, support each other through their difficulties, and even when they argue, it is always *"Schatzi."* They enjoy happy moments with my brother's and my successes at work and in school. They share our joys and disappointments with boy-and girlfriend problems, and with our experiences in becoming *Chileans.*

However, "No '**manana**' in this house," my father declares. "And no Spanish speaking here." This is still a "**today**" family. We leave nothing for the next day, if we can help it. I want you to keep the German language alive. Not because of the Germans, G-d forbid- but because speaking several languages is a great advantage."

***

1947

I just got married. My brother gets my bedroom and enjoys the extra space. He also welcomes the extra time he now gets on the telephone! He is nineteen and deserves a little more privacy. Bossy old sister is gone!

I speak to my parents every single day. My mother is still my best friend. I can talk to her about everything, my husband, living with my mother-in-law, being married, my work, my friends. She always has good advice and is honest and fair. I don't always agree with her.

"I have been your daughter all my life. Kurt is new to you," I remind her when she takes my husband's side.

"Why do you see his point and not mine?"

"Because he is right and you are not." This is my mother. Sometimes, too fair! She also says, "Do what your father and I have done. Find an endearing name for each other and always use it. *"Schatzi"* has kept us from ever losing our temper."

Kurt and I decide to call each other *"Liebchen"* (Little Love). My mother is right. It is hard to argue with a "Little Love."

***

August 3, 1958

My mother died today. She finally decided last week to have a benign tumor removed from her uterus. No cancer. The doctor insisted that it was necessary to stop the excessive bleeding that she had been having for several months. It was supposed to be minor surgery. She had the operation on Monday, came home from the hospital without complications on Saturday, her birthday, and died this morning, Sunday,

August 3rd, of a blood clot in her lung. She did not suffer, and it took only a few moments for her life to end.

I wasn't with her. I had seen her the evening before and, although she seemed weak, there was no reason to believe that anything was wrong.

August 3rd, 1943 was the date given to us by the Red Cross as the day my grandparents died in the Concentration Camp. Every year, around that date, my mother got sick and no doctor could ever find anything wrong with her. I don't want to believe that she willed herself to die the same day her parents were murdered, but I know she is finally at peace.

My father died with her. Not literally, but his soul went with her. One of the *"Schatzis"* was gone. Only together had they been able to face the tragedy of their time. One without the other was lost.

Sitting by her bed, she still and peaceful, I admire their love, their understanding and their empathy for each other.

After my mother's death, I caught my father often with the ribbon-tied package on his lap, reading and re-reading their letters to each other. He smiles and cries at the same time. These messages are testimony of such devotion, trust and friendship that they could be published as a guide to perfect relationships.

I pray that my children will feel about me as I have loved, admired and trusted my mother.

FELIX AND HERTHA

My Parent's Love Story

Santiago, Chile 1939

I sit next to my mother doing my homework and helping her with her sewing. We always talk. My mother is amazing. She can do several things at the same time, listen to my conversation, do her work and tell me *"Stories of her youth."* Mami is thirty-eight years old, and I am always surprised how many things she remembers from so long ago, when she was a little girl, the schools she went to, the dances she attended, her boyfriends and how she met my father. Their love story is my favorite. It is so romantic and I ask to hear it again and again.

My mother was born in Berlin, on August 1, 1901, and lived there with my grandparents and her younger brother, (my uncle John.) Her maiden name was **JACOBY**. My mother's grandmother, whom we called **Oma Feldblum**, also lived with them. Oma Feldblum was a widow and very old. She was sixty-five when my mother got married.

My mother had finished her studies at the University in Berlin, and was working as a secretary for a large international export company owned by Jewish people. She spoke English and French and, of course, German, and had learned shorthand, typing and secretarial skills. Although she now earned a good salary, she lived at home. In those days, girls stayed with their parents until they got married.

One day, in December of 1923—she was then 22 years old- one of her bosses called her into his office.

"My nephew is coming to spend New Year's with us. I would very much like you to meet him. We are planning to take him to the Adlon Hotel, you know, the annual "Adlon Ball?" Would you like to accompany us?"

My mother could not believe her luck. The Adlon Hotel was the most luxurious hotel in Berlin, and only the very rich could afford to go there. Although her parents were well off, they would never have taken her to the Adlon Hotel.

"Too ostentatious," her father said, "Not our style. No need to show off." But they gave her permission to go to the ball and meet **the nephew**.

She had a wonderful time, although the nephew turned out to be short and chubby with pudgy fingers and a big nose. He didn't dance so well either, but he was entertaining and pleasant. He seemed to like her a lot and showed her off to all his friends.

"Look who is here," he suddenly exclaimed, "My friend, Felix Raphael from Koeln. How did he get here? I didn't know he was in Berlin. Come, let me introduce you." And he took my mother over to meet Felix.

"This is Hertha Jacoby. You remember Joseph Schneider? She is his right hand."

"Very nice to meet you. I am Felix Raphael. I am visiting from Koeln."

There was an immediate magical attraction. Felix had a shy smile and a handsome face. He was thin and elegant. His demeanor was quiet and pensive. She saw tenderness and a certain sadness in his blue eyes. My mother was pretty, had a nice figure and exuded vitality and enthusiasm. Her brown curls danced on her head with every movement and her green eyes sparkled with life. Even in that first moment, it was obvious that they were opposites in personality, but perhaps that was the attraction.

Felix asked the Nephew for permission and invited my mother to dance. In his arms, her world stopped. She knew at once that this man would stay in her life. She had never felt so certain with any of the other young men she had gone out with. At the end of the evening, when they said goodbye, she knew that she would see Felix again, even if he was working in Koeln and only came to Berlin on short visits

The nephew took her home. He hadn't noticed anything! He loved his friend Felix, and was happy that Hertha had liked him also.

My mother and Felix exchanged letters every day. They told each other of their daily life, their dreams and hopes, and got to know each other quite well through correspondence.

He came to visit again in January, and asked my mother's parents for permission to take her out. My grandfather had reservations, of course. The NEPHEW was wealthy and belonged to one of Berlin's well-known Jewish families. He was working in a Bank in Frankfurt, learning the business and being groomed to take over his family's Bank in Switzerland later on.

Felix was an orphan. He was also born in Berlin. His parents had died some years before, both very young. His brother, Alfred and two sisters, Wally and Hannchen, lived in Berlin. Felix had studied Fashion Design and had been sent to Koeln for two years to work for a well-known women's clothing manufacturer. The Raphael family was well- educated, but didn't have **a situation**. "Situation" was a word tactfully used when speaking of money. Felix had none. He had a good job, but no fortune.

"You can see in his face what a good person he is," my mother pleaded with her father. "Just look into his eyes. There is nothing but tenderness in them. I don't care about the money if it comes in a chubby, big-nosed, fat-fingered person like the Nephew."

My grandmother understood. She convinced her husband that there was no harm in allowing Hertha to go out with Felix. "They are just friends. Who is talking about a serious relationship?"

In February of 1924, Felix asked for my mother's hand in marriage. Before my grandfather gave his consent, however, he made some discreet inquiries into Felix's background. He spoke to Felix's boss in Koeln.

"Felix Raphael is the most decent human being anybody would want for a son-in-law," he was told. "But I doubt that he will ever be rich. He is too much of a dreamer. He is an honest man, a man of character, kind and sensitive, and absolutely honest in his dealings with people. He is quiet, more of a listener than a talker, well-educated and a bit of a romantic. If I had a daughter, Felix would be my choice of husband for her."

Although my grandfather could not envision how a dreamer could make a good living and, as far as he was concerned, the "romantic" quality belonged in a book and not in everyday life, he was impressed with Felix's qualities.

Besides, my mother pleaded and persuaded him that Felix was the only man in the world for her, and if she couldn't marry him, she wouldn't marry anybody at all. I guess she convinced her father, or perhaps he didn't want his only daughter to be an old spinster, so he gave his approval.

Hertha and Felix got engaged on February 25, 1924, and were married a year later, on January 11, 1925. They never called themselves by name. They were both "**SCHATZI**" (Treasure).

Even when they argued, it was always, "No, Schatzi, you are wrong," or, "How can you say such a thing, Schatzi?"

My mother gave my father a key chain with the initials Z.E.A.E.G.D. They stand for: *Zur Erinnerung and einen gluecklichen Donnerstag.* (In remembrance of a lucky Thursday. (New Year 1924, the day they met, had fallen on a Thursday.) Through their entire life, Thursdays were their lucky days.

(My father used this key chain until the day he died. My brother kept it and gave it to his son Steven, who still has it.)

The Nephew became a very wealthy man. He emigrated in 1936, early on in the Nazi era, to Switzerland, where his money was. But for my mother, there wasn't a man in the world who compared to her Felix: gentle, friendly, shy and lovable.

I have heard this story often, but every time my mother tells me, I think it is the most romantic love story. I hope when I meet somebody, it will be like that for me.

But then, who knows? Living in Chile now, where will I meet a Felix? Will I ever be able to go to a dance? Will there be money for a beautiful dress and shoes and jewelry? I don't know, and there is really no rush. I'm only twelve now.

I just dream and hope for the best. Right now, we have other worries, and from what I can see already, my life will be very different from that of my parents in their youth.

My mother has kept all of my father's letters tied with a purple satin ribbon. Sometimes she shows them to me, but she never allows me to read any of them. "Not for children's eyes," she says. But her own eyes shine when she looks at them.

It's one of the rare moments when she forgets the present and re-lives a happy past.

***

117

My mother was the "social" one, and my father enjoyed her conversation and her entertaining of friends, although he was mostly a listener.

"We had a pleasant visit, don't you think?" he would say to my mother after an evening with friends. To which she would invariably answer,

"If everybody had spoken as little as you, it would have been quite boring. Somebody has to be the talker, for the others to have something to listen to. But I love your listening, Schatzi."

After they got married, my father moved back to Berlin and found a position as a designer for a ladies' apparel company. He was an artist and had excellent taste. He mainly designed women's coats and suits, all very original. My mother kept her job for two more years, until I was born, and then stayed home with me and my brother, who arrived a year and a half later.

My parents were active in the Jewish community, belonged to a Synagogue, volunteered at the Jewish old age home, had many friends and a lively social circle. They played Bridge, attended concerts and operas, and belonged to the B'nai B'rith Lodge, which her father had co-founded in Berlin. Their lives revolved around the family, with pleasant times, fun and culture.

Since my grandparents lived only a few streets from us, we saw them every day. My mother was very close to her parents, and everybody loved my father. My uncle John had left for Palestine in 1934, and my Omi always said, "Thank G-d for Felix. He is our second son."

My brother and I were the only grandchildren. My mother's cousins were younger, not yet married and, obviously, did not have children. Of course we were spoiled. Not with money, but with attention, love and food.

"What would you like for lunch today?" my Omi would ask. You got such a good grade in school today, we have to celebrate."

I always chose tomato soup and chocolate pudding. The main dish didn't matter.

The next day, good grades or not, it was my brother's day to choose the menu. He only wanted pudding instead of soup, and pudding instead of the main dish!

***

Life changed drastically in 1937, when my father lost his job. His Jewish boss, Mr. Pilpel, was arrested and his business was taken over by a Nazi who, of course, threw all the Jewish employees out. There was no way to find another job, nor to open your own business. Jews were not allowed to work.

My father, secretly at home, continued designing and made the patterns for the coats and suits, which he then sold secretly to other Jewish manufacturers, who were also working clandestinely from their homes. They all prayed that they would not be found out. It would mean immediate arrest and deportation. German cleaning ladies and maids were not allowed to work for Jews. At least there was no danger of betrayal from that side.

For all his imagination and creativity, my father was paid ridiculous amounts, but his pride did not allow him to sit and whine and go through his life savings, as some of his friends did.

My mother went to work, also secretly, as the assistant to an old lawyer friend of theirs, who tried to conduct whatever was left of his practice from his home. It was a very dangerous situation, but they had to survive.

My grandfather also continued to work covertly, with some of his old contacts, mainly to keep himself busy. There wasn't much money to be made under those circumstances, but by being constantly in touch with people, they **heard**; rumors, secrets, fear, hopes and sometimes good advice. They needed to stay in contact.

Slowly, my father's health began to decline. He had suffered from stomach ulcers for many years, but he was on medication and was periodically checked by his doctor. He was on a constant diet, but did not complain. Now, of course, he could not be treated, since Jewish doctors were no longer allowed to work, and German doctors would not attend Jews.

My mother continued to suffer from severe migraine headaches, which had started in her teen years and seemed to be hereditary. My grandmother also experienced these attacks regularly. The lack of medical care made everything worse.

Both my parents paid no attention to their ailments. Their main concern was to find a way to leave Germany with us children and my grandparents

***

Santiago, January 4, 1962

We buried my father today. He would have been 63 years old on the 16th of this month. Although he had no serious physical ailments, (his stomach ulcers had been improved with treatments in Chile), his spirit was broken when my mother died on August 3, 1958, two days after her fifty-seventh birthday. His will to live was gone. He couldn't face the days and long nights without his SCHATZI. He died, painlessly, of a broken heart.

The Shivah service (prayer service held for eight days after the funeral) for my father has just ended. Everybody has left. My brother, Kurt and I, sit in my parents' bedroom, empty now, each of us with our own memories.

I go to my mother's nightstand. I know it is there. The box tied with purple satin ribbon. This is where she has kept her love letters for thirty-three years.

I open the package, but I don't dare read the letters. It seems disrespectful, an intrusion into my parents' hearts, both silent now. But I look at the letters, touch them and feel my mother's and father's presence.

My heart aches for them, for the anguish and pain that had become the essence of their lives.

Like every other young couple in love, like Kurt and myself, they had made plans, had goals for a happy future and a vision of what their lives would be together. Their hopes and dreams, born in a world of normalcy and peace, succumbed to the terror of the Nazi era, and the happiness of their early years turned into an existence of pain and sadness. Their lives took a turn that nobody could have fathomed and demanded from them endurance, strength and valor that eclipsed any other feeling.

Sitting there with my parents' love letters in my lap, I am thankful for the wonderful, unique relationship that I have had with my parents. My mother was my friend and confidant, and she shared with me her innermost thoughts, worries and memories. I knew from her that she and my father were friends and lovers. There was never a secret between them. Their personalities complemented each other. In the good times, my mother was full of life, funny and practical. She loved people, made friends easily and was always available to help. My darling father, introverted and shy, adored and admired my mother and she loved his quiet ways, his wit and his need to be taken care of. They always spoke in "we", had their little quarrels, but never forgot to call each other "SCHATZI."

***

WHERE IS EVERYBODY?

(My Father's Family)

March 1997

Kurt and I have just returned from a trip to Israel where we, of course, visited YAD VASHEM, the Holocaust Memorial in Jerusalem. Among the documentation on exhibit is a memorial book published by the City of Berlin, Germany, where our entire family lived. The book lists 56,980 names of Jewish people who lived in Berlin in 1939, at the beginning of the war, and who were taken to concentration camps and killed. They do not publish the names of the survivors, only those who were gassed in the camps. 56,980 men, women and children, including babies, all from Berlin. There are additional books giving the number of victims from other cities in Germany, Holland, Belgium, France and Poland, which the Jews escaped, mistakenly thinking that they would be saved.

I found my father's entire family published in the Berlin book. Their birth dates are listed, their addresses in Berlin, the date they were deported, the number of the transport that took them, the name of the Concentration Camp they were taken to, and the date and manner of their end.

Deep in my heart, I had known all these years that my uncles, aunts, cousins and other relatives had not survived, but the glimmer of irrational hope persisted that some day, through one of these incredible, miraculous coincidences, I would meet somebody on a trip or somewhere in the world, who had known them or known of them. We had received information from the International Red Cross, after the war, about the deaths of my mother's parents in the Theresienstadt Camp, but we had never been able to find anything out about the fate of my father's family.

But now I saw their names in print under the heading, "Jews of Berlin who Perished in the Nazi Concentration Camps," and I know for sure. No more asking: "Where is everybody?"

My father was born on January 16, 1899. He always joked, "It is easy to remember my age. I am always a year older than the calendar."

His parents had died when he was eighteen-years old, and he had been on his own until he married my mother, who therefore never knew a mother-in-law.

As a child, I always felt cheated for not having two sets of grandparents like most of my friends, but as I grew older, I realized how my father must have felt not having parents of his own. He was always part of my mother's family. Her parents, aunts, uncles and assorted relatives adored my father. He was friendly, shy, quiet and introverted and totally devoted to my mother and to us, his children.

Not having grandparents on my father's side to check with, we had to believe his stories, "I wasn't the best in Latin and Algebra, but nobody could beat me in Drawing and History."

My Aunt Wally, father's oldest sister, had a different version. "He would come home, sit by the window and dream. He always had a pencil and paper handy, and would fill pages with the most elaborate costumes, gowns and faces. I ended up doing his homework at night so he wouldn't get bad grades.

Uncle Alfred, (his older brother), and I wanted him to have a good education. It was all we could give him."

Uncle Alfred was more specific. "Your father was a lousy student," he said, "but we knew that he would be a painter or designer one day. He had so much imagination and such a talent for drawing."

The stories Gert and I loved best were about his younger sister, Hanni, who had died at the age of twenty-six of pneumonia. My father's face would light up when he spoke of "Hannchen." "You don't remember her. You were too little when she died. But you are so like her." And he would study my face and shake his head, "So like her..."

Hannchen was, of course, spoiled by her brothers and sister, who took care of her after their parents died when she was sixteen.

"Nobody could tell Hannchen what to do," my father told us, "She was pretty, vivacious and clever. But she had a mind of her own, like you," he would add, his beautiful blue eyes taking in my face, "and look what happened."

Hannchen had a severe grippe in the winter of 1930, and refused to stay in bed because she had to go to a party. She wouldn't listen to anybody, went to her dance, and had a wonderful time. Her grippe turned into pneumonia and she could not be saved. And he then said, very softly, "Only parties in good weather for you, my darling. I don't want to lose another Hannchen."

He did not have to worry, although at the time he couldn't know it. There weren't many parties for us when we grew up, and it had nothing to do with the weather...

What a difference there was between my mother's family and the clan of the Raphaels! On my mother's side, we had our grandparents, great-grandmother, my Uncle John, (my mother's brother) who was single and lived with us, and dozens of great-aunts and great uncles. My brother and I were the only children in this enormous family. At all parties, <u>we</u> were the ones who had to recite poetry, sing, play the piano or otherwise perform, and we had nobody to play with. We always had a "Fraeulein" who came in the afternoons to do homework with us, and although she played with us, it wasn't the same. She was seventeen, too old to really play. She preferred to read to us, which was fine for a few afternoons, but reading is not playing!

Everything in my parents' and grandparents' houses was orderly and disciplined. There were things "you didn't do" (we never questioned why not), and other rules of behavior and etiquette that "always had to be followed." (We didn't question those either.) It wasn't that we were so good and obedient, but questions about manners and comportment always turned into long explanations of "because…" It wasn't worth asking. My brother and I were the center of everybody's universe, got attention and love from three generations of relatives, and they all spoiled us. Why ruin it?

My father's family was very different. There were four cousins our age, and the households were less formal than ours. In today's vocabulary, we would call their lifestyle "loose." Some of my maternal relatives, the older ones, used to make comments about my father's family by whispering, "gypsies."

Gert and I loved our cousins, uncles and aunts on the Raphael side. Since there were no grandparents, everybody was young and a lot less complicated. There were no great-aunts with powdered wigs and little lace shawls to remind you of what "was never done," and how "every nice girl should behave." In the Raphael clan, there were obviously less rules and regulations.

There was Uncle Alfred with his wife, Tante Klara, and Horst and Ellen, our cousins. Horst was three years older than I, and Ellen was a year younger. My middle name is also Ellen. We were both named after our father's mother, whose name was Ernestine, but my mother, as well as Tante Klara, decided that Ernestine was too old- fashioned a name for a little girl and modified it to Ellen.

My cousin, Horst, was gorgeous. I didn't know then that "tall, dark and handsome" is the highest standard for a boy/man. But that's what Horst was. I was so in love with him, that I begged my mother to buy me a boy doll so I could name him Horst. He was my most precious doll and I loved him as much as I loved the living Horst.

We saw a lot of Horst and Ellen. They lived in a different part of Berlin, but since Horst was older, and his parents were less complicated, he was allowed to take the Stadtbahn (city-train) by himself or with Ellen, and they came to visit often. Horst knew all kinds of stories and jokes, many of them "not for children's ears." My mother didn't like it because she knew what he was talking about. Of course, we pretended we did… we didn't want to be the "baby" cousins.

One day, Horst took me to the kitchen and whispered, "You know what sex is?" Did I know what sex was. What did he think! With all the pride of a ten-year old (in 1937!) I answered, "Of course I know, I have a brother, you know. He has a sex and I don't, so what's the big secret?" Only much later did I understand what made Horst laugh until tears ran down his face.

Uncle Alfred worked in the garment industry. Like my father, he was a designer, and while my father's skills were in creating coats and suits for women, Uncle Alfred designed ladies dresses.

Once in a while, either my father or Uncle Alfred would take us to their workplace, a fantasy land in our eyes. Hundreds of drawings on the walls of ladies without heads or legs, but wrapped in a coat; evening dresses that sat on mannequins with pins sticking out of their bosoms and behinds. Paper, pencils in all colors and sizes, photographs of famous artists, but most astonishing, the models. These were young ladies with ratty hair, ugly dresses, clotty shoes, no make-up, and who would run around the offices making coffee or picking up paperwork or keeping busy in some unimportant way. Once a garment was ready, the "Directrise" would be called in. She appeared with hairbrushes, lipstick, eye shadows, powders, high-heeled shoes, glittering silk stocking and dresses, and fixed up the girls.

Their transformation into princesses was so astonishing that we preferred to go to my father's or Uncle Alfred's office rather than go to the movies. At least here you dealt with real ladies whom you could touch and talk to. Then came the photographers who took pictures of each model. They looked fantastic. I decided that when I grew up, I would also wear eye shadow, pink make-up and lipstick, and be transformed into an exotic young woman like these models. To be sure, I did not mention this plan to anybody. I knew what the reaction would be!

My cousin Horst had decided that the garment industry was definitely not for him.

"I don't want to slave for somebody else," he said. "They steal your ideas and all that is left of your creation is a tiny initial at the bottom of the drawing." He wanted to become an architect and work for himself. He was very talented and drew the most fantastic buildings and houses.

"I will engrave my full name on the cornerstone of every building I create," he explained to us. "My full name will be visible for all to see as long as the buildings stand, and people will ask, "Who was this genius named Horst Raphael?"

(His name is engraved for everybody to see—but not where he had dreamed it would be.)

Ellen and my brother, who were the same age, didn't worry much about their future. They preferred to play. Horst and I made plans for when we were grown up. We decided to get married as soon as it was "proper" and be together all our lives. We didn't tell anybody. This was our secret. We had heard our parents talk about a friend who had married his first cousin, and they had used words like "incest" and "degeneration." We had looked these words up in the encyclopedia and did not like their meaning, so we decided to keep our plans to ourselves for the time being.

Horst's Bar Mitzvah was the first in the family. It was in an Orthodox synagogue. The Bima (altar) was in the middle of the sanctuary, and the men surrounded Horst during the entire service. The women, including the girl-cousins, sat upstairs behind curtains, and although we could see what was happening below, the men could not see us. I thought it was very sad. Tante Klara, Horst's mother, looked down with tears of happiness and pride in her eyes. But when she tried to catch Horst's or Uncle Alfred's attention, they could not see her at all, and Horst conducted the service without even a smile from his mother.

My parents were not Orthodox. We belonged to a Conservative synagogue and this Orthodox service seemed strange and very strict to us. Most Jews in Berlin were quite assimilated, and out of the conservative observance developed the liberal movement that is now known as "Reform."

After his Bar Mitzvah, Horst became completely obsessed with religion. He would not eat in any house that wasn't Kosher, and because not all of ours were, he became a vegetarian. Another idiosyncrasy that made him even more attractive. Vegetarian...how sophisticated! I loved it. His religious fanaticism lasted a couple of years, until one day, Tante Klara called excitedly to tell my mother that "he was normal again."

For the majority of the Jews in Berlin, who had lived there for generations and considered themselves Germans of Mosaic faith, the Orthodox community was a reminder of the ghetto times, of Poland and Russia, of pogroms and persecution, which they all wanted to forget.

My mother used to say, "Poor Ellen, she lives in the shadow of her older brother," but I couldn't see anything "poor" in living in Horst's shadow. It was such a beautiful shadow. He had a brilliant personality, while Ellen was shy and introverted. She wore glasses, which caused her enormous embarrassment. (I am sure, had she lived, she would have spent her first money on contact lenses as soon as they were invented.) She loved books and music, and the family had already decided that she would one day, G-d willing, become a composer, a scientist or anything else intellectual or spiritual.

(But the memorial book in Jerusalem, bearing her name, is proof that in her case G-d was not willing, or forgot about her.)

The other Raphael family was named "Gruen." My father's older sister, Wally, was married to Uncle Heinrich Gruen. They had two daughters. My cousin, Hertha, was five years older than I, and her sister, Eva, was three when I was born.

They were the most intriguing group. Although family matters were <u>never</u> discussed in front of us children, or my parents would speak French so we wouldn't understand, here and there we caught some remark, eye-brow lifting, or shoulder shrug, that indicated that the Gruens were "different." We adored them.

What was different about them was that there were almost no rules in their house. Everything was proper that wasn't definitely obscene. Their book of rules and regulations had lots of blank pages. But they had fun. The girls were good students, obeyed their parents and enjoyed their lives. Uncle Heinrich's philosophy was "enjoy life while you can." He didn't know how prophetic his turned out to be!

Hertha wanted to be an actress. She was tall and skinny and had curly black hair. And, oh jealousy, she wore dark red lipstick and red fingernails on weekends. When she spoke, she closed her eyes half-way "to look dramatic," in her words. Eva wrote stories and they dreamed of becoming movie stars, where Eva would write the script, and Hertha would be the actress. Whenever they came to our house or we went to visit, the Gruen girls were in costume. They wore their mother's hats and high heels and coats with fur collars, and both of them would curl their hair with a hot iron.

Sometimes they burned it a little, and they would then wear scarves or fix their hair with celluloid combs, like Spanish senoritas. Of course, they wore a little make-up. To me, they always looked terribly interesting and grown up, but my mother and Tante Wally rolled their eyes and shook their heads, and their sighs and whispers clearly indicated their disapproval. But the girls argued that they were not hurting anybody, and didn't their mother want them to be happy?

(Had our parents known how short-lived these games would be for all of us, they would have encouraged them, I am sure.)

The other relative on my father's side was an older uncle, whose name was Raphael Raphael. People would always wonder what had possessed his mother, whose family name was Raphael, to give her son the fist name Raphael. But he himself never asked, and rather loved the curiosity. He was called Uncle "Raffel-Raffel."

At the age of eighty-nine, Uncle Raffel-Raffel was also deported to the Concentration Camp in Maydanek, where he was gassed upon arrival. They had no use for old Jews with or without curious names.

***

The memorial book in Yad Vashem (Book of names at the Holocaust Museum in Jerusalem) states in its introduction that the Jews who were deported either were too poor to leave Germany, or too rich and afraid to leave their possessions behind, or they did not have connections that would have allowed them to emigrate and save their lives.

This is not entirely true. My father's family, like thousands and thousands others, were neither too rich, nor too poor. They were middle-class German citizens who did not believe that Hitler meant them when he spoke of eliminating all the Jews of Europe. They felt protected by the fact that they had been Germans for generations. Like my father, all of the men had fought for Germany in the First World War, and earned Iron Crosses of Valor, and only their religion differentiated them from the other Germans. Every family had another reason to stay, even after the attacks and brutality that started in 1936.

"It will pass," they said, "how long can this man last? How long before the decent people in Germany rebel against him?" The ones that emigrated early were considered "panic-stricken" or "overly pessimistic."

Even as late as 1938, both families, the Raphaels and the Gruens, thought they had a valid reason to stay. Horst was about to finish high school, so they decided to wait for his graduation before leaving. Besides, in their case, there was another reason—many countries around the world only accepted "perfect" people, and Ellen, with glasses, was considered imperfect.

They never made it out of Germany.

The Gruens had another problem: Uncle Heinrich's grandfather had been born in Poland, and although for three generations they had lived in Germany and were German citizens, by Hitler's race laws, they were considered "Poles" and were not given a German passport. The Gruens could not even apply anywhere in the world for an entry visa without a valid passport. They were doomed to stay.

***

March 1997. Coming from Israel two weeks ago, and having seen the names of my father's entire family engraved in the memory book, on memorial walls, and on trees planted in their honor, I know now with certainty WHERE EVERYBODY IS.

THE JEWISH HOUSE

ON 170 WASHINGTON AVENUE, SANTIAGO, CHILE

Santiago, August 1939

After living with Tante Jenny and Rodolfo since April, right after we arrived here, my father obtained a loan from the **HIZEM**, the Jewish organization that helps new immigrants getting settled. He rented a large house on Washington Avenue No. 170, located away from the city center, a district called **Nunoa**. It is a very nice area, close to our schools.

The house has two floors, with eight rooms, four on the first level and four on the second. Six of the rooms are rented to six different families, who came on the same ship with us from Europe. The two smallest rooms are occupied by us.

With an entire family living in every room, the house is crowded and noisy and nobody is happy. It is hard for everybody to live so crammed together. And they are all as depressed as my parents, and equally without money.

"Never say you are poor," my mother insists. "As long as we are together and in good health, we are not poor. We just don't have any money, which is very different. Don't forget that."

I keep thinking that there is so much I'm not supposed to forget, I better start a diary and write everything down. I am only twelve, and there are so many grown-up things to remember! But I promise not to forget, and I know I won't.

People call our house the **Jew-House**, but not maliciously. It is meant in fun. The neighbors have never seen seven families living in a one-family house, all speaking a different language from them. Not a Spanish word to be heard, ever! Also, their clothing is different. No grays, blacks or purple to be seen. The newcomers wear blues, greens, white suits, and colored shoes! And there isn't a maid to be seen, not even daytime help. We can't really blame them for being curious. We ourselves had never experienced such crowded, crowded living conditions. It seems so uncivilized!

One room is occupied by the Horwitzes. There are five of them: the parents, a grandmother and two girls, sixteen and twelve years old. The younger girl, Helga, goes to school with me. Her sister, Ellen, is working as a governess for a Chilean family, and Mr. Horwitz looks for work, like everybody else. He used to be a businessman in Berlin, but now, while he hasn't found a job, he goes from house to house in the neighborhood, selling sausages and marmalade which he carries with him in a basket. I hear him saying how humiliating this is for him, but "it is better than begging."

The grandmother does the cooking, and Mrs. Horwitz is constantly sick.

"She is very delicate," her old mother says, "she cannot face this kind of life." I repeat this to my mother, who tells me that it isn't nice to talk about other people, but says, "Some of us can bear more pain than others. Perhaps she is really delicate." I know Mrs. Horwitz isn't delicate; she is just lazy and lets her mother do all the work. She dresses beautifully every day and spends a lot of time "getting ready." But I'm keeping my mouth shut!

Helga, the younger sister, is really delicate. She is tall, very skinny and her Oma always cooks something special for her. Sometimes it is a dessert (which she often shares with me) or a piece of meat or a banana, anything to make Helga stronger. Since Mrs. Horwitz stays in bed until mid-morning, she'll never find out. And I am not going to say anything!

In another room live Susan Pick and her husband. She was a nurse in Germany, but cannot practice in Chile without passing the necessary tests. She plans on going to school to learn Spanish, and then go for the examination. In the meantime, she helps by taking care of all our illnesses and goes out to attend to old Jewish immigrants who need assistance. Mr. Pick, a very small, skinny man, sits around and does crossword puzzles in German. My father keeps saying, "How can he...? Isn't there anything he can help Susan with? I would go crazy sitting there with the puzzles day after day."

My mother, practical as she is, says, "At least he doesn't get on her nerves. He is nice and quiet and doesn't bother anybody. Everyone of us reacts differently under the circumstances."

When somebody gets sick, and eventually we all come down with diarrhea, or even typhus, we call on one of our immigrant Jewish doctors. Of course, they are not allowed to work in Chile unless they pass the state examination, which is almost impossible for most of them, given the difficulty of the language. Some of these doctors had been well known physicians in Germany or Austria. Many of them had been teachers to Chilean doctors, who had studied in German or Austrian Universities. These same students are now refusing to grant their one-time professors their licenses, for fear of competition.

Shamelessly, these Chilean physicians call on these unlicensed immigrant doctors, whose knowledge they respect, to treat high-standing Chilean personalities who need unusual surgery or treatment. Once the patient is under anesthesia, and has said his "good-byes" to his family, the illegal Jewish doctor is brought in, performs the operation and leaves. From the enormous fee that the Chilean doctors charge, the Jewish "doctor" gets a pittance, but he is proud to be needed!

How do I know all this? Because I keep my ears open and talk to everybody. Susan Pick explains this to me, and makes me promise not to repeat this to anybody, especially not when one of our immigrant, un-licensed doctors comes to the house to treat one of us. Of course, I don't tell. This way she trusts me and I get to hear more interesting stories.

Then we have Mr. and Mrs. Will. Her name is Inne and his is Hans. Very nice people. Elegant and sophisticated. I really like them. They have no children, but are planning to start a family as soon as they get settled. She takes in alterations from rich Chilean women.

"My mother should see me," she cries, "we had our own seamstress in our house for our needs. Look at me now, bloody fingers from needles and pins, and a bloody soul from the denigration."

I write *"bloody soul"* and *"denigration"* in my diary so I won't forget.

There are also Rose and Emil Kron. They are younger than the other people in the house. Newlyweds, they come from Austria. The trip to Chile was their **Honeymoon.** He found a job right away as a mechanic, and she went to work as a housekeeper for a rich Chilean family. Rosie gets up at four in the morning, cooks her evening meal, which is mostly rice with peas (called Reesi-Beesi in Vienna), puts the hot pot in newspaper, and then wraps it in blankets and leaves it under a down cover in her bed. When she comes home at night, it is still lukewarm and their dinner is ready.

"Could be worse," Rosie says. "We are fine." I don't see how much worse it could be, but at least the Krons are medium-happy all the time, not like the rest of the inhabitants of Washington No. 170. There aren't many smiling faces here! I like the Krons, but since they are gone most of the day, and I don't get up at four in the morning, I don't see them much. I'm sure they would be fun to be friends with.

In another room lives the family Leyde. His name is Walter, hers is Edith. They have a six-year-old daughter, also named Helga. Since we already have a Helga (Horwitz), we decided that the older Helga is *Helga One*, and the Leyde daughter is *Helga Two*, which she doesn't like. Mr. Leyde owned a shoe factory in Germany, and found a job as a worker in a factory that makes rain boots. He is not happy, but makes the best of it.

"The problem is," he says, "the Spanish I am learning from the workers at the factory cannot be used in decent company or in a civilized environment."

I immediately put the word "environment" in my diary. When I see my grandfather again, he will be sooo surprised at my vast knowledge of new words.

Mrs. Leyde could be fun, if she weren't constantly yelling at Helga Two. She doesn't work, but it seems she is very nervous, and "taking care of this child is a full time occupation." Poor Helga Two. She is too young to be our friend, but we try to play with her sometimes, to help Mrs. Leyde.

The last room is rented to a middle-aged gentleman, Mr. Grodner, with his mother, an old lady. They are also from Vienna. He is a little snobbish, and keeps telling everyone that "in his entire life, he never dreamt that things would so bad that <u>he, Mr. Grodner</u>, Bookkeeper at one of the largest industries in Vienna, would end up living like this."

My mother, again, stepped in to calm him down.

"This is only temporary, Mr. Grodner, soon you will find an adequate job for yourself. Just be a little patient. Look at us, with two children in school. At least it's just the two of you. Don't make it hard on your mother."

Mr. Grodner found a job as a helper in a clothing factory. His mother stays home. She is always knitting something "to calm her nerves" and worries constantly about her son, who has never married and always lived with her. He buys her the wool and sometimes sells a shawl to one of his co-workers. "What a relief that I can help him," says his mother.

I cannot believe my darling mother. Her own heart is semi-broken. She keeps half of it alive, only because she has us, my brother and myself. And she tries to be braver than she is, to calm these people, strangers to us. I promise again and again, that very soon I will be able to help her. At least I am making a great effort at school so that she can be proud of me. I just hope I turn out like my Mami, strong, practical and trying not to give in to these bad times. I know it isn't easy for her, but "there has to be peace in this Tower of Babel," she says, "otherwise how can this living arrangement ever work."

The house has two bathrooms, one on the second floor and a small one on the first level, and one kitchen on the lower floor. My father invented a system for the use of these facilities. The people who go to work early get to use the bathroom and kitchen first. Then, by alphabet, the others occupy these facilities, until everybody is ready and gone.

The women who stay home, get to go last. The bad part is that the toilets are in the bathrooms, and there is no way one could go pee, while somebody else washes up. We children are supposed to get clean in the evening, so that we spend as little time as possible in the bathrooms in the morning. Everything works quite well, unless somebody gets sick and needs to go urgently to the bathroom outside his turn! Then you need to knock at the door, ask to be let in right now!!! Most of the time, it works, sometimes it doesn't. For those emergencies, there are some chamber pots hidden in the garage...Some of the people complain a lot. Others, as my father says, "accept the inevitable" (I like that phrase) and hope to get back into a civilized life as soon as they can.

The kitchen, of course, is also under strict rules. Every family gets a certain time to prepare their food, cleans up and calls on the next "cook."

I wonder why they can't get together and make food for two families at the same time, by turns. This way, they would cook only every other day. But I am told to keep my mouth shut. Our own family lives mostly on sandwiches, so we don't really care. Sometimes, one of the ladies leaves a little dessert for us, which is nice.

The most important "system" is the house key. We all enter the house by the back door. It is open during the day, but gets locked in the evening. Some of the people never leave; others come in early, but some even go out at night, and the door stays open until the last person is in the house. My father built an "IN & OUT" board, which is attached to the inside of the backdoor. It has slots with the name of every occupant. During the day, most of the slots are "OUT," but in the evening, they are being pushed "IN," until the board is all "IN." The last one locks the door with the key. If anybody forgets to push himself "IN," and the "OUT" is still out, my darling father gets very frustrated. He checks the door every night, and the next morning there is a conference with the person who appeared "OUT" when he or she was really "IN," and had forgotten to lock the door.

My father, shy and friendly, who never argues with anybody, is now the "landlord" and obligated to keep everybody happy.

"There has to be order in such a crowded place," he pleads. "We are civilized, educated people and, with a little understanding and patience by everyone, we can make this work. It won't be forever, hopefully."

Although there are arguments and disagreements, all in all, the system works. The adults really have no choice and we, the kids, almost enjoy the commotion. Nobody has the time or the nerves to insist on the discipline we were used to in Berlin, and we do get away with breaking some rules.

My parents, my brother, and I occupy the last two rooms on the first floor. One is very small. It is my parents' bedroom, and my brother sleeps in there also, on a cot. The other is the living-dining-workroom, and I sleep on a folding bed in a corner. I am happy to have my own room—almost.

My father has a sewing machine on loan from the **HIZEM**, and is making bathing suits for a wholesale dealer. He is their workshop. Every week, they bring him the material, he cuts the bathing suits from a pattern that he made, and then my mother sews them together.

They are interesting bathing suits, not your normal kind. Not like the black tricot, one-piece suits that the German women wore, but colorful, crinkled suits. It is interesting how they are made and, of course, my brother and I have to learn how it works "just in case." The upper bobbin of the sewing machine is loaded with yarn, the lower one with an elastic thread. The needle is brought criss-cross through the material, covering little squares at a time, and the result is a shriveled suit that extends as you put it on. It looks a little like a quilt. These bathing suits are the hottest things on the market, and quite expensive. My father gets paid a few pennies for each.

It is really a family effort; my father cuts the material, my mother sews, and Gert and I help with the finishing touches by cutting the hanging threads and making knots at the end of each, so that the elastic doesn't unravel while a person is in the water. We laugh about the chance of some woman wearing such a suit and coming out of the water with just a piece of material hanging on her body, preferably covering important and embarrassing parts.

My parents work all day long and late into the night. What a change! My father was a designer of women's coats and suits. He has excellent taste and his drawings were always admired. My mother did not work outside the house until my father lost his job (for being Jewish) in 1937.

Like most other immigrants, we came to Chile with no money at all. In order to get permission to leave Germany, my mother told me, they were only allowed to take the equivalent of ten American dollars per person with them. In our case, that came to forty dollars. Therefore, here in Chile, everybody has to work at something. I don't know exactly what the other people in our house used to do in Germany, but here, they all have to make money to be able to eat. It's a pretty busy house.

Even my brother and I have jobs. I tutor a little Chilean girl, in German, after school. I also darn the socks of all the men in the house. My Omi showed me how to do it, and gave me a beautiful colored lacquer egg for darning. I didn't think then that I would ever use it, but now it comes in handy, and I have written to her telling her that I can now see how valuable her gift has turned out to be. I get paid one Chilean penny per hole. Some socks are badly torn, but some have tiny little holes and only need a few stitches, so it evens out.

I also deliver the clothes altered by Mrs. Will to her lady customers who live in the neighborhood, and some of them give me a little tip or cookies. Sometimes, they give me a blouse or shawl that they no longer wear, and when I bring these home, my mother shakes her head.

I think these ladies mean well. They want to be nice and don't realize that it is shameful for our parents to be in a "taking" position.

One of my Omi's favorite sayings is: "Always be proud. Rich or poor, your pride and self-assurance are your capital."

I keep reminding my mother that no matter what, I will always be proud and self-assured, if only to please my Omi, and the gifts from these ladies will never change this.

My brother, who will be eleven this year, also has a job. He works on a milk truck, delivering fresh milk on our street every day, early in the morning. He rides on the truck, then jumps off at every stop, rings the bell at the house and places the bottle on the front door. He does this before school, and the milkman pays him a few pennies per hour. We don't keep the money that we make. It all goes into the *family treasury* as we call it. It is a cardboard box and every night we shake it, just to hear the sound of our money.

***

LIFE IS IMPROVING

1941

It has been more than two years since we moved into this house on Washington Street with seven other families. By now, everybody has found work, and most of them have moved away to individual apartments or houses. There are only the Horwitzes, who now occupy the entire second floor, and we kept the lower part of the house. We still share the kitchen with grandmother Horwitz, but it is working very well. Mr. Horwitz found a job in an office, where he could use his German. Mrs. Horwitz knits baby sweaters and sells them. Helga One goes to school with me, and her sister is still working as a governess for the same Chilean family she started out with.

Susan Pick passed her examination and is working as a nurse in a hospital. Mr. Pick still does nothing!

Mr.& Mrs. Will became insurance salespeople and are doing quite well.

Mr. Kron got a much better job in a large metallurgic company, and Rosie works as a secretary. They dream of starting their own business, and working together sometime in the future.

Mr. Grodner took a job as an accountant in a large bookkeeping company. He is doing fine. The old Mrs. Grodner continues to worry about him. I guess she'll never stop.

Both Mr. and Mrs. Leyde are working in a textile company, he in the factory, and she helps in the office.

The house is quiet and normal.

"I am not sure we deserve this *luxury living*," my mother says,"It's almost obscene to have a half a house for ourselves."

My father's career has advanced, and instead of the bathing suits, he is again designing women's coats, jackets and suits, allowing him to be the artist he really is. He sells the patterns to clothing wholesalers who, in turn, deliver material to him, from which he makes the finished pieces. This is called a **Taller de Costura (sewing workshop.)** The work isn't easy, but he makes a little more money, and feels better creating real clothes instead of bathing suits.

The two larger rooms of the lower floor have become **The business.** They are filled with sewing machines, cutting tables, mannequins and the huge rolls of material, lining, cotton for shoulder pads, boxes full of buttons and large pyramids of threads in all colors. The three smaller rooms are being used as living quarters.

"**Opulent living,**" my Opa would ironically say, if he could see this setup, using one of his favorite encyclopedia words that I cherish so much.

There is still a great difference between the civilized living in Germany and this, but at least it is more normal than the beginning in this house, and we are not complaining.

In the meantime, my mother started to do alterations and by now, she is making new dresses for the wealthy ladies in the neighborhood.

My so-called bedroom has become the *Dressing Room,* which means that I have to leave it in perfect order every morning before school. It has a bed that folds into the wall, and I am not supposed to leave anything lying around, so that the lady-clients can make use of the room.

One great advantage is that my mother bought a large three-way mirror which covers half of one wall, and I enjoy that piece of furniture more than any other in the house. I can see myself from the front, both sides and the back, and although I don't like what I see (especially the lower back part), I love looking at myself.

By now, my parents have made some friends, mostly people who came on the same ship, and sometimes on the weekends they come to visit.

They have to live in the neighborhood, because they have to bring their own chairs, and each one a cup and saucer and a glass. We did bring some nice dishes from Germany, but they are put away (there is no room to display anything) and all my parents' friends are doing the same. They talk and reminisce and cry together, but very often, one has a new idea for a job or to make money and they share it.

By now, Gert and I have made friends in school. Mostly Jewish children, but as we are getting better and better with our Spanish, we do get together with some of the Chilean kids as well. What a difference there is in their way of life!

They look at us like people from other planets, but mostly they are interested in knowing about our "past" and how life was in Europe. Their parents treat us very nicely, but with some pity, and that is something that's hard to bear. We don't need "pity"—we know more than they, and even if our lifestyle is quite different from their Spanish/Catholic upbringing, there is a lot they can learn from us. Some do.

The Jewish Community has formed groups of immigrant children, by age, and organizes get-togethers and excursions that we very much enjoy.

They try by all means to keep us in touch, not only us children, but the entire families, to form a bond that will be the base for a new generation of immigrants.

My brother had his thirteenth birthday, and was supposed
to have his Bar Mitzvah. We don't have a Temple, but religious
services are performed in a Theater that is rented for the High
Holidays. Bar Mitzvahs are celebrated in a Jewish Center, near
where we live. It is Orthodox-Conservative, stricter than what
we were used to, and the melodies have been adapted from the
German, Polish, Hungarian and Czechoslovakian synagogues.
This way, everybody gets a bit of their music from "home."

We all hope to see our grandparents again, and my mother
decided to wait a year with Gert's Bar Mitzvah, praying that by
then my Omi and Opa are with us again. We understand her
and Gert doesn't mind.

1942

We haven't heard from my grandparents for over two
years, and although my mother has not given up hope, every
day that passes creates new anguish with the news that are
coming out of Europe.

With a broken heart, before Gert's 14th birthday, my
mother accepts that we celebrate his Bar Mitzvah in December
of this year. We have the ceremony in the "Temple," and having
learned to read Hebrew before, the boys do not need special
training. They participate in the regular service. There are no
speeches. "Aliyahs" (special calls to read from the Torah) are
given to the father of the boy, to the grandfather, if there is one,
or to good friends who participate in the service. My brother
knew all his prayers and did a very nice performance, singing
in the tune we knew from Berlin.

Everybody congratulated him and he was very proud.

After the ceremony, we go home. My mother tries to keep
her spirits up, for Gert's sake, but our thoughts are with our
entire large family, who has disappeared.

We have a little reception in our house, invited a few friends, have some cakes and sweets, and end up having a good time. My father told us in the morning, "We must celebrate the joys as they come. There are enough days to grieve. Laugh today, cry tomorrow. That should always be our guiding thought."

My mother really tries her best. She is a proud mother, a gracious hostess, and good friend to our visitors.

1945

We moved out of the "Jewish House" in 1943, and have been living in the apartment near the center of Santiago for two years now.

My parents' business is steady, they are making a living, but they are working much too hard. Physically too hard. The carrying of the heavy material up the steps (the apartment is on the fourth floor—no elevator) has gotten too difficult for my father.

They rented a small store in an old building, near the house on Irarrazaval Street. The back of the store is the workshop; the front is a display window. Besides making the coats and suits, they now also buy and sell additional articles, blouses, sweaters, gloves and such.

They have two women working in the back, and my mother takes care of the customers in the store, the books, the paperwork, and everything else that comes up. She has learned Spanish, and communicates very well with people. The clients and the workers love her. She doesn't demand, she <u>asks</u>.

She still has her private customers also. My father, sweet man, doesn't bother to learn much Spanish.

"Schatzi, please tell her to be more careful with the hems."

These are instructions for one of the seamstresses. His favorite expression is, "Someone has to call," (either the insurance, or the supplier, or a customer who owes money...) "Would you, Schatzi?" My mother was always the **SOMEONE**.

They work hard, but life got more normal.

My parents have quite a group of nice friends, play Bridge here and there and, with time, my mother has started to laugh again and be <u>almost</u> her old self.

My brother (who is by now called "GERARDO,") and I now belong to several Jewish organizations, organized by age. We go on excursions, go to movies, meet in houses to listen to music or dance, and have speakers come and talk to us about the situation in Europe and the possibility of emigrating to Palestine. When I tell my father, he gets very upset.

"We just made it alive to Chile. Nobody in this family is going to Palestine. You can make that decision when you are old enough to care for yourself."

Other parents feel that way too, although quite a few of our friends have become ardent Zionists and work toward going to Palestine, as soon as there is a chance.

Gert's group has similar activities, all geared to their age.

I am having a wonderful time and many, many friends, girls and especially boys!!

Life is getting exciting, and I am happy.

YOM KIPPUR

Berlin, Germany 1937

I am so excited! Now that I am ten-years old, I am allowed to go to the grown-up services in the big sanctuary. Up to now, my brother and I have had to attend the Youth Service. Not that this service is bad. In fact, it is very, very nice. Gert and I sing in the choir. We know all the prayers by heart and all of our friends are with us. The best part is that the Youth Service only lasts a few hours, not all day like the regular Yom Kippur service in the main Temple.

The Youth Service is held in the library, a large room in which rows of chairs have been placed theater-style. Girls and boys are together. There is an organ, a podium for the Cantor, and we have our own prayer books (just thinner than the regular ones, but all in Hebrew just the same) and one of the younger Rabbis preaches a sermon, which is appropriate for us kids. He speaks to us about the difficult times we are living in, and reminds us that we will have to assume greater responsibilities, and sooner than our parents had wished for us. It is quite different from the sermons that the old Rabbi used to preach in Temple on Friday nights. He would quote the Torah, the Prophets and the Sages, and never spoke of "modern" times. But we know from school that things are different now, so that even the Rabbis have had to change their "preachings."

However, all of last year I have been a little upset at being with the "children." From our tenth birthday on, we are allowed to attend the service in the big synagogue. My parents are there, my grandparents, all our relatives and I have always wondered, what do they do <u>all</u> <u>day</u>?

Do they really pray all day? We, of course, fast on Yom Kippur, so I know they don't go out and eat, but do they visit, do they talk, or do they really sit and pray all day? So this year is the first time I can go with them, get my own seat assignment, and sit with the grownups. I feel a bit sorry for my brother. He is now by himself at the "little" service, but I comforted him this morning. Next year, he will also be ten years old and can join us older ones.

Our Temple is called "**LEVETZOW-SYNAGOGUE.**" It is an impressive building, over 100 years old and, as my grandmother tells me, for three generations, our family has attended services here. How proud I am to continue the tradition! There are magnificent stained glass windows depicting scenes from the bible, the twelve tribes, Moses holding the tablets with the Ten Commandments (which we, of course, had to memorize and can recite in Hebrew!) The aisles are covered with thick red carpets, the seats are cushioned and the sanctuary is decorated with beautiful flower arrangements. It is very festive and yet solemn.

Everybody has his assigned seat. All the men and boys over ten years old sit on the main floor. The women and girls are seated on the balcony, which goes around the entire building. There are five rows. My grandmother, Oma Feldblum, and my mother sit in the first row, and we can look down and wave to my father and grandfather, who look up every so often and blow kisses to us.

The place is pretty quiet, but you do hear whispering among the women and a "Shhhh" from the ushers every now and then. Of course, the service here is more formal than the

Youth Service. Every page is read, every prayer said in Hebrew, and many of them repeated in German. I think it is a good idea. Not everybody speaks Hebrew, and what sense does it make to say a prayer when one does not understand what is being said. Especially those prayers where we ask for good health, long life, for a worry-free future, forgiveness for our sins and shortcomings. It is most important to clearly understand their meaning.

You stand up most of the time. Only old or sick people are allowed to stay seated. Luckily, I can follow the book and join in the singing of the beautiful prayers that we memorized years ago.

Because everyone fasts on Yom Kippur and the air is heavy, we brought flowers for my grandmother and Oma Feldblum for the perfume, and most older ladies bring a lemon spiked with clover, which they smell during the day for "sustenance." Some of the women keep a perfume bottle in their purse, and smell on it or dab little bits on their foreheads and temples. I think it is so sophisticated (word from Opa's encyclopedia,) to finally be part of the grownup world. Perhaps next year, my mother will allow me to bring my own spiked lemon.

We got new clothes for the High Holidays. We get something new every year. Most children do. Mine is a two-piece suit, lavender with a lace collar. Very pretty. I also got new shoes, white with a blue bow. I wished I could have worn stockings, but that was "too old" for me. Not my opinion. Socks look a little ridiculous with a two-piece suit, but I didn't fuss. Most of our mothers and grandmothers get a new hat. Nobody shows up at Temple without a hat. Last year, I got in trouble for saying that the High Holidays are almost a fashion show and was told, "Don't be a big mouth. This is just the way people honor the New Year."

The problem is that we <u>walk</u> to Temple on the holy days and new shoes, in my opinion, are not exactly an "honor" after forty-five minutes of walking.

The best part of the service is to see my mother and Omi show us off to their friends. Every time my Opa looks up to where we sit on the balcony, his face lights up, and he gestures to his friends around him and points to me. If you read his lips, he is saying: "This beautiful little girl is my love, my granddaughter, Mulli. Have you ever seen anything like her?" And my mother smiles and blows kisses to him, and turns to my aunts and cousins. It makes me feel so special to be part of such a loving family.

We stay in the synagogue until early afternoon. At that time, they have "Yiskor," the memorial service for the dead. By tradition, anybody whose parents are alive must leave the sanctuary. So we leave with my mother, whose parents are, thank G-d, alive. My father stays inside. His parents and one younger sister died long ago and he prays for their memory. This service lasts about one hour. We wait in the lobby. You can hear the wailing of the cantor from the outside halls and when we go back in, you can tell that most people were crying or had been crying. This is always very sad, and I am glad my parents are alive and I don't have to participate in this part of the service.

The day is over when the first star appears on the sky, which is around seven o'clock in the evening.

We then go home to my grandparents' house to break the fast, and the entire family, aunts, uncles, cousins and friends join us for a few hours. The food is the same every year. This is also a tradition. First, we eat herring, which supposedly is good on an empty stomach. Then we have a piece of Challah and coffee for the grownups. We kids get fruit juice. Egg salad and fruit is also served. Then comes the review of the day. Everybody has something to say.

"The Cantor was better this year than ever."

"How can you say this? By noon, his voice was a little hoarse. He is not what he used to be."

"What do you want from him? Aren't we all getting older?" And there is always somebody who says, "Who knows how long we will have services at all, the way things are going..." and the same worried looks that we see so often on our parents' faces are back again.

"Let's just pray for a healthy and peaceful year. That's all we can do at this time."

"I liked the Rabbi's sermon, my father says, "it's difficult for him to preach these days. The old biblical references and stories are so outdated now. He has to bring up current issues, even if they are not religious."

"He can't," says one of my uncles, "we would accuse him of being an "alarmist." (I like the word "alarmist." I hear it often these days) "and he doesn't know any more than we do."

"It's difficult for him to please everybody. He is so controlled by the "situation..."(Eyes are rolled at this point and gestures are made in the direction of us children)..."You know what I mean."

While this conversation goes on, my mother and grandmother are in the kitchen heating up Matzoball soup. The food was cooked and the table set the day before, and we now sit down to eat. Only soup.

"On an empty stomach, you don't pile up too much food at once."

These truths have also been handed down from generation to generation, so who is there to contradict them?

In spite of the undercurrent of worry and fear that is now with us at all festivities, gatherings and family affairs, I love the High Holidays. There is something about them that makes me feel safe and secure. I have already promised my Omi that I will continue the tradition and hand them down to any children that I might have.

"Don't you think it is a little early for you to talk of having children?" she says, smiling. "But I am proud of you for your promise."

Her pride in me is all I want.

***

Santiago, Chile, 1939

This is the first Yom Kippur since we left Germany. It is September. We have been here since May. Who is "we?" My mother, my father, my brother Gert, and I. No other family. They all stayed behind in Berlin, and we are still hoping to get them out. The war has just started and Hitler has invaded Poland. Who knows how long this war will last and when my grandparents can leave? I am twelve years old now, but as our mother says, "Under these circumstances, you grow older faster." And that applies to us children as well. The thought of a Yom Kippur without our Temple, without the family, is hard to bear. But, of course, we go to services. We now have so much more to pray for!

There is one Synagogue in Santiago. It belongs to the "natives," the Russian and Polish Jews who came to South America at the beginning of the century and speak Spanish or Yiddish. Their sanctuary is very small, outside the downtown area, and the spoken languages are Spanish, Russian or Yiddish, three idioms foreign to us. For the newly-arrived

German immigrants, the Jewish Agency has rented an old movie theater in Santiago for the High Holidays. We cannot walk there because it is much too far from where we live, so our first sin is to have to take a streetcar. The make-believe synagogue isn't even make-believe. It is an old, run-down building. Posters of the movies being shown (after our services are over) decorate the foyer. Beggars crowd the entrance, but although our religion teaches us to take care of the poor, we do not have enough money to share with them.

We go inside. The disappointment is an almost palpable pain.

No trace of beauty, no serenity, no feeling of exaltation. Absolutely depressing. Clark Gable and Vivien Leigh smile from life-size posters. What are they doing here on Yom Kippur, our most holy day? My brother whispers, "Are they Jewish?" and my mother whispers back, "No, but we don't belong here either."

The place is dirty. No flowers, no decorations, no biblical references.

Although all of us are nicely dressed (we still have all the new clothes we brought from Germany) there is a feeling of darkness, of sadness, of pain all around us. We sit all together on the lower level, men, women and children. There is no balcony from which to wave to your loved ones...

The Cantor is an immigrant from Czechoslovakia. His voice is nice, but his melodies are different from what we are used to. The Rabbi is a rabbinical student who did not have time to be ordained in Germany. He does not have the bearing or force of our darling Rabbi Lewkowitz, but he tries. His sermon speaks of our hopes and wishes for the future, of our prayers for the families that were left behind, of the need for our parents to be strong for their children.

I look at my mother and the mothers around me. They are desperately trying to keep up an appearance of fortitude for us, the children, while gripped by anguish, loneliness and fear.

I look at the other children. Instead of our parents showing us off with pride, here it is us, the older children, who lock eyes, giving each other strength to take over. We were told by our teachers in Germany in the last months before leaving, that it would be up to us to be our parents' support. We would be the ones to learn a new language quickly. While they were trying to find work, it would be up to us to help, be unselfish and grow up fast. I can see on this Yom Kippur day, in this "synagogue," that the days of our growing up fast are here.

The service is similar to ours in Berlin. The sermon is in German, the responsive reading also. For the memorial service, we leave and wait outside. This time, the wailing sounds do not come only from the Cantor's mouth, but most of the congregants are crying desperately.

As dictated by tradition, at the appearance of the first star, the Rabbi proclaims the end of Yom Kippur. We take the streetcar home. My brother and I do not even try to cheer up our parents. They were just too sad. We broke the fast with Challah, coffee and eggs, but the loneliness was worse than the hunger. We talked about the happy times we had spent in years past, and put into words the thought that had been with us all day, "Perhaps there will be a miracle and we will see them all again soon."

The next year, when it was clear that our families would not be able to leave Europe, and that it was doubtful that we would see any of them ever again, it was decided that we, the children, should be allowed to stay for the Memorial Service to pray for those who were lost to us, even if our parents were still alive.

That first time is one of the most stirring memories of my entire life.

***

A few years later, after most of the European immigrants had made a new life for themselves in Chile, a new Synagogue was built. It was small, unobtrusive and modest, but it was ours. It was furnished and equipped with many religious objects, Torah scrolls and memorabilia that had been saved and smuggled out of Europe, and therefore had a very special meaning for all of us.

Our beautiful Temple in Berlin, along with 340 synagogues throughout Germany, had been burned down by the Nazis in 1938, during what is called the "Kristallnacht" on November 9, 1938.

As we integrated into life in Chile, our Rabbis learned to speak Spanish and services in our new Synagogue changed somewhat, to accommodate the different customs of Western and Eastern European Jews.

Life was getting much better.

Look who's turning 80!!

My First Day of School
(Used in an invitation for my surprise 80th Birthday Party)

My Father, Felix Raphael

My Mother, Hertha Raphael

My Grandparents, Gertrude and Max Jacoby

Kurt's Mother, Julia Mostny

Kurt's Father, Paul Mostny

Kurt's Grandparents, His Mother, Kurt and Grete

Kurt's Sister Grete and Husband Juan Gomez

My Brother, Gert

Last Picture in Chile

My Brother's Wedding

Leaving Chile

Henrietta and Reuben Levetin
with Kurt and Marion

Kurt and Marion on a Cruise

Our 50th Anniversary

Our Grandchildren
Jen & Husband Tom, Steven & Rachel
—Pat's Children

Elke & Jeroen—Daniela's Children

Jordan, Renee & Julian—Yvonne's Children

Jacqueline—David's Daughter

Zoe Aliza

Great Grandchildren
Jen & Tom's Children—Abbie & Zoe

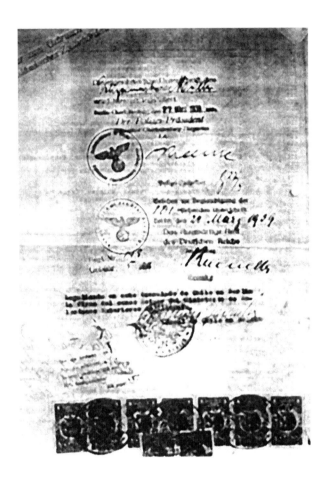

German Document
Partial list (52 pages total) of items my parents were allowed
to take out with permission from the German Police
Department

Reisegepäk - Verzeichnis
für Felix Israel Raphael und Familie   Frau und 2 Kinder

Nr.	Stück		Gegenstände
56	5	Mädchen	Rodelgarnituren
57	1	"	Strumpfbeutel
58	1	"	Schwimmkorken
59	2	"	Turnanzüge
70	6	Paar	Schuhe und Stiefel
71	1	"	Schlittschuhe
72	1	"	Rucksack
73	2	"	Hemdtaschen
74	1	"	Korselett
75	1	"	Stricküberzug
76 /77 je	2	"	Luftblusen und Hosen
78	1	"	Babykappe
79	3	"	Pullover
80	2	"	Strickkleider
81 /84	3	"	Dirndlkleider
82 /84	11	"	Kleider
82	8	"	Winterkleider
83 /84	4	"	Mäntel für Sommer und Winter
80	11	"	Blusen
81	1	"	Klubjacke
82/83	4	"	Röcke
84	1	"	Sommerjacke
85	2	"	Pebbhosen
86	1	"	Lufthose weiss
87	1	"	Trainingsanzug
88			einige medizinche Kleinigkeiten Kragen, Manschetten Gürtel Schleifen usw.
99/100	18 12	Dazen	Nachthemden
100	5	"	Pyjamas
101	3	"	Unterhemden weiss
102	10	"	Garnituren
103	8	"	Kunstseidengarnituren
104	4	"	Hemdhosen weiss
105	5	"	Kunstseidenhemdhosen
106	9	"	Hosen
107	6	"	Schlüpfer
108	4	"	Unterkleider
109	4	"	Büstenhalter
110	2	"	Hüftgürtel
111	3	"	Korselette
112	5	"	Untertaillen
113	4	"	Unterröcke
114	24	Paar	Strümpfe
115	5	"	Unterziehstrümpfe
116	48	"	Taschentücher weiss
117	12	"	" bunt
118	6	"	Tischtücher
119 /121	2	"	Morgenröcke
120 /124	13	"	Schürzen weiss und bunt
121	4	"	Kittel
122	1	"	Strandhose mit Jacke
123	1	"	Faltehose
124	5	"	Pusshirden
125	1	"	Überziehjacke
126	3	"	Seidenjacke
127	1	"	Sirformantel
128	8	"	Pullover
129	1	"	Wettjacke
130	1	"	Spitzenschal
131	1	"	Rodelgarnitur
132	1	"	Fussdecke

Page 2 of German Document

Page 3 of German Document

Kurt on Mostnystrasse, in commemoration of the Mostny
family in Linz, Austria

WILL YOU MARRY ME?

October 12, 1997

Today is our fiftieth wedding anniversary, and I am still waiting for my husband to ask me, "Will you marry me?" How can a girl be sure if she never had the chance to say yes or no?"

Ours was the most bizarre courtship. Love at first sight? Heavens, no. Matchmaker? No, no, those days were over and in 1947, we were independent and made our own decisions. With Kurt and me, there were no love poems, romantic secret meetings, moonlight serenades, or flowers with "I can't live without you" notes. Our relationship started with a <u>dirty towel</u>.

By all standards of compatibility, our marriage should never have worked. Had we consulted a psychologist, we would have been advised to stay as far as possible from each other. We were, and still are after fifty years, two people diametrically opposed in every way. Myself, vivacious, outgoing, loud, fast in movement and speech and full of mischief. Kurt, quiet, pensive, serious and introverted. How could it work? How did it?

This morning, after taking our assortment of geriatric pills and planning our low-cholesterol, non-fat dinner, Kurt and I took a critical look at each other. What a shock! Are we, two elderly, wrinkled, white-haired (or dyed!) people, a little lopsided from arthritis, a little stooped from osteoporosis, sagging in all the wrong places, are we the same pair that floated down the aisle of the Synagogue fifty years ago, tall, thin, exuding hope and happiness? We are still full of hope and happiness but the **Tall and Thin** is somewhat diminished.

"We made it because I always give in for the sake of peace and quiet," says my husband.

"No, it lasted because I was right most of the time and convinced you patiently," I countered.

"**Patiently?**" Kurt laughs. "I always thought I was the one with the patience. See, even after fifty years you have me brainwashed."

Undeniable, it took commitment, love, friendship and responsibility to make our marriage work. We added a generous overdose of flexibility, sense of humor and an "It's not that important" attitude to successfully share our lives and raise a family for half a century.

Our marriage was never dull. It has been exciting and full of adventure. We have always been known as "*The Gypsies*" for our informal ways, for making do with what was available, for bending organizational rules to adjust to our family's particular needs. We were, and still are at this time in our life, very uncomplicated.

I have always felt cheated for not being able to have a good fight with my husband and enjoy the making up afterwards. For all our married life, my mother-in-law lived with us and we never fought in front of her. Even our arguments had to be in whispers, and it is hard to quarrel with your spouse in a murmur; takes all the fun out of it and it doesn't work. We had to go to too much trouble to have a serious quarrel that most of the time we ended up laughing. Disagreements, we had many; differences of opinion, constantly. But there was never a fanatical insistence on points of view nor an irrational determination to get one's way, although it was more often than not, Kurt, who compromised for the sake of peace and tranquility.

***

My memory takes me back to Santiago. It is 1946.

I am eighteen-years old. My parents, Gert and I have been in Chile now for six years. Kurt, his widowed mother, and sister, Grete, had come the same year from Austria. We have been slowly adjusting to the South American way of life. Kurt is twenty-six.

To help the Jewish refugees from many European backgrounds settle in this new country, Jewish organizations have been formed to make sure that contact is maintained among the immigrants, particularly the younger generation. Different language groups have been formed, sport events have been organized, get-togethers are promoted to preserve the traditions and cultures from our past, to keep memories alive and to support those who have fled Europe without family. We are all driven by the need to stay together, to uphold our identity as Jews and Europeans in a strictly Catholic, Latin country and to find a replacement for the relatives that we have lost. Naturally, by now we all speak perfect Spanish.

My encounter with Kurt was anything but romantic. It was more a matter of convenience and necessity. We live next door to each other on Calle Passy, he at number 35 and we at number 17. We do not have an automobile, of course. Only a few wealthy immigrants who had been able to transfer money out of Germany to Switzerland, own a car, but we are not one of them! Our means of transportation are streetcars and buses.

A system has therefore been developed within our Group whereby, after a meeting or event, the young men will take home on public transportation those girls (or girl) who live closest to them. Girlfriends and boyfriends spend the day together, but lack of money for a taxi and transportation constraints dictate that one goes home with one's <u>neighbor</u>. And I am Kurt's neighbor. Willing or not, he has to take me home from wherever the group had met.

This particular Sunday has been no exception. The Group that Kurt and I belong to had gone to the beach. I know that Kurt will take the streetcar with me at the end of the day and walk me to our house, although I would much rather go home with my boyfriend, Salo. But this is how it works and there is no choice.

We spent a delightful day at the beach. I, with my Salo, and Kurt with his girlfriend (who remembers her name?) As we are leaving for home, Kurt hands me his towel full of sand and dirt. Very politely (he is always <u>sooo</u> polite) he says, "Would you do me a favor? I didn't bring a beach bag. Could you put my dirty towel in yours and I will then carry it." I did, but he didn't.

***

(I complained in later years about my husband being spoiled and accustomed to being catered to and, of course, blamed my mother-in-law for it. I got a glimpse into Kurt's nature that fateful Sunday, and should have known better, but young and impetuous, I ignored the warning. His friends called him *The Count Mostny*, the only one who always wore a tie, sat on the beach on a pillow! and brought his own food to picnics. His idea of <u>letting go</u> consisted of opening the top button of his shirt.)

***

I get home that night and empty the bag into the dirty laundry basket. A few days later, my mother, having done the wash, says, "Be sure to take this towel over to old Mrs. Mostny. We don't want them to say we kept one of their towels. It isn't even a nice one. Go return it."

Dutifully, the next Sunday morning, I march a few houses down to "old Mrs. Mostny." She is very proper and thanked me profusely for the return of the towel.

"I had already noticed it was missing," she says with a sigh, "It's not like in the old country, where I never had to count towels or anything else. Oh, how times have changed."

"Is Kurt here?" I ask, not so much because I wanted to see him, but rather to get away from old Mrs. Mostny's *kvetching* (whining).

He hears me and comes to the door. "What a surprise. Thanks for saving my life," he says. I then heard the saga of the lost towel.

"My family is not in the habit of keeping other people's property," I snicker. "That's the only reason I came." I am not going to give him any ideas!

"You doing anything important right now?" he asked. "I want to show you something. It's a surprise."

I have nothing better to do on this Sunday morning, so I say yes. I would like to see what it is that is so mysterious.

"It's a few blocks from here. Come on."

We walk down the street towards the commercial area. Kurt tells me that he has saved some money and gone into partnership with a shoemaker to manufacture sandals. I am impressed.

We go to see the workshop which Kurt, of course, calls "his factory." What ugly shoes! I can't see anybody buying, leave alone wearing, such monstrous creations. But Kurt is so proud and excited that I keep my opinion to myself.

"I want you to have a pair," he says, "take any type you like." I say, "No, thank you," but he insists, and gives me a pair of shoes, brown suede, clumsy-looking, which I know I will never wear (but eventually did!)

The gesture touches me. An entire pair of shoes must eat into his profit. I think, here I am, not even his girlfriend.

On the way home, we talk about how all of us are getting settled and making a living, and Kurt tells me about his life in Linz, Austria, and his dreams of entering his father's Liquor and Wine manufacturing plant, one of the largest industries in Linz. Kurt's father died when Kurt was nine-years-old, and his uncles ran the factory. He was supposed to get his inheritance at age eighteen and become a partner. But his hopes were shattered by Hitler.

I find that there is definitely more to this guy than I had thought. Truthfully, I have never given him much thought at all. He definitely isn't <u>fun</u>, but everything he says is judicious and makes sense. He isn't given to idle chatter, but his pride in his accomplishments is almost exuberant, a trait that I have never noticed in him before.

We make a date for the coming Sunday. My mother is in shock when I tell her. "But he is so serious and sedate. Won't you be bored? You are so impatient, and in constant motion. Besides, what are you going to tell Salo? I can see this is getting very complicated."

"I am only going to the movies with Kurt. I'm not going to marry him," I argue.

"Heavens, talking about marriage at eighteen. None of these boys can afford a wife yet, and we don't have money for a wedding." Typically, my darling, Jewish mother is already worried. Who wants to get married yet? I am having too good a time with the boys to even think of settling down.

We go to see *"The Seven Veils"* and again, I find that Kurt is more mature, more of a man than the boys I am going out with. But he sure has a lot of negatives against him, some perhaps *"unfixable."* He doesn't like to dance. "Too tiring." He doesn't much care for music. "Too noisy." He doesn't gossip. He only talks about meaningful matters. Too serious for me. He also speaks German with an Austrian accent. An absolute "No-No." He plays Bridge. Whoever heard of a young person playing an old folks' game?

Our romance didn't flourish, and I am back with Salo and then Peter, Alfred, and back to Salo.

A few months later, the Mostny family, Kurt, his mother and sister, move away. Grete just got married and her husband, very wealthy and quite a bit older than she, bought a house in the suburbs of Santiago. He insists that Mrs. Mostny move in with them, and since Kurt's mother won't hear of leaving her "little boy" behind, they are all moving into the new house, away from our neighborhood.

I personally think that Kurt is crazy to go and live with his new brother-in-law, whom he hardly knows. Although Paul (the new husband) is a very nice and loving person, he is only marrying one wife, not an entire family. But, I am sure when the word *Peacenick* was coined, they must have had Kurt in mind. He doesn't want to disturb the harmony of his family and "how bad can it be?" My opinion was not requested, but I tell him how bad I think it could be. But Paul, Kurt's mother, and Grete have made up their minds and Kurt doesn't like to argue.

A year has gone by. It is the beginning of 1947. I haven't seen Kurt since they moved away. One day I get a telephone call from him at the office where I work as a secretary.

"There is an emergency that I would like to discuss with you," he says, "Can we go out to dinner and talk—tonight, if possible?"

Kurt isn't one to use the word <u>emergency</u> lightly. I ask if it is his mother or Grete and he says, "No." I am intrigued and say yes, I will meet him.

He picks me up from work. My boss, also a Jewish immigrant and friend of the family, reproachfully comments: "<u>Him</u> again? What happened to Salo? You are playing with fire, my dear. Girls like you end up in trouble."

I am mad, but don't answer. After all, my boss is paying my salary and I need it. But, really, what is the matter with these people? I am only going to dinner with a friend. And one that is really only a friend, nothing more. So where is the problem?

We go to a little Swiss restaurant near my office. I am dying to hear about the emergency that prompted Kurt to call me again after all this time. I don't think he would use this as a pretext to see me. He isn't romantic enough for such a scheme, but I enjoy seeing him.

While we order dinner, we talk. He doesn't mention the emergency. I am sure he wants to wait until our food is served, so I refrain myself from asking. Not easy, but I make it! While we talk, I find myself amazed at how much Kurt has changed. He is still earnest, serious and calm, but somehow he appears to have loosened up since I saw him last year. What a difference between him and my other boyfriends! He is a man, they are boys. Or have I grown up in the meantime?

We talk about many things and there isn't a boring moment in our conversation. I don't think he is too mature for me, or have I suddenly turned from a girl into a woman? I haven't noticed any changes in myself, but Kurt has certainly become a different person.

The emergency has to do with my co-worker's husband, who is employed in the trucking company that Kurt manages. This young man, also a Jewish boy from our group, has given out bad checks and is in jail.

Kurt is looking for a way to help him and his wife, and wants me to intercede with my bosses to lend her some money to bail her husband out. How disappointing, I think, there is a real emergency. This was not a subterfuge to see me. No problem, though. I still have Salo and Alfred is waiting in the wings!

Kurt and I have several meetings concerning the Friedmanns, (the couple in question) and every time we get together, we have a lot to say to each other besides the matter of the jailbird (who, by the way, got out on bail, thanks to my bosses' help.)

Without noticing it, Kurt and I make date after date and start going out without mentioning the Friedmanns at all. My boyfriend, Salo, is appeased by thinking this is a business matter. Besides, he is so in love with me, he never doubts my intentions for a second. But I start doubting. I am not starry-eyed in love with Kurt, but there definitely is a strong attraction, physically and intellectually, although any intimate contact stops right there. Sex is out of the question. You remain a virgin until you marry. That is the rule. Standards allow a certain amount of necking, but that's all. Besides, leaving the moral issue aside, not having a car and living with your parents, where could we have an opportunity for anything <u>forbidden</u>? Perhaps we are not limited by our morals, but by lack of opportunity!

In May of 1947, on my twentieth birthday, Kurt gives me a gold bracelet.

"You take this right back," my mother insists. "This is a very compromising gift. Only a man with serious intentions would give a gift like this. Besides, can he afford such an expensive present? He has his mother to support, as you well know. This is an engagement gift. Besides, you haven't gotten rid of Salo, Peter and Alfred yet. Or did you secretly get engaged?"

I try to calm my mother, "I didn't get secretly engaged, and I am sure Kurt doesn't mean anything with this gift. Just don't say anything to Salo and the others until we are sure what's going on."

My mother has a migraine headache for a week over this, and I, reluctantly, get on the phone with Kurt. "I must return the bracelet to you. Such a gift implies serious intentions, which you and I don't have. Besides, my mother won't let me keep it."

Kurt is angry. "Throw it in the garbage," he says, "I don't want it back. Besides, who says I don't have serious intentions?" I am totally flabbergasted. He hasn't even said, "I love you" or something to that effect, nor has he asked me how I feel about him. And he has serious intentions? How about me?

"We need to discuss this in person," I say, hoping that I can talk Kurt out of his serious intentions and give myself a little more time to analyze my own feelings. I am strongly attracted to him, I admire and trust him. I love him as a person, but it isn't the love with flowers and blue skies and heartbeats and tears that you see in the movies. I am not "swept off my feet," but I do have strong feelings for him, I trust him and can imagine spending my life with him. Perhaps that is the real love.

"I want you to come to Paul's house for tea on Saturday," Kurt says, "I will pick you up." To his house for *tea*? With old Mrs. Mostny, his sister and brother-in-law?" How formal is this getting? But I say yes. I have already offended him by refusing his gift, so why make it worse by rejecting a perfectly proper invitation?

That Saturday is the First of June 1947. Kurt picks me up in his car, a 1936 Ford that he just bought. I think it is the epitome of elegance, since none of our other friends has an automobile. Paul's house is in the district of El Golf, a high-class neighborhood. It has a large front yard encircled by a fence. Kurt rings the bell and I expect the maid to come out and unlock the gate. To my never-to-be-forgotten surprise, it is <u>old</u> Mrs. Mostny who comes to the front, opens the gate and literally throws her arms around me in an embrace that is so untypical for her, that to this day I remember the feeling.

"My dear, dear girl," she exclaims, in a manner totally uncharacteristic for her. "You don't know how happy I am to see you." One has to know Mrs. Mostny to realize how extraordinary this display of emotion is for her. She is a very shy, proper and extremely reserved person who keeps her feelings always under control. I am speechless, which certainly is not my normal behavior. What is going on here? Have they all gone crazy?"

"It's very nice to see you also." I shake her hand and look at Kurt questioningly. Does <u>he</u> know what his mother's problem is? I get no response. He just looks amused. The next shock comes when I am greeted with the same passion by Kurt's sister, who normally is reserved and restrained like her mother, and Paul, who both kiss me and hug me like long lost lovers.

As we sit down to have tea, I decide to bring some sense into the situation.

"Would somebody please explain to me what all this means?" I ask nobody in particular but looking at all of them. "Your reception is very flattering and I thank you for it, but don't you think that I should be in on the secret that you all seem to know?"

"Kurt hasn't spoken to you?" Mrs. Mostny is utterly confused. "What a faux-pas! Kurt, I am so embarrassed. Please before we have tea, you must talk to Marion, now."

It turns out that my darling (now husband) has told his mother and sister that he is dating me again, and that this time it is serious and that he intends to marry me. Obviously, he has forgotten, or neglected, to tell them that he has not spoken to me yet, so they assumed that I have accepted and this is a so-called engagement party.

We have a very short tea and a very, very long conversation, Kurt and I. We come to the conclusion that we love each other, that our different personalities complement each other, and that we will make a happy and interesting couple.

I come home that night after midnight. My mother is hanging out the window of our apartment waiting for me.

"Thank G-d," she cries, "What happened? It is so late and you were only going out for tea in the afternoon. I was sure you were in an accident. Kurt's automobile always worries me. And you didn't call. Tell me, what happened?"

"I didn't call you because I couldn't talk from the Mostnys' house. I am sorry. I knew you would worry, but I just didn't know how to explain things to you from there. What happened is that I got engaged!"

My mother almost faints. "Engaged? To whom?" How could you get engaged to anybody while you were having tea with the Mostnys? Are you sure you are all right?"

"I guess I got engaged to Kurt Mostny, Mami, who else?"

"Who else? You are asking me who else? What about Salo and Alfred? What are you going to tell them? And your father, what do you think <u>he</u> is going to say?"

"Don't worry about Salo and Alfred, mother," I reassure her. I will talk to them. They may be surprised, even angry, but they will get over it. Besides, they are not your sons, let their mothers console them."

"But how about your father? He will never allow you to marry at twenty. I just hope his ulcer doesn't act up with this excitement."

"Don't worry about father," I say. "I will explain this to him. All he wants is for me to be happy. By the way, we should wake him now. Kurt is coming in the morning to talk to him and ask for permission to marry me."

"You want me to wake him up now? In the middle of the night?" My poor mother, the most level-headed woman I know, is now beside herself.

I try to calm her. "I think it's best. I am sure he has to prepare a speech or something and he will want to be ready in the morning. Besides, how could you go to sleep now when your daughter is planning to become the young Mrs. Mostny?"

We wake my father up. It takes a moment to tell him the news. He shakes his head, "I can't believe it. I just can't believe it. Typical of our family—these important decisions are made in the middle of the night. So let's analyze the situation." My father adores me. He doesn't want to lose me. He wants the very best for me and suffers because he cannot always give me what I want. He is now giving me all the reasons why I should wait, why I should enjoy my freedom a little longer, why I should not assume the responsibilities of a home and children at such a young age...and so on.

He cries. I convince him that I am sure (am I?) that I am ready to get married, that Kurt is whom I want to be married to, and that I know what I am doing.

We stay up all night talking. My parents giving me advice and worrying what kind of wife I will be. Me, reassuring them that everything will work out just fine. Finally, they say yes.

The next morning, Kurt shows up at our house with flowers for my mother. My father has taken two tranquilizers and is hoping that Kurt will ask him only if he can marry me. He will say yes, and it will be over.

My darling father, shy, almost timid, feels terribly uncomfortable asking Kurt how he intends to support me, what his plans are for the future, what would happen if something went wrong, questions that he feels are an intrusion in somebody else's life, and that nevertheless have to be asked to be sure that his darling daughter will have a happy life.

My brother and I are, of course, not present at this conversation. We listen through the keyhole in the adjacent room. I feel really sorry for both men. My father, saying to Kurt, "I guess I should say DU to you" (the familiar form in German) and Kurt replying, "I guess so, and I will try to call you <u>father</u>, which will be hard. I have not had a father since I was nine-years-old and haven't called anybody by that name since then. But I will try. Getting a father is an extra present that Marion is giving me."

We all survived that morning and got engaged officially on June 15, 1947, and married on October 12, 1947.

My only regret to this day, fifty years later, is that Kurt has never asked me:

"Will you marry me?"

THE BEGINNING OF MR. & MRS. MOSTNY

We got officially engaged on June 15, 1947. I was extremely happy, but also apprehensive. I was twenty years old. Was I ready to get married? Was I prepared to give up all my boyfriends? Would we, as a married couple, have as much fun as I was having by myself? Would I, from one day to the next, have to become a respectable married lady? At twenty…?

And Kurt, at twenty-eight, was so mature, so dignified, so serious, the exact opposite of me. But I loved him exactly for these qualities and hoped that our personalities would mesh and produce two perfect human beings

***

(As I am writing this, almost sixty years later, still happily married to the same Kurt, I can say: It has worked out beautifully. I could not have asked for a better husband and friend!)

My engagement ring was a golden band inscribed "Kurt 15 de Junio 1947." Kurt's ring was exactly the same and read "Marion 15 de Junio 1947."

Kurt had a pinky ring, with a diamond in it, from his father, the only piece of jewelry that he had been able to smuggle out of Austria, to be used as an emergency fund in case of necessity. He had it re-set as a wedding ring and gave it to me. In those days, wedding gifts were really not that important.

None of my married girlfriends had a diamond ring. (All the jewelry owned by Jews was taken by the Nazis in Germany and Austria in exchange for permission to leave.) And who had money in Chile to buy DIAMOND RINGS?

We set our wedding date for October 12th, because that was the date for commemorating the discovery of America, a national holiday in South America, and this way, we would always have a holiday on our anniversary. It so happened that in 1947, the 12th of October fell on a Sunday, a perfect day to get married. (It turned out that we enjoyed our anniversary-holiday every year until we came to America, the continent discovered by Columbus, and made a shocking discovery. Here in America, the 12th of October was just another day. It is called "Columbus Day," but certainly not a holiday.) Ironically, after eighteen years and such careful planning, our anniversary is now often celebrated on a regular weekday. What a disappointment!

We had an engagement party on July 13th, in our home. My parents could not afford a big wedding. Very few families could. It was customary to have an Open House to celebrate an engagement. It was a cocktail party in the afternoon. All our friends and acquaintances who could not be invited to the wedding, were invited instead to the engagement party. The celebration lasted until late at night. Everybody had a good time and there was happiness and joy in our house.

Besides small gifts, we got a lot of "advice" and had to listen to the "voices of experience" from the older couples.

After the party, I wore my diamond ring on the right ring finger and made sure everybody could see it. It worked miracles.

One night, Kurt and I were necking in his car (necking was the most you did in our days when you were "only" engaged; and only if nobody caught you) when a policeman approached the car with a flashlight and barked, "Nada de mariguanzas (no fooling around here.) Get out of the car." I promptly showed him my ring. "Officer we are engaged, we are not fooling around." He left. Good thing too. My mother would have been horrified had I shown up with a police officer at her door for engaging in "mariguanzas."

My grandfather's business in Germany was a sales agency for imported laces, brocades, decorative and embroidered fabrics, hand-woven silks and velvets from Switzerland, Belgium and Czechoslovakia. My parents took with them a supply of these beautiful materials hoping to sell them. Nobody wanted them and they ended up keeping them, waiting for the right opportunity to use them. The opportunity was October 12th.

My mother made my wedding dress, and also a beautiful outfit for herself and one for Tante Jenny. We were all were dressed "way beyond our means." We felt that this would be a symbol of my grandparents' presence at the celebration. More tears than yarn went into these clothes. The days that should have been the happiest of our lives, full of expectations, hopes and dreams, were clouded with memories and sad thoughts, and the loss of family tore at our hearts. Every one of our sentences began with, "If Omi and Opa could see you."

My father tried to console us. "Think how lucky we really are," he would say, "how many of our friends sent their children on Kinder-Transports to England or Holland and never saw them again. Or look at the Birnbaums. Their son spent the war in England and now that he finally came to join them, he is a stranger. He is an adult, and his parents don't even know him anymore. Aren't we fortunate to have our children with us? Our family is certainly not big. Just the four of us, no grandparents, no aunts and uncles, no cousins, none on my side, and just

Tante Jenny and Rodolfo on yours. A small group indeed. But a very close one, let's be grateful for that. Now, how is my princess' gown coming along?" My sweet father, whose heart was bleeding also, always worried about my mother.

Our wedding ceremony was at the Synagogue on Calle Monjitas, near the residence where we stayed on our arrival in Santiago, eight years before.

Afterwards, there was a dinner at the "Club Hungaro" with elegant food and a violin player. I was allowed to invite only my girlfriend, Eva Nathan. The other thirty guests were my three bosses with their wives, a few close friends of my parents, and, of course, Tante Jenny and Rodolfo.

Two of my bosses wished me "Masseltov." The third one, Mr. Suchestow, asked me to be sure to tell him immediately when I got pregnant so that they could look for a new secretary, whom I needed to train.

"I just got married," I told him. "And we don't plan on having children right away, so don't worry."

To think that this boss and his wife had to be invited to the wedding! I would have loved to have two of my friends instead. But that was the proper thing to do. Your bosses were invited to such celebrations. After all, you owed them your livelihood. At least that's how my parents felt.

I had one concern. I had to get used to the idea of being called "Mrs. Mostny." The only Mrs. Mostny I knew was Kurt's mother, and to think that I would now have to share my name with an old lady, wasn't a pleasant thought.

I made up my mind. I was going to be Marion Raphael forever, Marion Raphael married to Kurt Mostny. That would do it!

***

My ring brought another big change into our lives.

When Kurt asked my father for permission to marry me, he convinced him that he could support me with his job as manager of a large trucking company. Up to then, I had turned over my salary to my parents, who then gave me pocket money. Some of my friends got to keep the money they earned, but my parents needed it and I really didn't. But after the wedding, I would keep my salary, and I worried about how my parents would get along without it. They assured me that they would be able to manage. And Kurt and I would be fine with two salaries.

That was the plan, but when people noticed my engagement ring, they wanted to know all the details. Where were we going to live, was I staying at my job, were we planning to have a child right away? Among them was one of the customers of the company for which I worked. His name was Albert Meininger, an old Jewish man who loved to tell stories. Every purchase, even the smallest one, turned into an hour of visiting. My bosses liked him and didn't object.

Mr. Meininger saw my ring and said, "You are getting married? To whom? What does he do?" I told him and he declared, "Nonsense, trucking company. What nice Jewish boy works in the trucking industry? Your own business, that's what you want." I wasn't exactly shy. "Our own business? With what?" I asked him.

"Introduce me to your future husband" he said. "I have the idea of the century."

We all knew that he was a little crazy, but I thought there was no harm in listening to the "idea of the century."

Mr. Meininger was odd, there was no doubt. He was unmarried, had no children and drank a little too much. Basically, he was a lonely old man. But he was highly educated, had been a banker in Hamburg, Germany, was the proprietor of his own bank, and financial matters were his strength. He showed, however, the same traces of instability, from which many of the Jewish immigrants were suffering. We had seen these signs in many of our friends' parents. The higher their positions had been in Germany, the harder it was for them to get used to their new circumstances. Mr. Meininger was a typical example of a displaced intelligence, of someone utterly lost in this new world, half-genius, half-crazy.

Of course, Kurt and I were curious to hear about the "idea of the century." My bosses suggested that we should take it not only "with a grain of salt," but with an entire saltshaker.

Kurt and I met Mr. Meininger in a coffee shop a few days later. He told us that he had a business (he called it 'FACTORY') where he manufactured buttons and belts of leather. He was starting to make the same out of the new material called "Lucite," the latest discovery that was being imported from the United States. "I am old," he said, "I need a partner."

"We don't have any money," we told him. He dug out several used cigarette packages and matchbooks with pencil notes on them. This turned out to be his bookkeeping system. The numbers on the cigarette packages were the monies that customers owed him. The matchbook numbers indicated what he owed his suppliers. We were shocked. This was not the way we had learned accounting and bookkeeping. Mr. Meininger himself couldn't make heads or tails out of his figures, but he said, "Believe me, I make good money, but I am old and need a young partner to help me develop the business. You don't need any money. I make you a 50/50 partner. I put up the money and both of you do the work. Do we have a deal?"

We told him we had to think it over.

"O.K.," he said," let me know by tomorrow."

"It won't be tomorrow," we told him, "We don't live together and work during the day, so we will need some time to discuss this. We also need our parents' opinion. Anyway, before making any decision, we would like to see your factory."

"Sure," he said. Let's go right now." Kurt and I looked at each other. Either we were totally nuts or the man was really crazy, like everybody said. But what could we lose? We went. We took a taxi to a part of the city that I had never been to before.

Seeing it, I knew why. The whole district looked as if the Conquistadores had just left. The streets were paved with cobblestones. The buildings were old, dirty and one had the feeling that a strong wind would blow them apart. Number 1491 San Pablo Street, the address of Mr. Meininger's business, was one of the worst. The only mark that distinguished it from the rest of the neighbor houses was a sign that read, "FABRICA DE CUEROS ALBERTO MEININGER" (Leather factory Alberto Meininger).

The cars parked on the street were vintage 1930, maximum. Most of them had no fenders, bad paint, certainly no hubcaps, and clearly demonstrated the level of ownership pride the neighbors showed in their possessions.

Mr. Meininger—who wanted to be called "Don Alfredo"-said, with a pride undeserved by the surroundings, "This is it. Come in and look around. Isn't it something?" It sure was "something"!

The entrance was so narrow, I decided then and there that this was a plus. We could never get fat in this place because we wouldn't fit through the door if we gained as much as a pound or two.

The inside wasn't any better than we expected. The walls were partly covered with old wallpaper, partly with movie-star posters, partly with nothing. Everything was covered with dust that had been undisturbed for months, or years...? Naked light bulbs hung on wires, some isolated, some bare, criss-crossing the rooms.

Furniture...what furniture? Some old desks and chairs barely holding up.

I expected mice to come out of the upholstery to see what was disturbing their sleep. And the smell! There was an odor that pervaded the entire place. Smells of leather, which was O.K., of food, which was nauseating, of cats that I presumed were long dead, and of other undefined matters that I didn't attempt to identify.

"It isn't a very fancy office," Don Alfredo declared, but it does the job."

We had to take his word for it. The so-called warehouse was a little better. There was plenty of material lying around, unsorted, of course, but at least there was something tangible to look at. The machines and tools looked acceptable. The workbenches and workstations were of the type that would be any lawyer's dream for an "unsafe environment" claim. But in Chile, in those days, we didn't know about OSHA or working conditions or harassment suits. People were happy to have a job and to many workers, the place was not any worse than the slums they lived in. And they loved working for foreigners who treated them like the human beings they were, and paid them a lot better than the Chilean bosses, who still lived in the era of slavery as far as workers were concerned.

Our host opened a closet. From the FRAGANCE emanating from it, I expected to see dead rats staring at me. Thank G-d that was not the case.

"You get used to it," Mr. Meininger said. I doubted I ever would.

He then pointed at several large boxes overflowing with papers. "See, here you have the entire bookkeeping system. Anything you want to know is in these documents. My accountant hasn't been here in a while to sort them, but tax time is coming and he should appear pretty soon."

This was not exactly how the companies we worked for kept their books, but we didn't say anything.

There was a second floor, where the finished products were stored and displayed. It looked quite clean and one could see what the production consisted of. There were nicely finished belts, buttons and wallets, as well as samples of gloves and some display cases made of the new "Lucite" material that Mr. Meininger was planning to manufacture. It all looked quite organized, clean and businesslike.

"Nu?" Mr. Meininger asked. "What do you think?"

We told him we would let him know in a few days.

"Don't go by appearances," he said, "this is the opportunity of a lifetime for a young couple who wants to work and innovate." To us, it seemed more like the adventure and risk of a lifetime, but we wanted to think about it.

Before we mentioned the proposition to our parents, whom we knew would be aghast at the mere thought of giving up our jobs and starting our own business under these conditions, Kurt and I discussed the possibilities all through the night, and the next night, and the next...

What could we really lose? Only our jobs, and if everything failed, we would always find other employment. The situation in Chile at the time was such that anybody with a certain level of intelligence, education, knowledge of languages, with a desire to prosper and with energy and will to work, would find a good job. Chile was developing rapidly, in part thanks to the influx of foreigners, who had either escaped or survived the war in Europe, and there were opportunities everywhere in particular for young people. And we were young. Very young.

"This may be our chance to go into business by ourselves," Kurt said, and, naively, I added, "And we can work together and be together all the time." (Little did I know then that this should have been the most powerful reason not to do it!)

"And where else could we start our own business without any money?" was Kurt's reasoning. "We really have nothing to lose except a few years. We are young, and what are a few years compared to the chance of being in business by yourself for a lifetime"?

(Fifty years later, we are still in business by ourselves, still working full-time and far from young...)

We asked Mr. Meininger for the "books" and got the carton full of papers that we had seen in the closet. We poured over them for many hours, and came to the conclusion that with a lot of work and patience, we could straighten things out. The figures didn't exactly add up, but the potential for business was definitely there. Besides, if nothing else, we could learn a lot from the old man, and that was worth at least half a Masters degree in business, which we couldn't afford to get otherwise.

"Let's go tell our parents," Kurt sighed, after we had decided to take the gamble.

Kurt's mother was no problem. She lived with us, had no money worries, and whatever her adorable son did was fine with her. She wished us good luck.

With my parents, it was different.

"Be ready for a heart attack on my father's side," I said, "He thinks we can hardly live on our two salaries, and in his wildest dreams, he wouldn't dare do what we are embarking on."

I was right. My poor father almost fainted when we told him that we had decided to give up our jobs and work together in our own business.

"To have a partner is worse than having a boss," he said, "A boss you can leave, but a partner is forever. You know we don't have enough money to help you if something goes wrong," he lamented, "You will be entirely on your own. I surely wouldn't do it." My mother agreed with him. "Why take such a chance when there is no need for it," she added. "If you don't like your jobs anymore, you will always find new ones. Why take such a risk?"

We understood their concern, but assured them that everything would work out fine.

It was September 1947. We were planning our wedding in October, and instead of spending our engagement time in carefree dreaming and planning, we worked during the day at our jobs, and spent the nights sorting the "books" of the business, the inventory, the customer lists, the debts and assets—if you could call them that. We worked weekends in the factory, cleaning and straightening out, but we were happy because we did it together.

After a while, we saw the great improvements that could be made to the dismal conditions of the place, and felt that we had made the right decision.

In the meantime, Mr. Meininger had adopted us. He was a lonely old man, very happy that he now had some young company, and never stopped talking about "who he had been" in the old country. We learned a lot from him, and a little patience on our side made him quite acceptable as a friend.

We gave notice at our jobs, left with doubtful wishes on the part of our bosses, and after a four-day honeymoon, started to work on October 16, 1947, as co-owners and partners of the "Industry" which was immediately re-baptized "Fabrica de Cueros Alberto Meininger y Compania." (Alberto Meininger & Company).

***

KURT'S FAMILY

HIS PARENTS

Kurt's parents were Paul Mostny, born on April 26, 1887 in Linz, Austria, and Julia Glaser, born on February 14, 1894, in Gruenburg, a small town in Austria. They got married in 1913. Paul, his brothers Ludwig and Richard, purchased the liquor factory founded by their uncle Leopold Mostny, and produced all kinds of hard liquor, vinegar and fruit juice.

They had the monopoly for alcohol production in Austria and became quite wealthy. The name 'MOSTNY' was a known and respected name in "Upper Austria."

In 1904, Paul's parents had another child, a son, Hans, who, because of the age difference with his older brothers, became more a friend than an uncle to Kurt.

Kurt's father served in the First World War in the Austrian Army. Because he owned an automobile, he became the chauffeur of a General named Redl. Once they found out that he was a prosperous businessman, he was elevated to Business Manager of the General.

Julia, Kurt's mother, was an only child. After grade school in Gruenburg, she was sent to the next big city, called Steyr, to finish her education. She lived with the Rabbi's family, who also instructed her in the observance of the Jewish faith.

Paul and Julia had two children; Grete, born in 1914, and Kurt, born on March 3, 1919.

Kurt's father died very young, at age forty-one, of liver and stomach cancer. Julia, who was then only thirty-three years old, was left with the two children, fortunately in a very comfortable financial situation.

Kurt's uncles became the children's guardians, and provided them with the best upbringing, education and family love. Money was never a problem.

Leopold Mostny, the founder of the factory, and the head of the entire family, was a very wealthy man. He believed in giving part of his fortune to philanthropic endeavors, and donated a large piece of land that he owned, along the river Danube, to the city of Urfahr (which became later part of the city of Linz.) He was named advisor to Emperor Franz Joseph, and was given the title of 'Honorary Citizen of Linz'.

However, all his benevolence and charity for his country did not help him. When the Nazis overtook Austria, he was arrested at the age of one hundred years, and died on an open truck on its way to the Concentration Camp. He lived from January 5, 1842 to June 19, 1942.

After the war, the city of Linz named a street in his honor, the "Leopold Mostny Strasse." It did not bring him back to life, but at least, the name Mostny is remembered in Austria.

Most of the Mostny brothers survived the Holocaust. One of them emigrated to the United States; another, went to Brazil, and Hans, the youngest, left for Argentina. He and his wife, Isolde, had a son, Mario, born in Mendoza, with whom we are still in contact. The uncle in Brazil had managed to get his money out of Austria before the German invasion. He started a new industry in Sao Paulo and became very successful. After the war, he returned to Austria. With documents attesting to his ownership of the business, which he was able to produce, he achieved to get the factory back from the Austrian Government (which was then under Russian occupation) and recuperated the fortune that they had lost. However, he did not make an effort to stay in touch with his relatives. Money, perhaps?

***

KURT'S SISTER GRETE

Grete was the "famous" one in the family. She graduated from High School as Valedictorian, entered the University of Vienna, and studied Archeology. She had to learn seventeen languages, mostly dead languages, and succeeded in getting a job as an archeologist with the Italian Mission in Egypt. She took part in the excavation in Luxor, and was ready to get her PH.D. from the University. She returned to Vienna on March 9th, 1938 to receive her title on March 15th. However, Hitler had invaded Austria on the 13th of March 1938, and because she was Jewish, her title was denied.

She immediately left Austria and went to Italy, where Kurt followed her a few months later. They applied for a visa for Chile, which was not granted.

Grete then managed to get a job at the Museum of Brussels, Belgium, and insisted on taking her "secretary" (Kurt) along.

Through connections, they were able to get their mother out of Austria, and, via Czechoslovakia, into Brussels. They finally got their visa for Chile, and Kurt left immediately. Grete stayed to finish her studies and obtain her PH.D. title. Julia stayed with her.

There is a story that goes with Kurt's leaving Belgium that would have been funny had it not been so disturbing.

He had an Austrian passport that had to be replaced by a German one, now that Austria was part of the 'Great Germany.' The German Consul in Brussels issued the new one. With it,

Kurt went to the Chilean Consulate to get his visa for Chile. The Consul looked at his new German passport. He turned red.

"You said you are a Jew and need to escape from Europe. Where is your "J" in the passport? (All passports for Jews were stamped with a large letter "J"). "If you are not Jewish, why do you need to leave?"

Kurt took his passport back to the German Consulate. "You forgot to stamp a "J" in my passport. I insist on it. I'm entitled to it. Please add it now," he told the officer. The consular employee was aghast. "It was my mistake, sorry. But why do you want to be brandished as a Jew?" "Because it is my right," said Kurt, "I deserve it!" The German stamped a large "J" all across the passport, shook his head, and said, "You Jews are insane."

Kurt went back to the Chilean Consul, proudly showed him the passport with his "J" and got his visa.

Kurt's mother and Grete arrived in Chile just two weeks before World War II broke out. Grete immediately found a job as Secretary of the Director of the National Museum of History in Santiago. She was the only archeologist in Chile, and after the Director retired, she got his job. Later, she became a professor at the University of Chile, published many books and at a Science Congress held in Cuzco, Peru, was honored with an honorary PH.D. Her name was constantly in the newspapers, she became a member of Mensa and was appointed Curator of the Easter Islands.

It was Grete who gave permission to the author of the world famous book, <u>Kon Tiki</u>, Mr. Thor Heyerdahl, to land on the Easter Island on his voyage from the South Sea Islands.

After the war, the Austrian Government sent her the diploma of her PH.D. which they had denied her in 1938, and offered her an honorary job at the University of Vienna, which she declined.

Grete was married twice. Her first husband was a European refugee.

Grete died in 1991 of liver cancer. The President of Chile ordered that the House of Representatives, and the Senate, in full session, keep one minute of silence in her honor. The National Museum dedicated the archeological section to her, which is now known as the "Dr. Grete Mostny Department."

Kurt was born on March 3, 1919, in Linz. He attended grade school and middle school and finished High School in 1937. While Grete was the exemplary student, Kurt felt that it was enough to have one genius in the family, and did not aspire to become Valedictorian. He registered at the University in Vienna to study chemistry. It was understood that he, and his cousins, would eventually take over the liquor factory.

Destiny is pre-ordained. Kurt's destiny was, thank G-d, to survive. He owned a motorcycle, which he had been allowed to take to the barracks, and which sometimes was used for Army purposes. After the Hitler parade, he picked up his motorcycle and drove home.

The Germans, in the meantime, had taken away every single automobile, bicycle and motorbike owned by Jews. There wasn't a vehicle left in Jewish hands.

As Kurt drove through the city, he was stopped by a German policeman, who, with a gun in his hand, asked, "Are you a stinking Jew?" to which Kurt answered, angrily, but shaking inside, "Would I be riding a motorcycle if I were one of those?" The German let him go.

On the ship, he met some interesting "Chilean-Germans," non-Jews who had lived in Chile for generations and were on their way back from Europe. They traveled in first class and still spoke German fluently. Kurt was traveling in third class, but this group of gentlemen knew that on the lower decks were educated emigrants, and they needed a fourth for a game of bridge. They found Kurt, who, of course, had excellent manners, was well-dressed and loved to play bridge. One of these men, Heriberto Horst, offered Kurt a job in his printing company. He owned one of the largest publication companies in Chile.

Kurt worked for him as an apprentice in the chemical section, learned Spanish, was promoted to cashier, and stayed there for several years, until a much better job was offered to him as manager of a transportation company, of which he later became the CEO. He earned a very good salary, made a lot of friends and girlfriends, and had a great social life.

He then met and married Marion, and started his own business, which he kept until his family emigrated to the United States. Through all his life, Kurt has been an honest, pleasant, educated man, a wonderful son and son-in-law, a loving husband and a dedicated, responsible father, grandfather and great-grandfather. This chapter is written by his wife, Marion, who loves him today as much as she did SIXTY years ago.

HAVING CHILDREN

We had been married for two years, and decided it was time to have children. We didn't want to be old parents (although at twenty-two, I wasn't exactly past my prime) but we wanted a large family to make up for the loss of our own relatives. Kurt's sister had decided not to have children, and my brother was younger than I, and single. so there was no assurance of family continuity to be expected from either one of them. We felt it was up to us to fill the world with new children, who would have children of their own, and thus make certain that the line of Mostnys and Raphaels would continue to exist in spite of Hitler's plans to eliminate all of us.

I got pregnant right away. All my friends were having children, and there wasn't much fuss in finding out. You missed a period. Then another one. You knew you were pregnant! I went to the gynecologist, who was taking care of all my friends, and had the "rabbit test" done. In those days, we didn't know about fertility drugs, amniocentesis and sonograms. The rabbit died, and you knew for sure. It was also customary to wait until about the third or fourth month, when it showed, to tell people that you were expecting.

Nine months is a long time, and keeping it a secret for a few months made the waiting a little shorter. Besides, we wanted to make sure nothing went wrong during the first three months. We kept our secret as long as possible, except, of course, from the immediate family. And, in true Jewish tradition, we had to put up with their superstitions.

"First, have a healthy baby, then we tell people. G-d forbid, something should go wrong. Let the baby be born first, then we will announce it."

We did not buy maternity dresses until none of our regular clothing fit anymore. We removed the belts first, then leaving the zipper down a little, wearing a sweater or shawl even when the weather didn't call for it. We did not make much fuss.

I had a wonderful pregnancy and never felt sick. The best part was the planning and dreaming. The sweet mystery: a boy or a girl? We thought of names, but did not decide on anything definite until the baby was born. In grandmother's words: "Don't tempt fate!"

After the initial visit to the doctor, who confirmed that I was pregnant, I went to the midwife, who would in time deliver the baby. Only deliveries with problems were handled by a doctor in a hospital. Normal pregnancies were checked by a midwife. Ours was Mrs. Victoria Rousseau. She owned a private maternity clinic and had by then delivered more than five thousand babies during her career.

I went to her every two or three months, until the seventh month, and then once every four weeks until the day of delivery. We never heard about Lamaze. None of us expecting mothers would dream of including our husbands in any of the prenatal visits. Being pregnant was <u>my</u> (<u>the mother's</u>), own marvelous experience.

Mrs. Rousseau was known in all circles and we trusted her implicitly. Every gynecologist knew and recommended her. She was a motherly type, middle-aged, patient, kind and down-to-earth. She never scared me with mention of possible birth defects, genes that could interfere or grim possibilities that anything could go wrong. She loved all of us expectant mothers and our unborn babies as if we were her own daughters.

"Don't eat for two," she said, "try to watch your weight and keep your regular life style. Having a baby is the most normal thing in the world and the most exciting and rewarding." And she was right.

I continued working until the last day and never felt sick during the entire nine months. I loved being pregnant!

Victoria's maternity clinic was in the old part of Santiago. It was a one-story building, painted in light colors in contrast with the red brick houses around it. The furniture was in the old Spanish style, but the medical equipment was modern and up-to-date. The decorations were strictly religious. Paintings of Jesus Christ and various Saints hung everywhere, and crosses adorned the walls. Although the religious aspects of the clinic had no meaning for me and my friends, we drew comfort from the fact that two Gods were watching over us; our own Jewish G-d, and Victoria Rousseau's Catholic trinity.

Our first daughter was born on December 12th, 1950.

Early in my pregnancy, I had made up my mind that neither of our mothers would come with us to the clinic for the delivery. In those days, husbands were not allowed in the delivery room. Lamaze, coaching and breathing exercises were unknown. Photography during delivery was unheard of. It was the mother, and the mother alone, who delivered her baby, without visitors, witnesses, camcorders and other distractions. The question was how to keep our mothers from coming along "to help." My mother-in-law, Julia, was living with us. She was the dowry I got when we were married. (I must say, though, that I got along with her extremely well.) My parents lived across the street. It would take some planning!

The baby was due sometime between December tenth and fifteenth. The afternoon of the eleventh, I was in the office where I worked, and felt what I thought must be labor pains. It wasn't really a pain, just a discomfort, and although the date was right, I knew it would take hours or days until the baby came. That's how it was supposed to be, at least with the first child!

I didn't say anything to anybody. Not to my husband, nor my boss.

Instead, I called my mother in the early evening, and invited both my parents to the movies.

"They are playing *Sayonara* with Marlon Brando and I just have to see it. Who knows when the next time will be that I can go to a movie, with a baby in the house?" I told my mother on the telephone.

"Are you sure you want to spend time in a movie house so close to the date?" My mother sounded doubtful. "And why should we come along? Your father is not much of a movie-goer, you know."

I had to insist. "Oh, come on, mother, we invited Julia, too. This way we can all go out together before the baby comes. Besides, if anything happens, we will have plenty time to go to Victoria's. Have you ever heard of a baby being born in a theater?" My mother had to admit she had never seen any.

"I still worry," she said, "but alright, we will go with you. Just in case, we will leave our car on the street in front of your house when we get home, so in case the baby comes tonight, you can wake us up and we go to the clinic together."

Exactly what I wanted to avoid.

"Sure, Mami, very good idea." I felt bad lying to her.

We had no intentions of using my parents' car, although we did not have one of our own. I knew that my mother would sleep with both ears open, waiting for the car to start and rush down to go with us. I adored my mother, but I couldn't see having company on the birth of my first child.

We all went to the theater. I hadn't told my husband that I felt the baby would be born that night. He would have never let me visit with Marlon Brando that evening.

I don't remember much of the movie. My pains started coming in shorter and shorter intervals, and while Brando was making love to the Japanese girl, I thought, "If you only knew how you will feel nine months from now!"

The movie finished. We all went home. My parents, as promised, left the car on the street and gave us the keys. I checked. They also left the window to their bedroom, facing the entrance door to our building, open, just in case.

We said goodnight to my mother-in-law who was, as planned by me, "awfully tired" and went straight to bed.

My husband started to undress. I said, "Wait a minute. I think we should go to Victoria's. I am having pains. Seems that the baby will come soon."

"No, no, no," Kurt was smiling, "you know that first babies take a long time. Let' go to bed, and we will see in the morning how you feel. There is plenty of time."

"I don't think so. My pains started at four in the afternoon and it is now two in the morning. I don't think there is that much time."

"And you insisted on going to the movies?" Kurt asked incredulously, "Why?" I pointed at his mother's bedroom door. He understood and grabbed the suitcase that had been ready for weeks—since the seventh month to be exact, "because you never know with first babies", one of my mother-in-law's favorite admonitions.

We tiptoed out of the apartment, down the stairs. The street was empty, empty of people, and empty of taxis. Victoria's clinic was about twenty blocks from where we lived. I started to walk.

"Are you crazy?" Now, my husband was getting a little nervous. (It took a long time to make him nervous, but this wasn't our everyday <u>little</u> <u>matter</u>, as he used to call things that happened, but were not worth worrying about.)

"Let's walk until we see a taxi," I suggested. Fortunately, there was no need for a hike at this hour and in our condition. A taxi appeared. We gestured wildly, and it stopped. There was a passenger in it. One look at me and the driver turned to his fare, "She needs a taxi more than you. Get out and wait here. I will drive them to the hospital and come back to pick you up later."

The poor passenger didn't have a chance. "I guess it's O.K. I am not having a baby...Name it after me, will you?"

We didn't ask what his name was, but thanked him and drove off.

Our daughter was born at seven in the morning. She was gorgeous, and the pains were not half as bad as I had been told.

"Call my mother and let her know," I said to Kurt. Since we did not have a telephone in our apartment, he would ask my mother to run over to tell my mother-in-law.

He called. The telephone rang only once.

"Mother, we just had a little girl." My mother's answer later made the rounds through Santiago:

"WHY"?

"I can't explain it to you now," Kurt never lost his patience. "Would you please run over to my mother's?"

In the meantime, my mother-in-law had woken up, saw our bedroom door open, nobody there, the suitcase gone. She wanted to be the first to tell my parents, dressed in a hurry, ran down the stairs—only to meet my mother on the way up.

"They left for..." My mother immediately interrupted, "I already know. It's a girl."

From that moment on, my mother-in-law hoped that we would have a second child soon, so that the next time, <u>she</u> could be the one to know first. This little competition went on until my mother died, eight years later. Julia then became not only the first one to know anything, but the <u>only</u> one. I must say, however, that she did not enjoy that status, having acquired it through the loss of my own mother. They had liked each other.

We named our daughter Patricia Ruth. The middle name in memory of my own grandmother, Gertrud, killed in a concentration camp.

When Patty was nine months old, I was pregnant again. Our second child was due by the end of June 1952. My visits to Victoria's clinic were now even less frequent. We already knew what pregnant meant, and after having had such a smooth time with the first one, the second, we felt, should even be easier, if that was possible.

I was still working in the Office of Senator Tomic, my prestigious job that I loved. The fact that Kurt's mother lived with us, if not a perfect solution in the eyes of others, allowed me to work and earn a substantial income. Our baby was in the best of hands. Nobody in our circle of friends was that lucky. We did not need a nanny. We couldn't afford one, in any case. With a loving *OMI* around her, our daughter Patty's life was heaven. My mother-in-law looked forward to a second grandchild, even if it meant more work for her. My being away during the day made her the most important person for our child—and soon, children.

In June 1952, my boss was in Europe. This baby was due at the end of June. I had been training a replacement to take over while I was on maternity leave. It was the sixteenth, and I still had two weeks to finish my work. I awoke at six in the morning, all wet. My water had broken. No pain whatsoever, but I knew this baby would come earlier than expected. I felt like saying to my mother-in-law, "You said first babies were always early, not the second one," but I didn't think that waking her up to tell her this would make any difference. How unreliable babies are! Never punctual. <u>The end of June is the end of June and not the sixteenth!</u>

Didn't this child know that I had not finished signing documents and checks for which I was responsible in my boss' absence? I could already see that whatever this baby was going to be, it would have to learn responsibility. You announce yourself for the thirtieth, you don't show up on the sixteenth! But right now, there was no time to dwell on the education that I would have to give this kid. It had to come into the world first!

I didn't say anything to anybody. After the experience of *Sayonara*, they would never let me go to work. I got dressed and as usual, Kurt drove me to the office downtown, on his way to his business. I tried to finish as much as I could. It didn't last long. The pains were now coming faster and faster. At eleven in the morning, I closed the office and had the secretary drive me to Victoria's. Before we left, I called Kurt at work and told him to meet me at the clinic.

"Don't ask questions," I said, "there is no time." Kurt had given up trying to make me act as the rational woman I really was. A crazy strain ran on my side of the family. All the women were daring, independent and rather unconventional .We women were the "Meschuggenes" (that's what you call it in Yiddish.) We were UNIQUE! Besides, had Kurt not promised to love me "for better or for worse?"

"Are you all right?" he asked, "Sure you don't want me to come and get you? I don't know about Cristina driving you..."

"I will be fine. Just don't take one of your famous shortcuts through downtown. It will take you twice as long to get to Victoria's." (My husband loved shortcuts. We got to know the entire city by taking shortcuts and getting lost!)

During the ride to the clinic, I thought the baby would be born in the car. I imagined that we would then have to call it "Chevy", which sure didn't go well with Mostny. Besides, no baby of mine was going to make its entrance into the world in an old rusty automobile!

We made it to the clinic. There was no time for registration nor for the usual preparations. Before they could even undress me, my baby made its appearance. It was another girl. Tiny, like a miniature doll.

Kurt got to the clinic twenty minutes after our daughter was born. He had stopped to buy flowers. Otherwise, he would have just made it. Victoria sent him home immediately to get the suitcase with the baby clothes, which I, of course, had not taken to the office in the morning. In those days, you had to bring your own baby clothes and wraps to the maternity. They did not provide (or even lend) blankets, diapers or anything else. They only gave you medicines, if needed.

While Kurt ran home to get the baby's things, the nurses borrowed a blanket from another new mother, who was very happy to oblige. She had wanted a girl and all her baby clothes were pink. However, she delivered a boy, and no respectable mother would dress a boy in pink! At least her tiny, pink baby clothes got some use. Her own family would have to bring a blue wardrobe for her baby.

Kurt's mother got her wish. She was, this time, the first to know about this baby, and it gave her immense pleasure to run over to my mother's to tell her, "It's another girl."

We named her Daniela Paulette, after Kurt's father, Paul.

***

MORE CHILDREN

February 1954

Twenty months after the birth of our second daughter, Daniela, we awaited the arrival of child number three. This one was due on February 12, 1954.

In the meantime, we had started the construction of our house, which was supposed to be finished by the end of 1953. This, of course, did not happen, but the construction was coming along, and we could hardly stay in our apartment with three children. Patty, our oldest, was still sleeping in our bedroom and woke us up every night at four in the morning by advising us that she was "listo tuto" (finished with sleeping) and wanted to play. Having to get up at seven to go to work, this announcement was not exactly what I was dreaming of, and we had a hard time getting her back to sleep. Daniela, still sleeping in the playpen in the living room, did not bother anybody, but her "bed" was getting a bit uncomfortable for her. It was therefore time to move, whether the house was completely finished or not.

Although the new baby's arrival had been announced for the twelfth of February, I was told to "give or take a few days." According to the midwife, it could be the fifteenth! Considering that January to March are the hottest months in Chile, I was not too happy about even a few days more than necessary. There were already two babies to take care of. I therefore discussed with my unborn third child that it better be exactly on time. I had no desire to carry it one minute longer than absolutely necessary.

The twelfth of February came and went. So did the thirteenth, fourteenth and fifteenth. I decided to do something about it. Victoria (the midwife), by now a household name, was sympathetic.

"Let's wait until the eighteenth," she said, "if it isn't here by then, we will extend it a special invitation by inducing labor."

I tried to convince this baby that it would be far better for it to show up by itself. It didn't listen, and in a prenatal display of my maternal authority, I took the baby, surrounded by myself, to the clinic on February eighteenth, at seven in the morning. One more warning went unheeded, and they gave it (through me) the inducing shot. The baby was born an hour later. It had been ready all along, but I guess it didn't feel like coming out to face the world. As it was born, Victoria said, "Ah, the House of the Three Girls, in honor of their father." (There is a famous Austrian Operetta "The House of the Three Girls," which was, and still is, Kurt's favorite piece of music.)

She was the biggest of the three babies, blue-eyed with a mane of black hair. We named her Yvonne Susana. We picked "Susana" by using letters of the names of our lost cousins.

This time, both grandmothers knew at the same moment when the baby was born. They both knew that I had given it a deadline of February eighteenth, and by now they were used to running back and forth from one house to the other, announcing a birth every year and a half. The great novelty was gone, and they were thinking, "How often are they going to do this?"

As it turned out, we did it again, and then again.

***

1955

We now had three adorable little girls and showed them off, all dressed alike, wherever we could. But we wanted a boy to make the family complete. One day, our daughters would marry and change last names. It was important that there be another MOSTNY in the world. Although three children were already a handful (or several hands full!) one more would surely not be a problem.

In the meantime, we had moved into our new home right after Yvonne's arrival. The few details that still had to be finished were done while we were living in the house. Not the perfect solution, but it worked out very well. We are, by nature, uncomplicated and easy-going, and the small discomforts were worthwhile. The house was perfect, two stories, big and beautiful.

My mother-in-law had her comfortable room, the older two girls shared one bedroom, and there was a third bedroom for Yvonne and a future baby. We had our bedroom— without a baby bed in it—and enjoyed the privacy. There were maid quarters, three bathrooms, and of course, a kitchen and pantry. We had a large garden that was planted with trees and flowers, and a playground with a doll house for the girls. We were as happy as any young couple could be.

The only drawback was the distance from our parents and our workplace. It took us about an hour to get to downtown Santiago, and we had no telephone! Being in a new development, our house had a waiting time of about seven to eight years for a telephone, unless you had "**connections**." We were fortunate to have a friend living a few blocks away, Erika Gibian. She had a telephone, and a maid to take and bring messages to us in case of emergency. All our other calls were made from our Offices. Not perfect, but this was not an unusual situation.

We all made do with these "small" inconveniences.

On Yvonne's first birthday, I announced to my husband pregnancy number four. The first three times we had no specific preference for either sex. All we wanted were healthy babies. This time, we really hoped for a boy. I checked myself for different feelings, different physical signs, anything that would indicate a male baby. No such signs were evident. I felt as good as I had through the other pregnancies, and nothing was different. This time, I advised the midwife that I was pregnant again, that I knew what to do, and that I would see her around September/October, the baby being due end of October of 1955.

Everything was fine. I was busy working at my job and taking care of the three girls, with the help of my mother-in-law, and a nanny, which we were then able to afford.

The first five months went quickly and without any trouble. I hardly noticed that I was pregnant. It had become a "normal" condition for me. No need for visits to the midwife, I knew by now what to do.

I was about to make an appointment with Victoria, when suddenly, on September 5th in the afternoon, I started hemorrhaging in the office. In a few minutes, I sat in a pool of blood. My boss, having had eleven children, was not surprised about anything related to childbirth, nor did it make him lose control. He phoned Kurt at his factory, and told him that he didn't think there was time to wait for him to pick me up, and that he himself would immediately take me to Victoria Rousseau's clinic.

On the way there, I worried that I would now have to stay in bed for the remaining two months of pregnancy, and mentally started to plan for such an emergency. It would, obviously, affect my household and my work.

Fortunately, the trip to the clinic didn't take very long, and my anxiety subsided as soon as we reached Victoria's bungalow. She was utterly surprised to see me, and more so when she saw the state I was in.

An examination established that I was suffering from "placenta previa" (instead of being attached <u>behind</u> the baby in the womb, a placenta previa sits in front of the baby, disengages itself from the fetus, and prevents it from receiving nourishment. By leaving the mother's body before the baby, it produces hemorrhages, often fatal.)

Kurt had arrived in the meantime, and Victoria decided to call the doctor who worked with her in cases such as this. Normal deliveries were handled by her; problems were immediately turned over to the doctor. While we waited for Dr. Cabrera to arrive, I felt my life rushing out of my body. I was alert and conscious, and more worried about my little girls than about myself or this new baby. I felt the blood flowing out in waves, and my energy and strength ebbed with every stream. I knew I was dying.

The doctor came within a very short time. He was wearing a tuxedo, and had obviously been called from a party. He examined me for s short moment. I heard him say, a voice coming from far, far away, "Her water broke also…not a second to lose." I remember saying to him, in a whisper that I didn't recognize as my own, "Can't we do a Cesarean? I have three little girls at home who need me!" He assured me that "everything will be done," and called an ambulance, which took me to the Hospital Santa Maria, the best hospital in Santiago, and, luckily, the closest.

Dr. Cabrera was not only gentle, but also extremely good-looking, and in my half-consciousness, I thought for a moment, how nice it would be to die in the arms of such an attractive man.

On the way to the hospital, with Kurt at my side in the ambulance, I knew my end was near. I felt my body emptying out and leaving only a shell, but there was peace, no pain, as if all my worries and senses had left with the blood. Then I passed out.

When I came to, I was in a bed in the hospital. Several faces loomed over me. I recognized Kurt and Dr. Cabrera, who gently stroke my forehead and said, "We tried to induce labor, but the baby isn't ready to be born. It also has the umbilical cord wrapped around his neck and is positioned feet first. We will do a Cesarean and try to save it." I could only nod. I was awake, and although I heard the voices coming from far away, my mind was clear. "Please think of my little daughters—save me for them."

They took me to the operating room. I asked what time it was. "A little after midnight," somebody said. As the anesthesiologist was putting a mask on my face, the last words I heard were, "She is so young and leaves three little girls."

I woke up two days later from a deep coma. I recognized Kurt anxiously looking at me.

"Am I alive?" I asked him. I had to make sure I hadn't died.

"Yes, yes, yes. You are alive, thank G-d", he said. He was crying. I noticed hoses and needles sticking out of my arms, and a blood transfusion post next to my bed. Reassured, I went back to sleep. It took me another two days to wake up completely. Drained, weak, in pain and unable to move, but awake. Four days had passed since the surgery. I looked around the room and did not see the little crib with the baby that normally sat next to the bed.

"Did the baby live?" I asked.

"Yes."

"Where is it?"

"In the incubator. It is very tiny and weak."

I did not believe Kurt, but was too sick to argue. My mind wasn't functioning at full speed yet.

They gave me blood transfusions every day; I was fed through tubes, and most of the time, I slept under heavy sedation. I didn't dare ask for the baby again.

On the sixth day, Kurt went home. I wasn't aware that he had stayed at the hospital during all that time. I also hadn't realized that my mother and father, or Julia, hadn't been there. I had no sense of the time passed, and thought that perhaps everybody had been to see me and I just didn't have any recollection of it.

The night Kurt left, I lost it! I had an anxiety attack. I screamed to see my baby. Since the nurse refused to bring it to me, I tried to get out of the bed, which was impossible because of the hoses, IV's and apparatus attached to my body. I tore at the restraints, screaming all the time, "I want to see my baby, show me my baby, if there is one. Don't lie to me any longer." I was sure by now that the baby didn't make it, but I wanted the truth. I continued screaming and crying. The room was filling with nurses and doctors. They all told me that the baby was too sick to be taken out of the incubator, which, of course, I did not believe. Dr. Cabrera was called and rushed to me room. He decided to call Kurt to come back to the hospital.

Calling Kurt was impossible, since we did not have a telephone in our house. Tired of crying, I passed out. Fearing for my sanity, the doctor called the police and asked them to go to our house in the suburbs, in the middle of the night, to bring Kurt back to the hospital. He arrived in about an hour, during which time I was put under sedation again. When I saw him, I pleaded with him to tell me the truth. If the baby was alive, I wanted to see it. If it wasn't, I wanted to know. Given my state of mind, the doctor relented and wheeled my bed, with the attached paraphernalia, into the nursery.

There, in one of the cribs, laid this tiny heap. They lifted it. It looked like a naked small chicken, with spindly little legs, thin little arms, no bigger than a man's middle finger. It had no eyebrows and no fingernails. But it was alive, and the armband on his tiny, tiny wrist read "Mostny."

Only then did I ask, "What is it, a boy or a girl?"

When told it was a boy, the boy we had wanted, it no longer made any difference. I had my fourth child, and it would live. That was all that mattered.

I went home twelve days after the baby was born. He stayed in the incubator for another two weeks, and we then brought him home. We hired a nurse to take care of him until he was a little stronger and I had regained some of my strength. She stayed for about a month.

Kurt told me afterwards what had really happened in the hospital. When we arrived in the ambulance, Dr. Cabrera told him that the baby was probably dead, and that there was a fifty/fifty chance that I wouldn't make it. I had lost too much blood. He suggested that Kurt call my parents, in case I did not survive the operation. Fortunately, my loving, thinking husband did not make such a call.

We had never had our parents present at any of the other births, and he decided that there was nothing they could do at this time. He would only create a desperate situation for them. My mother-in-law was another matter. Since she lived with us and expected us for dinner every night, she would be worried sick by now. It was past eleven o'clock at night, and we usually got home by eight.

Our friend, Erika, who lived only a few blocks from us, and was the lucky owner of a telephone, had offered her help in case of an emergency. This certainly was one, and Kurt called her and asked that she go to our house and let Julia know that we were all right, but that the baby might be premature and that we had gone to the hospital to be checked, no reason to worry.

Before the surgery, they called for a conference at the hospital. Kurt pleaded with the doctors to save me. "We have three little daughters. They need their mother—and I need my wife. Please, do whatever is necessary and possible to keep her alive." They promised him that they would. And they did. I am a living example of the doctor's skills and G-d's will.

It took over a year for me to fully recover from this pregnancy. Our son, whom we named Alejandro David, strong names to make him a strong man, developed normally and in good health, and the difficulty of his birth left no consequences. We all adored him. He was handsome, sweet and funny, and a joy to have around.

***

A year went by, and I longed for yet another baby. Another boy to keep our *Lalo* (the diminutive for Alejandro) company. Kurt was not convinced.

"We have four children now. We do have a boy. This last time was very difficult. Let's not try again." But I really wanted another child. We had always planned a large family, to make up for all our lost relatives and give our children the joy and strength to belong to a large "clan." And so, in March of 1957, a year and a half after our son's arrival, I was pregnant again.

This time, though, I took no chances. Having had a Cesarean birth only eighteen months earlier, I went for a checkup to Dr. Cabrera, besides faithfully going to Victoria's clinic. Unbeknownst to me, she had spent two days at the hospital watching over me the year before, and had made a "Manda" (a promise) to her Church, asking that nothing like Lalo's birth would ever happen again.

Dr. Cabrera advised us that this would be another Cesarean. They did not take chances with a natural birth so soon after this last pregnancy. I took good care of myself during the nine months. Again, no trouble whatsoever. I felt wonderful and, even with four children to care for, I enjoyed every day of the pregnancy.

The doctor set the day for the delivery, December seventh, which was a Saturday, and therefore a good day to have a Jewish baby. Besides, the nine months were up, and I had been pregnant long enough, in my view. Of course, we did not know whether this would be a girl or a boy. Truthfully, I admitted to my family that, although it would be nice to have another boy, my main concern was to have a healthy child, girl or boy.

Surgery was scheduled for noon, December 7th. I arrived at the hospital in the morning and walked up to the registration desk. I asked Kurt to wait in the lobby. I felt so good that I wanted to do something playful with the nurse. I said to her, "I am Dr. Cabrera's patient, scheduled for delivery at noon." The woman looked at me and with that "yeah-dear" expression that one reserves for a person with limited intelligence, she said, "Noon of what month, may I ask? Babies take nine months to be born. You will have to be a little patient. How far are you? Six, seven months?"

I loved it. My goal had been, through all my pregnancies, not to gain much weight, and I enjoyed the nurse's miscalculation.

"Just take the information," I said, "and let Dr. Cabrera know I am here." She shook her head and left to get the doctor, who confirmed that, yes, I was delivering that day and, yes, it was a nine-months baby.

The delivery took about an hour. Everything went well. The baby was a girl, perfectly formed, with long hair and large dark eyes. Having been born by C-section, she was not wrinkled, or squashed, or red. She was perfect. Beautiful long fingers, a mouth like a little heart. We loved her even if she didn't have what it took to qualify as a boy!

We named her Andrea Esther, the middle name representing all the proud women of our history.

Our family was now complete. Kurt made me promise not to mention the word "pregnancy" again, and I was obedient and didn't.

There was no greater happiness for us than being surrounded, and touched, and loved, by this cluster of little faces and voices.

Our life was complete and fulfilled.

***

CAREER MOVES

San Francisco, 1994

We just bought a computer in the office and I am working on our balance sheet, fascinated again with this unbelievable technology. One click with the mouse, and here is our updated inventory for the year. Another touch, and our bank statement appears, up to date. Who could have imagined such innovations fifty years ago when I started to work? My mind wanders away from the figures on the screen...

Secretary

It was 1942. At fifteen, this was my first job, still going to school, but with permission from the principal to attend classes only in the morning, to allow me to work in the afternoons. My parents needed the extra income, little as it was. It was in the office of a nail factory owned by three Jewish immigrants. The place was quite far from my school, and I had to take two buses to get there.

One of the owners, Mr. Goetzl, from Vienna, lived in a house adjacent to the factory. My parents had arranged for Mrs. Goetzl to give me lunch, since I got there right after school. The Goetzls had been in Chile for several years already and were "established," meaning they were making money and not considered newcomers any longer. They did not charge for my food.

The office was a single room in an old building, loud and smelly. The noise of the nail cutting machines was deafening, and the smell of oil pervaded the surroundings. There were several mechanics employed in the factory and, once I started working, they came to "visit" the office under one pretext or another. I enjoyed it!

The office manager was Mrs. Goetzl's sister. She was a spinster, but called herself Mrs. Collin. She had been engaged in Germany, but had to leave her fiancé behind when she emigrated. Not having a husband nor children to take care of, her entire life revolved around the business. This was her world! She was stern, inflexible and meticulous, and had no understanding of the mind of a young girl, nor did she care. Our teachers in Germany had been strict, and I was used to discipline, but nothing compared to Mrs. Collin's demands. There was no conversation in the office. Personal telephone calls were not allowed.

"We concentrate on our jobs," she said, "and you have a lot to concentrate on."

Her only smiles were for Mr. Goetzl, when he walked through the office. I used that opportunity to smile at him also. I knew he liked me, but I could tell he was afraid of Mrs. Collin and never visited with me when she was around. And she was always around!

One of her many rules was a prohibition of erasers. ("White–Out" to correct typing errors didn't exist.) If I made a mistake in a letter, I had to re-do the entire page. I hated it, but from necessity, I learned to become a perfect typist. My typewriter was the latest model of an IBM manual, and Mrs. Collin reminded me every day of how much it cost.

"It is an investment," she repeated often. "You must take care of it."

Mrs. Collin sat across from me and watched me constantly. I was not allowed to use her pencils or pens. She arranged them in a certain order on her desk, and noticed immediately if they had been moved. I didn't like working for her, but I learned a lot. She also taught me concepts of accounting. When I complained to my mother, she says, "One day all this knowledge will come in handy. And you get paid while you learn. You are very lucky." I had to believe her.

***

(Mrs. Collin left me with an obsession for detail and order for the rest of my adult life, to the chagrin of my husband and children, who call this "paranoid." On occasions, I catch myself thinking, "Mrs. Collin would have screamed" when I do a job that is not perfect.)

***

As I think about these early years, sitting in my office in San Francisco, I hear the noise of the nail machines, I smell the oil and hot metal, I see Mrs. Collin's face and wonder what turn my life would have taken had I been born in a different time. Could I have become a university professor, a scientist, somebody important?

***

My mind wanders back to Santiago. It was 1943. I had just had my sixteenth birthday, and had finished the fourth year of Humanidades (equivalent to High School) with the highest grades. There were two more years to go to a University. Although the school fees were low, my parents could not afford to let me study two more years, with expenses for books, clothing and transportation. The painful decision was made that I quit school and work full time for the Goetzls. They were now paying me a decent salary.

I was very disappointed at not being able to finish my studies, but tried not to show it. I knew it had been a difficult choice for my parents, and didn't want to make it any harder for them. But I envied the few lucky friends who were allowed to finish school.

To make up for the unfinished Humanidades, my parents suggested that I register for English lessons at the Chilean-American Institute, three evenings a week. I also signed up for classes of accounting at the University of Chile, once a week. They charged a minimal tuition. Although these classes also cost money, my father said, "This will prepare you for a career as a tri-lingual secretary. The effort is well worth it. Don't worry."

But I did worry. Constantly. I promised myself to make it up to them and did, by turning over my paychecks to them in exchange for pocket money.

***

Santiago 1947

Five years have gone by. In the meantime, the other two partners of Mr. Goetzl, Mr. Reich from Czechoslovakia, and Mr. Suchestow, from Poland, have opened an office in the center of Santiago, and started an import business called <u>ARTICAL LTDA.</u>, mainly products and machinery for the shoe industry. They took me with them, and even bought me an electric typewriter! Mr. Goetzl continued to manage the nail factory with Mrs. Collin.

My knowledge of English and accounting came in very handy, and I had also learned shorthand. I became the "Head

Secretary" of ARTICAL and they hired a girl to help me. I was in charge of the correspondence with foreign countries and the bank transactions, and I also dealt with local customers. It was a very responsible and demanding job. I loved it and got paid very well.

***

Businesswoman

In October of 1947, my life changed. I got married and left ARTICAL LTDA. to work with my husband, who had just gone into business with a partner, Mr. Meininger. In exchange for half of his business, Mr. Meininger had demanded that both Kurt and I work with him. I was to manage their office. This was difficult, since there was no <u>office</u>!

There was a large table in the middle of the workshop and an old manual typewriter. Receipts, invoices and letters were piled up underneath leather sheets, used envelopes served as notepads, and used cartons as filing cabinets. The smell of the workers, who didn't have bathing facilities in their homes, wafted through the place. Our everyday guests were ten-inch long rats!

This was a place for men, not gentlemen, and definitely not for a woman. I felt betrayed. For this I had given up my sophisticated job?

I agreed that this was our chance to have our own business and didn't mind working, but not under these conditions. I tried to be patient, but this was not a place for a <u>secretary</u>! Kurt and my personal relationship was perfect, we loved each other and wanted to be together into our old age. At this factory, we would never make it.

The decision was obvious, and I started to look for another job. We explained the situation to our partner, who didn't like it, but understood.

Public figure

Employment agencies did not exist in Chile at that time. Jobs were found through the want ads in the newspaper, or by recommendation from a friend.

I studied the ads. The very first day, still working at Kurt's factory, I saw the perfect job for me. It read:

"Male, Chilean citizen with experience in politics, needed as assistant to a Senator. Salary offered $6000 (Chil.pesos.) Apply in person between 2:00 and 3:00 PM at Calle Huerfanos 1147."

At my former job, I had made $2000 monthly, which was a very good salary. $6000 was unheard of!

It was 2:15 in the afternoon. If I hurried, I could still make it to the interview.

Obviously, I was not of the male gender, neither was I a Chilean citizen yet. Knowing absolutely nothing about politics, reason would have dictated to continue looking for an appropriate job. My guts, however, told me, "GO!GO!" and I announced to Kurt and Mr. Meininger, "I found the perfect job and I am leaving now for an interview, if you don't mind."

They looked at the ad, looked at me and both shook their heads. Mr. Meininger said, "Crazy, totally crazy. An insult to the man searching for an assistant, not to speak of the waste of time." Kurt said nothing. He knew me and my ambitions.

The address indicated the commercial center of Santiago. I took a taxi.

The elevator took me to the eighth floor, and I knocked at office number 836.

An elegantly dressed gentleman opened the door.

"Yes?"

"I came about the ad in "El Mercurio.""

"Excuse me...?

I mentioned my name. Being young and blond, and having a foreign-sounding name, is always a "door opener" in South America.

"Oh, I know I am not a male, but would you explain the job to me anyway?"

With typical Latin courtesy, he let me in and offered me a chair. The office was elegantly furnished. I visualized working there...

"My name is Radomiro Tomic. I am the Senator for the province of Iquique. As long as you are not a man, which I can clearly see, I assume you have extensive experience in political work, campaigns, speeches and press interviews?"

My guts came into play.

"No," I said. "I have no experience whatsoever in politics, and I am not even a Chilean citizen yet. I am Jewish, an immigrant from Germany, and my citizenship is *Stateless.*

Mr. Tomic wasn't only elegant, but also very good-looking, and he spoke a beautiful, sophisticated Spanish. I knew I had to have this job. He looked at me, amused and curious.

"Tell me about yourself," he said. "And why do you think you can fill this position if you have none of the requirements?"

"This is it," I said to myself. "Remember, you are a female. Use all your guts and flirt a little and it should work."

So I told him about my background, the persecution in Germany, my qualifications, the fact that I was married, and my ambition to be successful in life, in spite of the disadvantages we had had to contend with.

I could tell he was interested. Obviously, I was different from his other applicants.

"Why do you think in your case, a woman cannot do the same job as a man?" I smiled at him. "Are there tasks involved that require the strength of a man? I thought this is an intellectual position, not a physical one. Besides, I can learn about politics. In fact, I can learn anything." I smiled at him again.

He looked puzzled and did not respond. I took this as a good sign and went on. "It took me six months to learn Spanish and have full command of the language. Would you have known that my mother tongue is German?"

Again, he looked perplexed. I could tell that I got him thinking.

Finally, he answered. "This is rather absurd, but if you consent to take a test, I might consider giving you a try for a week or so. Could you come back tomorrow to take a test?"

"I am sorry, I said, smiling again, "As I told you, I have my own business with my husband, which I cannot neglect even for a week. I am intrigued by this job. It would be a challenge to prove to you that a woman can fill this position as well as any man."

"You are an aggressive lady, but I like that," he answered, very curious now. If you wish, you can start next Monday and we will work on a trial basis for three months. Is that acceptable?"

(Was that acceptable? I couldn't believe I did it.) "Yes," I said, "that is perfectly acceptable."

I started that next Monday, and worked for Mr. Tomic for **sixteen years**, until the day we left for the United States. I became his assistant, secretary and confidant, an expert in Chilean politics, a seasoned campaigner. He relied on my female intuition, and I benefitted from his enormous knowledge of international affairs and world history. He remained a Senator for three consecutive periods; then became Chilean Consul in Belgrade, Yugoslavia; Ambassador to Ghana, Africa, and Ambassador of Chile in Washington, D.C.

"We" won and lost election campaigns, and I met many famous world politicians who came to see him. Hubert Humphrey, Eleanor Roosevelt, Salvador Allende, and Marshall Tito, of Yugoslavia. While Mr. Tomic was out of the country, I continued my work in the office in Santiago.

The provinces that Mr. Tomic represented are in the North of Chile, where the large copper and saltpeter mines still exist. There has always been a serious water problem. He became very interested in Israel and their success in the cultivation of the land. I introduced him to the Israeli Ambassador in Santiago, who was a friend of ours. He arranged for an official visit to Israel for Mr. Tomic, from which he returned, highly impressed and surprised. He spoke at several Jewish organizations to express his admiration for Israel and the Jewish people.

He was a great influence in my life and over the years, became a personal friend.

Our five children were born in the years that I worked for him.

He had eleven children, and the sight of a pregnant woman was nothing unusual for him. During my maternity leave (five times!) he would come by our house, which was close to his, and leave work for me to do.

He paid me the greatest compliment when I left him and Chile to emigrate to the United States. He insisted that I hire another woman to take my place.

"You convinced me," he said, "that a woman can do as good a job, or better, than a man. I don't think I would have trusted a man as I trust you."

Kurt and I remained friends with him, visited him in

Geneva, Switzerland, where he had been appointed President of the Economic Council delegation to the United Nations, and in Chile, where he returned to retire. He died in 1991. I have kept in touch with his family to this day.

Secretary Again

The extra doses of Chutzpah I was blessed with came to play again, when I looked for a job in San Francisco, shortly after we arrived. We were still struggling with our English, and had no idea how to begin finding worthwhile jobs for both of us. Kurt had decided to go to Real Estate school and had an offer to work in Ed Nazal's office in the Mission District, where he could use his Spanish. He was "established."

As for me, I asked the Chilean consul in San Francisco for advice. He suggested going through an employment agency. "But I warn you," he added. "Even people with your experience have a hard time finding the right job. Your English is not perfect, your knowledge of office machines, telex, telephone switchboards, duplicating machines and so on, is non-existent. Besides, you are unfamiliar with the business environment in this country."

While Kurt went to school, I took a trip downtown to an employment agency whose name I took from the telephone book. I decided to do my own research. I just couldn't believe the consul's pessimistic assessment.

The girl at the agency gave me a form to fill out that listed more than a dozen or more office machines. I was supposed to check the ones with which I had experience. Experience? I didn't even know the purpose of some of these machines. Nothing was spelled out. All the equipment was listed by initials: 10-Key, NCR, T.T. I checked five of them, just in case.

She asked me for personal information, work experience, previous employers. No use. It wasn't surprising that she didn't know any of the companies or places, since they were all in South America!

"No local references?" She was getting impatient and I was getting gutsier by the minute. I needed a job, and I knew I could perform, and learn, if given the chance. So, I offered, "Why don't you give me a test? That should show my qualifications and experience."

She called her supervisor and they had a whispered conference right in front of me. They decided to give me a test.

"You say you take shorthand?" the girl asked me. "Then take <u>this</u> down." She handed me a pad and a pencil and proceeded to read a newspaper article as fast as she could. In English, of course. She put a timer on, and the thing ticked away while I was trying to listen. Half of what she said, I didn't hear and of the other half, I only understood a small part. But I was taken notes like a wild woman. The pencil flew over the paper and I turned page after page without looking up. What I wrote down didn't make sense. I could have never transcribed these notes, but I was going to worry about that when the time came.

After a while, she stopped, checked her timer and said, astonished, "My, you take shorthand at hundred words per minute. Fantastic!" She never asked me to transcribe these notes.

Her next test was a typing test. "I assume you touch-type," she asked. You know that's typing without looking at the keyboard." I didn't blink. In Chile, you learned to type as fast and accurately as you could with as many fingers as you wanted to use. Mainly, we left the thumb and little finger out.

Was she going to watch me? I hoped she wouldn't, but, of course, she did. She gave me a sample letter to copy.

As soon as she saw me type with six fingers, she uttered a cry, as if I had tried to attack her. "Heavens, you don't use all ten fingers. How am I going to find a job for you?"

This was the moment I had to call up all the guts I was born with, and new ones that I had developed over the years. I stopped typing, looked at her with indignation and said, disdainfully, "It surprises me that in this advanced country you are not up to the latest scientific findings. Even the underdeveloped Chileans know that by using your little fingers, you stretch the ligament of your hands and endanger your wrists. In some cases, the damage goes all the way to the elbow."

With this, I shut off the typewriter, stood up and said, "I will have to look for a more up-to-date agency. Thanks for your time. I have no interest in continuing this test."

"No, no, wait," she cried. "Let me call some of the other examiners. I am sure I'm not the only one who didn't know this. Please don't be upset. Just wait a second."

She then called three other women and told them the valuable medical lesson I had given her. "You should see this woman type," she exclaimed. "Six fingers so as not to hurt her wrists and elbows. Unbelievable."

I was the center of attention for a while and they collectively decided that such a wonder woman deserved a chance. They sent me on a job interview with an import firm doing business in South America. I was hired after an interesting twenty-minute conversation with the vice-president of the company. I started working immediately, without even going home!

In the afternoon, at closing, I remembered that I had

absolutely no idea of the location of the office. It was on Sansome Street, but I had taken a taxi to get there and did not know how to get home. I called Kurt at home, and my boss explained to him exactly where I was, and waited with me until Kurt picked me up.

I stayed at that job for eight months and learned to use the telex and fax machines, practiced how to put people on hold on the telephone, was introduced to coffee breaks and office gossip, and did homework for my boss, who was taking Spanish lessons.

The president of a large international trading company hired me away from this first job. He met me at an office meeting and offered me a much more stimulating position. I worked with him for four years. I loved the work and the people, had my own office, total independence, and was paid very well.

In the meantime, Kurt had done quite well in real estate, but was still a sales agent on commission. The broker made the "big" money, but foreigners could not become brokers at that time. My husband was yearning to be independent again and asked me to work with him—again—and we decided to go into business by ourselves—one more time.

JOHN AND ALICE

My mother's only brother, John, was three years younger than she. He left Germany in 1925, aged 21, for New York, where a far-related uncle had offered him a job in his company. He did very well, but when I was born, in 1927, he decided to come back to Berlin "to meet the baby." He stayed, lived with my parents and spoiled me rotten. I adored him. My mother had a hard time saying "no" to me. Whatever it was, John would plead with her to "let her have it," or "don't be so strict with the little doll." He and I were allies.

In 1933, when Hitler came on the scene, he decided to leave Germany again, with his fiancée, Alice Damman. Her mother was French, her father, German, and an admirer of Hitler. John and Alice went to Paris, stayed there for three years and then decided to go to Palestine as "Pioneers." Alice converted to Judaism, and they got married in 1936, in Tel-Aviv. John joined the British Army, and worked as a translator at the Lidda Airport.

After going to war against the Arabs, then fighting for the State of Israel, and being in the military most of his life, in 1950, he decided to leave Israel. My aunt Alice adored him and agreed with all his decisions. They had no children. Both of them felt that they were too attuned to each other, and too selfish, to share their lives with children.

He stayed in constant contact with my mother and, by pictures of his apartment, his workplace and his friends, she was able to share his life. I also kept him up on our family, my husband, the children, and we were able to maintain our loving relationship, even at such a great distance.

My mother longed to see her brother, and tried to get an entry visa for them to join us in Chile. I couldn't wait to meet John again as an adult.

However, the Secretary of the Interior, the same one who denied the visas to my grandparents, was still in the Chilean Government and not willing to ease up on the immigration of Jews. There were no visas for Jews, particularly from Israel. My mother was devastated, and so was John. Determined to leave Israel, he decided to go to Germany to visit Alice's family and wait there for a visa to Canada, where Alice had some old friends. Canada was open for immigration.

Their stay in Berlin was not very successful. Alice's father had never approved of Alice's marrying a Jew and converting. Her brother had been a prisoner in Russia, and was a typical German, with no understanding for Israel or the Holocaust. But Alice's had a wonderful reunion with her mother, who loved seeing her daughter and John.

They left for Canada and lived there until 1963. Knowing that we were in the United States, he decided that he wanted to be with us, and came to live in San Francisco the next year. My mother never got to see him again. She had wanted to visit him in Canada, but the trip for her and my father was too expensive, and she wouldn't hear of going alone.

We had the most wonderful relationship with John and Alice. We were their children, our kids their grandchildren, and they shared our lives in every way. I loved him and respected him, the only survivor of the entire family, and became very good friends with Alice, who was an extraordinary woman. John was not easy to handle, but she adored him and did everything he wanted. They made many friends, got involved in charitable organizations and led a peaceful life. We saw them frequently and spent several vacations with them.

This all ended on December 27, 1986. We were called in the middle of the night by the manager of the building in Palo Alto, where Alice and John were living, who advised us that there were lights on and a radio going in their apartment, and that a phone call from him had not been answered.

We "flew" to Palo Alto and found both John and Alice dead in their beds. They both had committed suicide. There were notes for me all over the apartment, signs on their beds asking us not to revive them, and letters addressed to me and other friends. I was devastated! Although I understood his mood swings and idiosyncrasies, and was sure that he talked Alice into going with him, I never dreamed that he would take it that far.

The most horrible consequence of their deaths was even harder to bear. We found out that our children had told us the truth: John had molested two of our younger daughters, who sometimes spent weekends at their swimming pool. At the time, we were aghast, but did not believe them. We had confronted John. He vehemently denied it.

"Perhaps they saw some pictures, or a program on television. How could you accuse me of such an act? They are very friendly with our neighbors, maybe one of them touched them? You know how children are. They fantasize."

Had we known then what we know now, we would definitely have investigated this horrible accusation more intensively. But, given our high esteem of my uncle, we did nothing more than question him, again and again, only to get a negative response. (I wish we had pursued this charge to the bitter end.) Forty years ago, the word "pedophile" was not an everyday expression and, in our ignorance, we decided not to dwell on it. Over the years, we have apologized to our daughters and hope that they have forgiven us!

We faced the second disillusion on the occasion of the probate of John and Alice's will. It showed that he had deceived us in his dealings with the German government, who was paying some restitution to persecuted Jews. He took mine and my brother's share of it, always denying that anything had been recovered. Had he needed it for his own living expenses, I could have forgiven him. But he had money of his own, and defrauded us by keeping our part. He left everything, including our share, to Alice's German relatives in Germany!

My memory of him is forever tarnished, and the pain in my heart will be there as long as I live. My genuine love for John has been destroyed. I feel wounded and violated, and cannot get myself to forgive him.

***

MOVING IN, OUT AND UP

October 1947

Our first "home" was a single furnished room in a
boarding house (Pension Goldmann) owned by
German Jewish immigrants on Calle Moneda,
downtown Santiago. It was accessible by foot to our workplaces
and not expensive. Most importantly, it included all meals, so
that I did not have to learn to cook right away. We knew this
place was temporary. We were waiting for an apartment that
would be available in a short time, across the street from my
parents' house, on Calle Passy No.591.

They lived on Passy 017, and we wanted to be near them
and share the part-time household help my mother had.
Besides, my parents were fortunate to have a telephone, a rarity
impossible to obtain in their neighborhood. Installation of
a new phone for us could take eight to ten years. Therefore,
while waiting for the vacancy near my parents, the "Pension
Goldmann" was the next best thing.

All the guests at the residence were European Jews, mostly
our parents' age. We were the only young couple and, of course,
"adopted" by the older ones, who provided us with unsolicited
advise on "how to be married." They figured that a twenty-
year-old wife had a lot to learn. At least we brought some life
into the place.

One day at lunch, Kurt was out of town on business, the telephone rang and Mrs. Goldmann called through the dining room, "Call for Mrs. Mostny."

Nobody answered. She repeated the announcement. Still no answer.

I sat there, eating my lunch and thinking, typical for old people, they complain that nobody calls them and when somebody does, they don't answer.

At that, Mrs. Goldmann cried out, "Marion Raphael, it's your husband. Did you forget that you are Mrs. Mostny now?"

Everybody was highly amused, and several of the guests proceeded to accompany me to the telephone in a corner of the dining room to listen to my conversation with Kurt. Fortunately, I spoke Spanish to him, which left most of the curious ones disappointed and guessing.

We stayed at the Goldmann's for almost six months, waiting for our apartment.

During this time, my mother-in-law, Julia, was living with her daughter, Grete, and son-in-law, Paul, in a large, luxurious house in a suburb of Santiago. Kurt's mother, widowed at thirty-three in Austria, had joined her son and daughter in Chile, after a horror-filled escape through Europe. The three had been living together, until Grete got married a year before us.

Julia had lost everything in Austria, had no income of her own, and her son was her only support. Although Kurt didn't think that living with Grete and her husband was a perfect idea, at least his mother had a beautiful home and was not alone, now that he was also married and gone.

One afternoon, we all were having tea in Grete's house. My parents had also been invited. We talked about the difficulty of finding an apartment, when Grete's husband, Paul, said, in front of Julia, "You might as well look for one with an extra bedroom and take your mother with you. I don't want her here anymore."

Grete said nothing. My mother-in-law, obviously stunned and hurt, started to cry. My parents, embarrassed to witness such unbelievable, hurtful behavior, looked at each other and shook their heads. The anguish in Kurt's eyes prompted me to immediately say, "Of course, Mama (that's what I called her) "You will come and live with us. It will be wonderful to have you teach me to cook, and I can go to work without starving your son."

I looked at my mother, and saw her nod of approval. My mother-in-law, a shy, withdrawn woman by nature, went to her room without a word. My parents left.

The tea party was over, but my life would change forever. Julia came to live with us, and thus became the "dowry" that I got at my wedding. She lived with us for eighteen years, and we always got along. We liked each other very much. She was very different from my mother, but she was gracious and sensitive and, like myself, made every effort to please. I always felt sorry for her, for her dependence on us and for the life that she led, so different from what she was used to.

Julia never blamed her daughter for this incident and its consequences, but she never forgave her son-in-law.

***

The apartment across the street from my parents finally became available. My mother could look from her fourth floor window into our second floor living room. When we had our first child, Patricia, long conversations between her and her Omi took place across the noise of the street. Sometimes,

259

when Pat's little face appeared at our window and my mother wasn't at hers, a passing neighbor, who knew our family, would ring the bell at my parent's apartment to alert them to their granddaughter's presence.

Having my parents nearby was wonderful. We had a very close relationship with them, and we helped them as much as they helped us. We used their telephone, we shared their maid, and it gave us comfort to know that Kurt's mother had a friend close by. Living across the street had all the benefits of living together and still afforded us privacy, which was limited anyway, due to my mother-in-law's presence. The good part was that Kurt and I couldn't fight. There was a "witness" in the house, and any difference of opinion between both of us was, obviously, only expressed in a very low voice.

By 1952, we had two little daughters. I went out to work, and Julia took care of the babies. She loved being in charge of the little girls, and I could maintain my job without ever having to worry. It worked very well for all of us. The only problem was that the house was getting too small. It was time to move.

Inflation in Chile was rampant. We had a comfortable life, but could not save any money. Prices went up from month to month and, although earnings also climbed accordingly, it became a vicious circle, and the only security for the future was to invest in property.

We fantasized about owning a house, but bank loans or thirty-year mortgages did not exist. We had to have the cash to buy or build a house. And we didn't have it, nor could my parents help us. They barely made a living with their "business." My brother, who was eighteen years old and living at home, helped them with his earnings as a mechanic. My mother-in-law depended entirely on us.

Young and optimistic and willing to make any sacrifice, we countered the objections of those who thought we were crazy with, "There is nothing wrong with wishing and dreaming," and set out to look for "our" house.

We owned half an automobile. Kurt and his partner had bought, with shared funds, an old Peugeot, which they used during the week for the business, and each of them got it every other weekend. On "our" Sundays, we took our two babies and drove to the newer suburbs of Santiago that were being developed. We visited one in particular over and over again. It was the most beautiful area, near the Cordillera (Los Andes Mountain) and the plans for development promised a luxurious neighborhood. Just as we got there one weekend, a developer was putting up a sign on a large corner lot that we had been "ogling" for several weekends. He offered four years' credit on the purchase of the lot to any buyer who committed to building a house immediately. We spent several sleepless nights, played with numbers until they danced in front of our eyes, talked each other in and out of doubts, said nothing to any of our parents, and made an appointment with the developer. With nothing to lose and everything to gain, we negotiated with him.

"Instead of forty-eight equal quotas, we offer to make very small payments for the first two years, and larger ones for the last twenty-four months. If you can recommend an architect who can help us finance the building, we could start construction at once."

Our optimism was based on the principle that inflation would work in our favor. With the price fixed for the lot, we counted on inflation-increased income. On the other hand, the developer was willing to help. It was his first venture, and we convinced him of the benefits of having the first building on his parcel, which would surely attract new buyers; adventurous, daring people like ourselves. A few meetings later, he agreed.

My parents were in shock. Conservative and careful by nature, they were alarmed, "How will you pay for the land and build a house at the same time? If we could help you, we gladly would, but you know..." This coming from my mother.

"What if business gets bad, or you lose your job, what then?" argued my father.

Not only did my parents worry about the financial risk we were taking, they were also apprehensive about losing us to the suburbs, a distance of about forty minutes by car, which would make our daily visits impossible. And the babies...No more window talks!

But they saw our excitement and happiness and did not verbalize their disappointment. We knew how they felt and loved them for their generosity of spirit.

My mother-in-law made no comments. She would live wherever we decided to go and, secretly, she loved the idea of becoming Omi Julia without the competition of the other grandparents.

It took a year and a half to build the house. It was not easy. We saved every penny we could. We no longer went out to dinner; then we stopped going to the movies; the word "vacation" was eliminated from our vocabulary. We took the streetcar, where under normal circumstances we would have taken a taxi. We did not buy new clothes, chocolates or pastries, and spent money only on absolute necessities. In those days, I had never gone to a beauty salon to get my hair done, so that was not something that I missed. Fingernails were done at home. We had agreed to make any sacrifice and, seeing our house growing, we knew it was worth it.

In the meantime, we were expecting child number three and, although the house was not entirely finished, we moved in just a month before the new baby was born. She started her life in "luxury."

Omi Julia, of course, moved in with us. I was working full time in a very important position, and she was such a great help with the children that I could not envision my life without her.

The house was a two-story building, had four bedrooms with balconies, three bathrooms, huge living room, separate dining room, an "Escritorio" (a combination of sitting room and office) kitchen and pantry.

All the rooms had huge windows, sliding doors and a beautiful view of the outside.

There was also a separate room and bathroom for the maid.

We had a large garden in the front of the house, which took a while to landscape, and a large backyard, where we built a playground and doll house for the kids. We planted fruit trees, rose bushes and an array of flower beds. Our garden was our paradise.   Unfortunately, we never got to taste the fruit of our trees, plums, apricots and cherries. The children never let them ripen. As soon as they appeared on the trees, green, hard and sour, they "harvested" them. We ended up buying the ripe ones in the market!

Moving into our own beautiful home was the culmination of our dream. The address of our "palace" was Vaticano No.4391 esquina Americo Vespucio.

Our calculations turned out to be right. By the time we paid the last installment on the lot, four years later, the amount was equivalent to the price of a winter coat.

MY BROTHER'S WEDDING

1962 Santiago

My brother wants to get married. Or he thinks he wants to get married. All his friends are settled with wives and children. and he wants a family of his own before it is too late. He is thirty-four years old, not too bad by Chilean standards, but just on the border of confirmed bachelorhood.

He has been so choosy that we think his wife will have to be made to order to please him.

He adores our children and is the world's most loved uncle. His name, Gert, had been changed to the Spanish *Gerardo,* but our kids call him "Uncle Pitze." This was a tradition invented by our own grandfather who, one day, when my brother was three years old, said, "You look like a Pitze to me." It meant absolutely nothing, not to my brother or anyone else, it was something that our Opa made up. But it went down from one generation to the next. When our first daughter was born, my brother immediately called himself "Uncle Pitze," to continue this non sequitur in memory of our grandfather. Over the years, most of his friends got used to calling him "Pitze."

I love my brother. I also like him very much. To my husband, Gert is the brother he never had. He is kind, loving and honest, and has a wonderful personality. I don't think there is a girl out there who deserves him, but I do understand his loneliness. I always worry about him.

He lived with my parents until my mother died, and, of course, continues staying with my father. He would never let him live by himself.

The custom in Chile is that sons and daughters live with their parents until they get married. It isn't a matter of money, it is a matter of family. One stays home until one gets married.

For some time, after my mother died, Gert has had a semi-serious relationship with a girl named Evi Singer. She is very nice and perhaps the right one for him. She lost her mother a short time ago. Her father is definitely unpleasant!

Gert's decision to continue living with our father ended the love affair with Evi. I think it became a good excuse for him. He just wasn't sure.

In January of this year (1962) my father dies suddenly and leaves our "Pitze" all by himself. Oh, he has all seven of us, and plenty of girlfriends, but he now really wants a home and yearns for a family of his own.

My brother loves to show off his nieces, and give Kurt and me a little quiet time with only two children. He picks up the three older girls some Sunday mornings to "visit a friend."

"Uncle Pitze," they plead. "Take us to your girl friend, the one with the gold bracelet on her ankle, the one with the pretty long hair." My daughters are fascinated with Gert's lady friends. They are all skinny, brunette, elegant and very beautiful.

"Okay, come on, but please don't ask embarrassing questions!"

I find out that my girls have made comments to these young ladies on prior visits, such as, "Oh, the mess in your room!" or, "We always have to put our clothes away at home. The maid is not supposed to help us. She has other things to do!"

The girls have a fascination for Gert's romantic adventures. But they will embarrass him, intentionally, by asking him, "Is this a NEW one?" when introduced to a young lady that they have not met before.

One day, a few weeks later, my brother calls me. "Can I come out tonight?" His tone sounds urgent. "I think I have found the girl I want to marry. I want you and Kurt to meet her. She is 25 years old and very sweet. She is not spoiled at all and I really, really like her." In typical male logic, he explains how he met Miryam. In reality, she has made every effort to meet him. (Much later, she herself tells me how she did it.)

The story is, that on the High Holidays, a few months ago, Miryam saw Gert and myself in the Synagogue. She asked somebody whether I was his wife. She was told that, no, I was his sister. There was no wife!

Miryam then arranged with her Jewish friends to be invited to several parties, which Gert also attended, and that is how HE met HER.

Being as close as we are, Gert wants us to meet Miryam so we can tell him what we think. It is a great responsibility, but Kurt and I agree that we will have to be honest. Gert's happiness is at stake.

The four of us go out to dinner somewhere in the Center of Santiago.

Miryam is pretty, very nice and pleasant and obviously in love with my brother. She is Jewish, born in Chile and doesn't speak German. One little flaw that can be forgiven!

She seems somewhat intimidated by me, as I must have represented the part of "mother-in-law" in her mind.

Both Kurt and I feel that she is right for my brother if he is sure of his own emotions.

Before meeting Miryam, Gert had planned a trip to Canada to see our Uncle John Jacoby. Miryam tells him that she intends to go to Israel, for good, and lets him know that she already has her airline tickets. She can only wait for his decision until her date of travel.

Gert comes back from a 3-week trip to Canada, where he had time to think, and decides he cannot live without her. He proposes and she "cancels" her (non)-existing tickets to Israel...

Things get serious. We meet Miryam's parents, Flora and Enrique Rubinstein, and her three brothers, Tito, Ricardo and Pepe. They are very nice people, low-key, and we get along very well.

The wedding is planned for the second of March 1963. We want to wait for the year of mourning after my father has passed, before having such a celebration.

The custom in Chile is that both the parents of the bride and the groom decide on the wedding plans, and the financial side of it. Because our parents are gone and our joy is mixed with sadness, Gert's wishes are not to have a big Temple wedding as is customary, but to get married in our house, in an intimate circle. How my mother would have loved to see her Pitze under the Chuppah! I am now taking the role of mother-in-law rather than sister-in-law. Not that I enjoy the connotation, but there needs to be a mother to take care of everything.

Our daughters are ecstatic! Pitze getting married! How romantic! And to have the wedding in our house, with them involved in all the preparations, makes it so much more poetic!

"Of course, we are going to be the bridesmaids," my daughters decide. "What are we going to wear? Can we get our hair done?" It is yes for the first question, no for the last.

Of course, we have four identical dresses made for them, pink with little flowers, and garlands of roses for their hair. David will wear a gray suit with long pants, a white silk shirt and a tie.

Miryam's brothers are unmarried and there are no little children on her side of the family. There is no competition!

March being the end of summer in Chile, we plan to hold the wedding in our garden in the late afternoon. The weather is just perfect. Not too hot, no wind. We have a large terrace, and order the Chupah and chairs for the ceremony. Afterwards, we will have a reception in the garden. Later, we will have a dinner-dance at the Hungarian-Jewish Club nearby.

The invitations go out. There will be about seventy people, family and friends of Miryam and Gert, as well as our own friends, and old friends of my parents who continue to share our lives. Every one of them has a meaning for us and is part of our extended, albeit adopted, family.

Given that we have often had sudden surprises of electrical failure due to the excess use of electricity in the neighborhood, I take precautions. I buy one hundred white candles and place them in foil cups. We might have to have a candlelight ceremony, if necessary. For now, I just want to be prepared. Worst case, I own one hundred white candles!

"What can go wrong?" Kurt, always serene and level headed, tries to calm me down. "Why would the lights go out the day of the wedding? Our **dark** day is Wednesday, and we haven't had a problem for months. You are just a worry-body!"

But I know better...

March 2, 1963. The house looks gorgeous. All the guests are there. The Rabbi has just arrived. He is the one who married

Kurt and me, did Gert's Bar Mitzvah and was with us at the funeral services for our parents.

It is six o'clock and we are all waiting for Gert and Miryam to arrive. Our kids are lined up at the front gate. So are the maids.

"There is the car, a big, black automobile." My son's excitement is real, not for the loving couple, but for the lovely car! "Here they are. Oh, look how handsome Uncle Pitze looks."

Under any circumstance, our children have only eyes for their Pitze. Genuine love! I pray that his new wife adores him like my girls do.

Miryam looks beautiful in a long, white dress, a veil, and a flower crown on her dark hair. She is radiant.

Suddenly, all lights go out. The neighborhood is dark. Our house is dark.

"How well you planned this," my brother says. "This is really romantic. Thank you."

"Thank you—nothing!" The lights went out all over. Another one of our usual little failures in the system.

There is consternation and "what to do now" from friends who have come to the front in the dark—surprised.

THIS IS MY MOMENT! "Everybody inside. We have a hundred candles, ready to be lit. This will be a most romantic wedding, a unique experience, a personal touch." I knew all along that something had to happen, so here I am right in my element, and widely admired for being so well prepared.

All the kids get a candle. "Careful, keep the candle straight up and walk in a single file, like Indians. Move very slowly. This is a very important occasion," I tell them.

My children lead the parade into the house, and from there to the outside terrace. Miryam and Gert follow. It is highly emotional and festive. We couldn't have planned it any better. The maids have lit all the candles and each guest is holding one. Miryam's parents, Kurt and I are under the Chupah, holding candles. This is a moment of great wonder and awe. The ceremony is beautiful. The sun is starting to go down and the sky begins to turn pink. The flicker of the candles gives the ambience a supernatural feeling.

After the reception in the house, we leave for the Club. There is music, a lovely dinner and speeches. I had prepared a poem about Gert's life for each one of our children, which they present, some singing, some spoken, to the entertainment and laughter of the guests.

Whenever I look at Gert, I know he is happy, but I can tell, that he, like myself, is thinking of our parents and how perfect the night would be if they had been with us.

We come back from the party at dawn the next morning. The lights are still out. We experience one more wondrous moment. Before going to bed, one of my younger daughters says, "I have been thinking. Do you believe that perhaps Omi and Opi from heaven made the light go out to show us that they want to be with us?"

I am almost sure they did.

***

Gert and Miryam had a daughter, Jeanette, in 1964. The next year, they decided to join us in San Francisco. We had missed each other terribly and wanted nothing more than being all together again.

They had another baby, their son Steven, the first American in our family. Gert found a job, worked hard and soon they were making a living and buying a house.

***

Life can be cruel, however. Gert got very sick and was diagnosed with melanoma, a deadly cancer that had already spread through his system. He had several surgeries, chemotherapy treatments, but it was too late. When he could no longer work at his job at Western Piping, Kurt and I took him into our business as Office Manager, to give him at least some hope and self-esteem. We couldn't cure his sickness. He died on August 24, 1981, at the age of fifty-three, after suffering indescribable pain. Our hearts are broken, and there isn't a day that we don't talk about him.

Over the years, Miryam and I been not only good friends, but *SISTERS*. We have dropped the "in-law" a long time ago. She and her children and grandchildren are part of our extended family. I could not ask for a more generous and loving relative.

ANOTHER EMIGRATION?

March 1963 - Santiago, Chile

Our personal world seems as perfect as we can wish for. Kurt's business is doing very well. My job as secretary to Senator Tomic is challenging, interesting and very well paid, and because of it, I have acquired a certain status in the Jewish community. Mr. Tomic is a very influential person in Chilean politics. He will be the candidate of the Christian-Democratic party for the Presidency of Chile in September of next year.

Being connected with him makes me an "insider" with access to secrets that are inaccessible to the general public. Since the Jewish community (about 30,000 between the "natives," born in Chile, and the immigrants from 1935-1945) generally stays out of politics, my belonging to the inner circle of the Government has afforded me a certain "position" among our people.

Our children are happy and healthy, doing well in school, and only giving us the everyday worries that every parent lives with.

However, little dark clouds have appeared on the beautiful blue Chilean sky. At least, in our minds.

"I can't believe that we have been married for fifteen years," I say to one of my girlfriends, also a refugee from Germany. "Everything just seems to be too good to be true."

"It must be our Jewish insecurity," she counters. "Why can't we ever enjoy anything without this flicker of fear in the back of our minds? You know what they say here, 'In Chile, nothing major ever happens!' Why can't we just believe that and stop worrying?"

"Because we know better—that's why," is my pessimistic answer.

There are reasons to worry. The country is beginning to show disquieting signs, not entirely unexpected, but nevertheless troubling.

Chile is a democracy. For the last six years, the governing party has been the Christian-Democratic Party, deeply religious (Catholic) somewhat leaning to the left of the political spectrum. There is total freedom of expression, of press, of religion, free commerce, and liberty to belong to any political party, of which we have sixteen at this time; three major ones and an assortment of smaller movements. However, there is a tremendous difference in the living standard of the Chilean population. A large segment lives in abject poverty, while a small minority belongs to the "Society," the rich people, who own and have everything: money, houses, industries, education, family connections and business and employment opportunities.

A middle class is slowly developing and the Jewish community of immigrants certainly belongs to it. We have brought with us from Europe industrialists, businessmen, doctors, architects, fashion experts, accountants and lawyers. Although few of them have found work in their exact specialty, their high degree of education and experience gave them opportunities for jobs in different fields, jobs for which the majority of native Chileans were not prepared, or not willing to take. To get ahead faster, all the Jewish immigrant women went to work. Some very successfully, others just helping to bring their living standards to a higher level. The worst part is that one does not have to be a millionaire to be considered rich. Owning a house, a car, a refrigerator and a washing machine puts us in the "rich class." We belong to the privileged class if our children go to private school and if we can afford a maid to help with the housework and the children.

The social structure isn't fair, and the crass difference between the "society" and the "people" is starting to permeate our everyday life. The murmurs of discontent are becoming louder and louder.

Next year, we will have presidential elections, and the negative mood of the poorer people is being used to great advantage by the political elements, who are seeking to turn Chile over to the Communists and follow the example of Fidel Castro in Cuba.

The election campaigns for President, for Senators, and candidates for the House of Representatives (Camara de Diputados) are just beginning, but we don't like what we hear.

I have been working for Mr. Tomic for sixteen years and know him to be a close friend and most honest politician; a man committed to his convictions. But his politics and convictions are inspired by socialism, and in order to gain the Presidency, any candidate of the center-left needs the votes and help of the communists.

These are obvious reasons to worry. And worrying is a Jewish character trait. Given our background, there is a certain paranoia inherent in our Jewish soul. There is a German saying: "Ein verbranntes Kind scheut das Feuer" (in English: "Once burned, twice shy.") We want to stay as far away as possible, not only from fire, but also from any glimmer that could develop into one. We worry. We ask ourselves and our circle of friends, "Have we been too complacent all these years? Taken for granted the happiness, peace and success that we enjoy? Is this a sign from above to move on...?"

After suffering the loss of all that was dear to us, we were fortunate to escape alive from Germany. Fate allowed us to start a new life in Chile, to raise our families in freedom and tranquility. Are we, again, put to a test of survival? Should we wait for another annihilation, this time perhaps not because of our religion but because of the "class" we belong to? Or are we, typically, exaggerating? Are we so negatively conditioned that we can only see black or white? Could there not be a gray that we are overlooking? Is our inherent Jewish pessimism getting the best of us?

We spend many sleepless nights and uncounted hours debating with my brother and our friends. Do we leave? Where to? Do we stay and wait? . Could this bring, G-d forbid, a new wave of anti-Semitism?

And, always in the back of our minds, is the lesson from 1939, a generation ago. There were those who believed in Hitler's threats and they left. They were considered crazy and paranoid by their families and friends, but they were right. They survived! The others, millions of them, did not. They refused to believe until it was too late, and they paid with their lives.

We do not know what will happen now here in Chile, nobody does. But we **do know** that it is safer not to wait until another 1939. This time, we have choices; we are free to go. And it isn't just Kurt and myself. Five children depend on us, and for them, we want a secure future.

"If we leave, where do we go?" I ask.

"Out of South America, for sure," Kurt says. And definitely not Europe. The United States or Canada or, perhaps, Australia."

"Shouldn't we consider Israel, and once and for all end up where we belong?"

Kurt is a realist. "Why do we <u>belong</u> in Israel? We are not pioneers, we are too old to learn such a difficult new language, and I, personally, am not idealistic enough to have my children live in constant fear of war. Israel is not an option."

My parents are both dead, but we will take Kurt's mother with us if she want to go, otherwise we would have to find living arrangements for her...another worry to deal with.

Are we taking on a greater responsibility than we can bear?

For ourselves, we are not worried. We will make it anywhere in the world. We are hard-working, intelligent, flexible, uncomplicated and used to taking risks.

A decision must be made. We are in limbo, making no additional investments in our business for fear of losing everything. Like everybody else in our situation, we are buying American dollars at horrendously high exchange rates and sending the money out of Chile. This is still legal, but we know from experience that this can change overnight.

Kurt and I take a day off from work and go to our Estadio Israelita (Jewish Country Club). It is a weekday in March. Very few people, beautiful weather, a quiet atmosphere. Peace. Perfect for making a life-changing decision. (The Estadio Israelita had been built with money from the Jewish Community and was our "home" on weekends. It was luxurious; perfectly built with swimming pools, tennis courts, restaurants, playground for the kids. It was the place where all our friends met and our children spent most of their free time. By law, we were allowed to only accept Jews as members.)

After a refreshing swim, we lie on the grass. It's been a long time since we have been alone like this.

"We don't have relatives anywhere in the world, so the decision of where to go has to be based on factors other than family." This is Kurt's reasoning.

"Two hundred million people live in North America. If they can make it, so can we!" One of my favorite arguments. "Besides, the time is right for the children. They are too young to be asked, and they are not leaving any jobs or connections. They will make friends anywhere in the world. They are **our** children!"

"Americans work hard, but so do we," Kurt says. "Besides, we wouldn't have a problem with the language. We know some English already and would be fluent in no time."

I feel that the choice is made easier by a system of elimination.

"Australia is too far away from everywhere. Canada demands an affidavit, or several hundred thousand dollars in bank deposits, which cannot be touched for a certain time. Let's not consider those countries as possibilities."

And then it occurs to me. "Here we are making plans to emigrate to the United States without knowing whether they even want us. I suggest that we go to the American Consulate and find out what the requirements are and whether we qualify."

"Right now you want to go to the Consulate?" Kurt asks. "Right now, just like this, in sports clothes?"

"Why not? We must make a decision soon. Either we stay in Chile and forget this notion of danger and leaving…or, we find out what it would take to transplant all of us to yet another continent. We did it before, why not again?" Let's go." I am already standing up.

Kurt agrees. "This is as good a time as any to find out what our options are. Ready?"

We get dressed, debate whether to go home first and change into more businesslike attire, but are afraid that we will lose our nerve if we don't go straight downtown to the Consulate.

"We will only get the forms today and see what the situation is. It's not as if we are to be interviewed. Perhaps they don't even give information without an appointment." We decide to go as we are. Casual, like tourists.

There is a Jewish saying: "Man proposes, G-d disposes." At the American Consulate, we are told that the Consul is free and willing to talk to us. No going back now. We explain that we came unprepared, brought no documents with us, apologize for our informal appearance (unacceptable in Chilean business circles) and find out that the United States would be happy to accept us provided we meet certain criteria.

The criteria involves a system of quotas, which are assigned to prospective immigrants according to their country of birth. Kurt, born in Austria, did not do well. The Austrian quota is closed. I would fall under the German quota, which at this time is open. A change in this quota would only occur if problems arise with the Berlin Wall situation, where there have been several hostile encounters a few weeks ago between the West Germans on one side, and the Russians on the other.

"Even if the German quota should be closed, you would qualify for the Chilean quota because of your five Chilean-born children," the Consul assures us and adds, "We seldom have a request for emigration to the United States from Chilean nationals. You wouldn't have any problem."

We are always practical. "Why don't you give us the forms and documents that need to be filled out, and we will make an appointment in a week or so and come back to you with all the facts.

"I want to warn you," the Consul replies. "If you qualify and your application for permanent immigration is approved, you will have six months to set foot on American soil. Otherwise, your visas will be cancelled and you will not be eligible to apply again."

We thank him for his time and frankness and leave with an armful of papers to ponder not only our own future, but that of our children as well.

THE CONSUL

Santiago, Chile, April 1963

W e are standing in front of the American Consulate in an elegant suburb of Santiago.

"Now, remember, children, not one word unless you are spoken to. No fighting. No screaming. No running around. Our future is being decided in here!"

"What's a future?" Our five-year old daughter Andrea wants to know.

"Not now, come on, we don't have time for big talk now." We always call important words "**BIG TALK**," and since our children speak two languages interchangeably, there is a lot of "**BIG TALK**" in our house.

We are ready to be interviewed by the Consul, on whose decision it depends whether we will be granted a visa for permanent residence in the United States. Afraid of the upcoming presidential elections that might bring a communist regime into power, we have decided to leave Chile. With five young children, we do not want to take any chances. We have not forgotten the lesson learned in 1939 in Germany. Once there is a panic, the leaving becomes difficult. There is no panic here in Chile, at least not yet.

We sent our application to the American Consulate a few weeks ago, not sure whether we should hope for approval or refusal. The decision to leave has been monumental, and doubts have been assailing us since the day we mailed the letter with the application to "Consul General de los Estados Unidos de America", an ominous title in itself. Who can say whether we are doing the right thing? At least the decision has been mutual for Kurt and myself. I did not push to convince him, nor has he put pressure on me.

We are both hoping that our prophecy will come true; the Communist Party will win the election, we will be safely out of Chile and we will be proven right for leaving on time. Our friends think we are crazy, anyway.

It has gone much faster than we thought. Since we received the notice for the appointment with the Consul, my mind has been on a roller coaster, up and down and sideways. I haven't been able to eat or sleep. What adventure are we embarking on, or is it an adventure...?

But here are the children, scared, excited and totally confident that their Mami and Papi, who always know what's best for them (like oatmeal for breakfast) will take care of everything. I wish I had the same certainty.

I assume my posture of self-assurance; boobs out, stomach in, back straight, chin up—and ring the bell. The answer comes from a box in the door frame. We had never heard an intercom in action. The children are thrilled. "Walls that talk? Is that what America is like?"

"The kids in school will never believe this!" they shout. The noise is somewhat unusual in the quiet, elegant street, although not unusual for our five lively children.

"Shhh, kids, we have to give the impression that we are civilized people. The Gringos call us Indians, anyway."

"But we are not Indians, Mami, we speak German."

"Shhh, pleaaaase, be quiet!"

Two uniformed guards greet us in English. "Good morning, the Consul is waiting for you."

Our son, seven years old, is ecstatic. "Wow, I'll tell my teacher that the man spoke to us in English and I understood. I didn't think English is so easy." "Good morning" sounds a lot like the German "Guten Morgen," so it was no big deal, but my conceited children are ready to swear that they now speak three languages.

We are led into a waiting room that looks like a fancy travel agency. Huge photos of San Francisco, New York, Washington and the Grand Canyon adorn two of the walls. A large portrait of President John F. Kennedy occupies most of another. What a good-looking young man, I think. If he is the prototype of the Americans, in whose midst we will hopefully soon be living, we are okay; young, energetic, elegant and full of life. Nothing to worry about. America is the land for us.

There are three beige leather sofas and several little tables full of magazines, brochures and information booklets. Everything is in perfect order. American efficiency, I muse. Cream-colored Persian rugs with American flower motifs cover the polished hardwood floors. I had made sure that the kids had wiped their shoes before coming up. There wasn't a detail that I hadn't thought of!

Just to be on the safe side, we divide our five children into little groups. In small numbers, they can't think of as many tricks as they can invent when they are all together. Two are on one sofa, another two on the second couch, and the youngest one sits with me while we wait to be called into the Consul's sanctum.

We have been notified that we will be interviewed, each one separately, including the children. They will be called first, one at a time, for a conversation that will only last about fifteen minutes, and they will then be sent back to the waiting room, at which time Kurt and I will meet with him for about an hour. I asked, alarmed, if the Consul knew what he was doing. Leave five children alone in the waiting room for an entire hour? Is he sure that the Consulate's furniture, walls and carpets are insured against crayons or other damage?

"Madam," he said on the telephone, when we made the appointment. "These are the rules. We Americans are very fond of children, and what can they really do in one hour?" I asked him if he had children of his own. (Obviously not).

Finally, it is our turn. There is nobody else waiting for the Consul, and while the children parade in and out of his office, one by one, scared and timid, I am not too concerned. Kurt and I are still in the waiting room, keeping an eye on the remaining four.

"Where will we be living?" our oldest daughter, Patty, wants to know. "I want Florida. It has a beach," statement by Yvonne, our number three. "No, stupid, we have to live in a city, where Papi can do business," our daughter, Daniela, replies.

Our son Alejandro, (called Lalo) eight years old, of course also has an opinion. "I want to live there, that picture with the snowy mountains, so we can go skiing."

"Shhh, children, please!"

The last one to be called is our youngest daughter, Andrea, five years old. She is, of course, petrified. I go into the Consul's office with her. He is looking at an enormous pile of papers and documents on his desk. Our application. We have had to fill out dozens and dozens of forms "with black pen, press hard, you are making nine copies," had made photocopies of each, wiped the smudges from carbon paper off our dining room table, and supported the Chilean paper mills to the tune of several hundred pesos. "Is he looking at every one of these forms?" I silently ask. "Can he even digest all of them?"

"Now, Mrs. Mostny," the Consul says, peering over his granny glasses. "The forms for Andrea Esther (her middle name) are not completely filled out. The child left out some vital information."

"The child cannot write. I filled out the forms for her. What's missing?"

"Well, points No.111, 112 and 113 are left blank."

I give him what I hope is a shocked look, shake my head and say:

"You mean the questions about subversive activities?"

He nods, earnestly. The fact that this applicant is five years old seems to have eluded him. Almost vehemently he says, "Yes, I need these questions answered for everybody, no matter what the age of the visa-seeker." (My baby, a *Visa Seeker*)

He reads, "The questions are: Do you swear not to engage in prostitution or other immoral activities? Do you swear to uphold the Constitution of the United States of America? Do you swear not to participate in any subversive movement with the intention to overthrow the Government of the United States?"

I smile, incredulously. He can't be serious. But, yes, he is. "So what are these child's answers?"

I keep my voice low, ladylike, but astonished.

"You mean to say that this five-year-old should know today, whether she wants to be a prostitute or an agitator when she grows up? She has no idea what a prostitute or an agitator is. Not that she is stupid," I add for good measure, "She does speak Spanish and German!"

The Consul himself speaks only English, of course, like most of the diplomats, which is part of the reason why they never get to really know the South American mentality. They memorize the questions in Spanish to handle these interviews. At this point, though, I decide not to dwell on that subject or discuss it with him.

"Well, Mrs. Mostny, regulations are regulations," the Consul says solemnly, "You will have to vouch for your daughter then. The questions must be answered."

For a moment, I am ready to forget the whole emigration idea right then and there. What a ridiculous demand! But I behave according to the circumstances and fill out the forms in nice printed letters:

"As far as I can predict today, May 24 of 1963, my daughter, Andrea Esther Mostny Raphael, age five, will not engage in either subversive activities or in prostitution. However, I will only be responsible for her behavior, and that with reservations, until her 18th birthday. What she decides after that is her own business."

"Here," I say to the Consul "this is the best I can do."

"Dear lady," he protests, "this is highly irregular." He spreads his thumb and middle finger across his forehead as if to squeeze a new idea out of his head. "I don't know what to do with this child."

I am now enjoying the situation. "Honorable Sir," I say in my most polite and convincing voice. "You can either deny the application for the entire family, because a five-year-old is not sure whether she will turn into a street walker or a revolutionary when she grows up. Or you can allow an innovative, self-assured, hard-working family of seven immigrants to go to the United States where we will, I assure you, not be a burden to anybody. On the contrary, we will make a contribution of value to your country, as we have done here in Chile for twenty-four years."

I wait. It takes him a few minutes to ponder this. I am sure this approach had not been used on him before. Finally, he initials Andrea's application, smiles and says, "You may have a point here, and I like people who stand up for their beliefs. Have the little girl wait outside. I will now go through the interview with you and your husband. We should be done in about an hour."

I remind him, once more, politely, "You are absolutely sure that you want these five children out there by themselves in the waiting room for an hour?"

No answer from him; just a look. "Please, no more arguments, dear Mrs. Mostny, let's get this over with."

I take Andrea back to the outer room. In the meantime, two ladies have come in. From their quiet conversation in Spanish, I hear that they are waiting for another consular official.

I admonish my kids one last time to please be quiet, hopefully, our conversation with the Consul will not be long, and add pleadingly to the two women, "Would you do me a personal tremendous favor and make sure that these children do not leave the room while we are with the Consul?"

"Don't worry, we will keep them entertained," the older lady says, "Are you emigrating to the United States? Why?"

"Too long to explain," I answer, "But thanks, thanks a lot for watching them."

Our interview with the Consul lasts an hour-and-a half. Since our English, although far from perfect, is better than the Consul's pathetic attempts at Spanish, we make a good impression. Our past experience, our present occupations, recommendations, financial standing, health certificates and other requirements pass muster, and we end up having a lively and interesting visit. Strange, how the reason for wanting to leave Chile is so clear when you explain it to somebody else. Only in the solitude of sleepless nights do doubts creep up...

During the entire meeting, I strain to hear noises from the waiting room. Not a sound! Have our children decided to leave by themselves? Are they outside on the street? Have they killed each other? Or the two women? What is going on out there? Several times during the interview, I have to say, "Beg your pardon?" to the Consul. My mind and half my hearing are outside his office.

Not a sound. Not even the voices of the two ladies. I am getting panicky, but I don't want to give the impression of a nervous, out-of-control person. After the perfect performance with Andrea and our own interview, I don't want to ruin the good relationship that we have just established with the Consul, but my heart is beating at double speed.

Finally, the meeting is over. It is to be one of three interviews, we find out. I can't believe it. <u>Two more visits like this</u>? I don't think I can go through this one more time, leave alone <u>twice</u>! What more can they squeeze out of us? It is a shock.

We open the door to the waiting room cautiously, and prepared for the worst. Here are our five children neatly sitting on one sofa, all of them together in harmony, looking innocently at us with an angelical expression of, "See, we were sooo good!" The two women are gone. One look around the room explains the silence that hit my eardrums while we were inside with the Consul. Every magazine and brochure has been cut into doilies, hats, little ships and other folded objects. Fortunately, they haven't touched President Kennedy's portrait, nor drawn on the San Francisco, New York or Florida posters. Those look fine, thank G-d.

"Guess what, Mami. The nice lady showed us how to make these and helped us. Look, look, I made this one and Patty made that big doily." Daniela is very proud. "And I made ships out of newspapers like you taught me, look." Our son points to a pile of folded papers. "Can we take them home?"

We don't waste a minute, not even to put their coats on. I grab all our belongings, gather the paper art work and stuff it into my bag, and we hurry out the door. Instead of waiting for the elevator, we run down the stairs. I can't wait to get out of the building.

1999

Evidently, our visit to the Consul was successful, since we are here in San Francisco thirty-six years later, and I am writing this story for my grandchildren.

We never received a bill from the American Consulate in Santiago for the wasted magazines and leaflets. Living in the United States, we soon learned that wasting paper is a habit inherent to all Americans. My worries that day at the Consulate were therefore unfounded.

***

Our daughter, Andrea, decided to honor my pledge and has not, to my knowledge, become a prostitute, nor has she lead a revolution against the government of the U.S.

I guess you might say everything turned out for the best.

IMMIGRANTS

September 1963

We left Santiago on August 31st, on a propeller plane that stopped in Peru, Ecuador and Mexico, where we got off. Full of passengers with packages, wine bottles and food, we stuck out by our clothes and mannerisms. Our children behaved extremely well. It was, after all, their first trip on an airplane, and all the good-byes had lowered their spirits. There was no air conditioning, and after one of Pat's neighbors spilled a whole jug of wine over her brand new dress, they got, understandably, somewhat impatient.

As a matter of security, I wore light chains on my wrists, attached to which were David and Andrea, the youngest ones. Kurt had Daniela and Yvonne hanging on his elbows, and Patty, the oldest, walked by herself in front of us. All our friends in Chile thought we were crazy, but with the plane stopping several times for a few hours, we were afraid that one of our children could walk away, curious to check out the scenery, and wouldn't know how to find us again.

We had planned to spend a week in Mexico, knowing it would be our last vacation before starting our new life in the United States. We enjoyed some carefree days, went sightseeing and recovered from the turmoil of leaving our home of 24 years and not yet burdened with the problems of beginning all over again in a new country.

We arrived at Los Angeles Airport on September 6th, two adults, five children and nineteen pieces of luggage. It was eleven o'clock at night as we went through Customs. There were not many people on the flight from Mexico City, and we hoped that the customs inspector would be tired enough not to order us to open every one of our suitcases. As one after another of our bags tumbled onto the conveyor belt, the inspector's eyes grew rounder and rounder.

"This all yours?"

"Yes, sir. We are immigrants to the United States, you see, and all these children are ours also."

He wasn't impressed. "Open this one," he said, pointing at one of the larger bags.

We had marked the suitcases with code numbers to know what was inside, so we wouldn't have to open them all before we reached San Francisco, our final destination. The number of the bag that the customs official had chosen indicated that it contained dirty laundry. What luck! No inspector, or for that matter anybody else, would want to go through loads of soiled children's underwear, stained overalls, stinky socks or heavily used handkerchiefs. So, hoping for the best, Kurt opened the suitcase. One look and the man said, "No good. Take this one," pointing at a smaller bag. I opened it, he checked it, found nothing of interest, and asked, "You smuggling anything?"

Our English wasn't very good, and we thought we heard him say, "You smuggling anything?" We must have misunderstood. Why would he think we were smuggling anything? Or expect us to admit it if we were?

Our papers were in order. We looked well-dressed, perhaps too well-dressed, compared to the other people around us in shorts over behinds and thighs that one would definitely <u>hide</u>

in South America. Even the most bizarre imagination could not have taken us for smugglers.

"Smuggling?" I repeated. "Why would we be smuggling anything? We are legitimate, legal immigrants, decent, law-abiding people. Here are our X-rays and medical reports."

Kurt whispers to me, "Don't aggravate the man and don't argue with him. We want to get out of here as soon as we can."

We had been instructed by the American Consul in Santiago to carry our chest X-rays and medical reports, all seven of them, by hand, and to produce them to the first immigration officer in Los Angeles immediately after arriving. I presented them to the Customs now. I figured he would be impressed with our efficiency and leave our bags alone. Not that we had anything to hide, but we did not feel like opening nineteen suitcases packed to the gills and try to re-pack them on the narrow benches at Customs. At the same time, we had to keep one or all four eyes on our children to make sure the entire family got to San Francisco without losing a member somewhere along the way.

The expression on the inspector's face confirmed my gut feeling. He wanted to get rid of us. "This is Customs, lady," he declared. "I know nothing about X-rays and medical stuff. I hope you are not sick, but that's not my business either. Just take your luggage out of here and good luck!"

He stamped our papers and disappeared.

The immigration officer who then came to check our papers was more sympathetic. It was now almost midnight; the children were exhausted and impatient. He must have felt sorry for us. He inspected our passports, visas, health certificates and bank statements, gave the children some candy and admired our son's hat. David was wearing a suit and tie and hat, formally dressed for travel. The girls wore dresses with matching jackets, proper attire for "young ladies." After commenting on their looks, he said, "Welcome to the United States. Good luck to all seven of you. You are ready to go."

Suddenly, there were shouts from the top of the escalator, "Hello, Mostnys, hello!" Surprised, we looked up and saw the three children of our friends, Lore and Bert Zanders, who had emigrated from Chile to Los Angeles a few months before us. Bert was working as a chef in a Hotel and Lore had gone to Switzerland to visit her mother. They sent their twelve and thirteen-year-old daughters, Evelyn and Susie, and their son, Ralph, who were friends of our children in Chile, as a welcoming committee, a gesture of friendship that we have never forgotten. They had made reservations at a motel for us, and we found a basket of fruit and sweets with a note, "Welcome to your new life" from Lore and Bert.

We spent a week in Los Angeles, rented a station wagon, and visited some relatives of our Chilean friends whose addresses were given to us in case we needed help. It was interesting to learn the experiences of people who have been in this country a long time. We took a tour through the city, visited some landmarks, learned to eat hamburgers with lettuce, and meat dishes with Jell-O—unheard of in Chile—and got a taste of *American* life and language.

We were now ready to take the final step, San Francisco.

We packed our five children and nineteen suitcases in the car and took off.

To this day, I don't know how our children lasted for eight hours, crowded like sardines in the car. It was hot, muggy and there was definitely no room to play. I guess the newness of it all allowed them to bear the situation that, under normal circumstances, would have been cause for complaining and fighting. Kurt and I had to watch the road and follow the map that had been given to us. We pleaded with the kids to be patient. And they were.

After driving for about an hour, I'm panic-stricken.

"We are driving around in circles, I say to Kurt. "We just passed a street called ONE WAY a little while ago and here it is again. And look at this gas station right ahead called 'RICHFIELD'. We passed that one half an hour ago, and we are back here again. We are lost!"

Kurt, always patient, says, "I am following the map exactly. We are going in the right direction. Or at least, I think so. Let's drive a while longer and see if the next town is where we are supposed to be." I agree.

"Lost, lost, we don't know where we are." Our children are excited.

I didn't think it was exciting at all and convinced Kurt to stop at the next gas station and ask how best go to San Francisco.

"Fill 'er up?" the attendant asks.

"Who is ER?" I ask in return. "We would like to put some gasoline in this car and then ask you to show us the way to San Francisco. We have been driving around in circles and come back to the same street ONE WAY all the time.

The man must have thought we were idiots. "I can't show you the way to San Francisco. You are six hours away from it. I'll explain to you what road to take." He shook his head while pumping gas.

"Cash or credit card?"

Again I get nervous. What is a credit card? "No, we don't know what a credit card is. But we have money. Do you take money?"

The station attendant now was convinced that he was dealing with escapees from a mental institution, dressed in winter clothes in September—the hottest September in Los Angeles in 15 years. We had been told that in San Francisco, it is <u>always</u> cold and windy, and didn't think it was necessary to dig for light clothing in our luggage.

He looked into the car one more time, checked out the number of children and the piles of luggage, and called the manager. By his expression, I guess that he explained his frustration to him. His boss, an elderly man, knew how to handle the situation. He addressed us in a <u>loud</u> voice to make sure we understood, "You are going in the right direction. Take the Coast Highway. It is a nicer drive, and you can let the kids out to get some air every so often," he said. "Just follow the signs on the road, you can't get lost." He obviously did not know us well.

"The Coast Highway? I ask, alarmed. "Does that mean it costs to go on it? We would rather take a road where we don't have to pay," I say.

What is the sense of spending money right away just to get to San Francisco on a nicer road? We will have to spend enough once we get there.

Kurt shakes his head. "Don't argue with him. We are spending too much time here. How much can it cost? A few dollars? Makes no difference any more."

"No, lady, it's called Coast Highway because it goes along the coast. You know, water...ocean...coast?"

"Ah, now I understand. Thank you." I feel much better. But Kurt and I decide right then and there that we will have to take some courses in English right away. Otherwise, we will be treated like morons everywhere.

We laugh about the manager speaking as loud as he could, as if the <u>volume</u> could clarify the meaning of words.

***

It was midnight on September 12th when we arrived in San Francisco, exhausted and drained. Our kids had meanwhile named the car "Sardine Can," which was an appropriate description. We couldn't wait to get out of it.

We drove through downtown, map in hand, in search of a hotel, but found out that the Jehovah's Witnesses were in town and, after driving from one hotel to the other, discovered that there wasn't a room to be had.

"Treat, treat, let's sleep on the street," our children chanted. Our son had a better idea.

"Let's sleep in the car. We have been in it for so long, a few more days won't matter."

The only way to survive this situation was to make jokes about it.

Kurt came up with a novel idea. "Why don't we play beggars and sit on a street corner. We look dirty enough."

I failed to see the humor in all this. Was San Francisco <u>that</u> small that one convention could take up every available room in the city? And who were the Jehovah's Witnesses anyway? Jewish, maybe? That would be great. We would find people like us right away. Or were they a sect of some kind?

Whatever and whoever they were, I deeply resented them, but more than resentment against this group of people, of whom we knew nothing, was the heaviness of doubt in my heart, as so many times on this voyage. What had we done? What had possessed us to give up a normal, comfortable life, our family and friends, all the things known and dear to us, for this adventure?

Or, had we been right in our decision that our children's future was more secure in the U.S.A. than in Chile? Without knowing a single person in this new country, would our lives ever again follow a steady course? The word "fear" was not in my vocabulary; "forward" was more like it. There was no sense in dwelling on what could or would happen. We would face the problems as they presented themselves, one at a time. <u>NOW</u> we had to find a place to stay and not think of anything else.

Finally, after being turned down everywhere, one of the night clerks at a hotel on Sutter Street, who had also claimed not to have a vacancy, took pity on us. He made some phone calls.

"Go back to Market Street. Drive up a little further north. On Gough and Market, there is a motel that has rooms available. Look for the sign "Executive Motel." We thanked the young man, gave him a tip and drove on. Executive Motel, I thought, can't be all bad. We didn't know what neighborhood we were in, nor did "Gough and Market" have any significance for us. Years later, when we drove by there, I shuddered at the thought of having lived there with our children. But that night, everything was dark, the streets were empty, and to us one street looked like the other. What did we know?

Mr. King, the owner of the motel, was expecting us. In the dark, we didn't see how dilapidated the building was, how dirty the street, how gloomy the neighborhood. And the promise of a bed eclipsed all other thoughts.

We rented two rooms for a week. Even if the place was not what we would have chosen under normal circumstances, we didn't know how long the Jehovah Witnesses were going to occupy San Francisco, and we were not about to repeat the search for another place until we knew what we were going to do next. We paid for the week in advance, in cash. This turned out to be a wise move. By the utter disbelief on Mr. King's face when we emptied the car of five disheveled kids, nineteen pieces of luggage, toys, papers and other paraphernalia, we could tell that he would have gladly changed his mind, and regretted not having put up his "No Vacancy" sign before we arrived. But money talks and he led us to our rooms.

In a matter of fifteen minutes, the place resembled a gypsy camp, but nobody cared. We needed to go to the bathroom, clean up a little and go to sleep.

The next morning, each one of us checked on his or her height. We all looked normal. After the long trip in the car, bunched up and curled around suitcases, we were sure we each had lost a few inches in height. Fortunately, we had stretched out overnight, and were again seven normal-sized people. It felt good.

After breakfast at the corner coffee shop, we went back to the motel for a family counsel. Truly democratic. Kurt and I represented the Government, the ones that made the rules. We decided what to do and brainwashed our children into believing that it was their idea.

"We need to go out and look for a place to live. We also need to go to Immigration to register, and we must contact the Chilean consulate to find out about schools for you," we explained to the kids. "There is no way we can take all five of you everywhere. We will ask Mr. King if he can recommend a person to come in and stay with you for a few hours, or perhaps Mr. King himself may be nice enough to keep an eye on you while we are out. We will check on you every hour or so."

My kids exchanged looks that spelled trouble. I could see that they were thoroughly enjoying this promise of unexpected freedom. I came up with a contingency plan.

"I hope you understand that you will not be able to leave this place. You will have to stay in the rooms at all times." They knew I meant it. "You don't speak English and cannot wander around the streets." Had we known what neighborhood we were in, we wouldn't even have considered leaving them alone.

We made a deal with Mr. King, who, for fifty dollars extra, would go up to the rooms at regular intervals and see if our children were still alive. We left the telephone number of the Chilean Consulate with him, left coins for the Coke machine, an invention that we were unfamiliar with, and Mrs. King offered to order pizza for lunch. We left with a prayer on our lips. If G-d wanted us to live in San Francisco, He would see to it that nothing happened to our children. Besides, Mr. and Mrs. King were older people who looked grandparent-like and responsible. Nevertheless, we felt guilty and uneasy.

Again, the nagging thought, "Should we have stayed in Chile where our daily existence had been regulated and pleasant? " And, again, the logical answer, "Too late now." We had sold our home in Santiago, sold our business, sent our money out of the country, and basically burned our bridges behind us. There was nothing to go back to. Straight ahead was the only way.

Our first visit to the Chilean Consulate proved to be catastrophic. After admiring our guts to emigrate to a strange country with such a large family, the Consul embarked on a lengthy political speech, discussed with me the possibilities of my ex-boss, Mr. Tomic, becoming the next President of Chile, gave us a detailed account of his accomplishments—in case I still had an influence on Mr. Tomic, and in essence, got on my nerves.

"We need a place to live," we told him. "How does one go about finding a house to rent in San Francisco?"

"Easy. Let's look at the newspaper ads and make a few phone calls. No problem."

It turned out to be a big problem. When people heard that we had five small children, they either hung up or said something like, "You must be kidding." The Consul was not in the least perturbed.

"O.K. That's it. You won't be able to rent a house. Maybe you should buy one. What else can I help you with?"

Deeply perturbed with the inefficiency of our diplomatic representation, I vowed to write a letter to my connections in Chile as soon as I could lay hands on a typewriter. Kurt, more practical and less aggressive than I, decided that the <u>very first thing</u> to do was to find a place to live. From there I could write all the letters I wanted…

Given the lack of interest or brains of the Consul, we decided not to ask him about schools. We were concerned that he would give us the wrong information just to get rid of us.

We decided to take matters into our own hands. Although Kurt and I are very, very different in character, we agree on most things that are important to our lives. We may have a discussion first, but in the end, our decisions have always been taken with the full support of both of us.

In the lobby of the Consulate building, we had seen a billboard with business cards offering various services. We picked the telephone number of a Real Estate office that advertised in Spanish, contacted them and made an appointment for the next day.

We called our children at the motel, spoke to all five. They sounded healthy and normal.

Our next step was the Immigration Office. The formalities didn't take too long and we headed back to the motel. The building hadn't improved in looks, but neither had it been destroyed. The doors to our rooms were closed, curtains drawn, no noise to be heard.

We entered with trepidation. Anybody with a weaker constitution would have had a heart attack. But we were glad to see all five of our dear children alive and well. And then we looked around...The kids had unpacked the nineteen suitcases and were playing with the clothes. They were wearing each other's garments, some of ours, my shoes, and Kurt's hat. They had painted their faces with make-up and the girls had modernized their hairdos. The television set was on and the kids were dancing to the tune of used car commercials. But all five were in good shape. The place looked like a gypsy camp, but who cared?

We had a choice to either cry or laugh, and opted for the latter when the children announced, "We were <u>sooo</u> good, we didn't leave the room for a minute. We didn't fight much either, or make a mess with the pizza. All we did was go downstairs a few times to get a few Coca-Colas. Aren't you proud of us?"

***

Our interview with the real estate man the next day was an exercise in creativity. He not only spoke Spanish, but was also from Chile, which made the whole conversation easy and uncomplicated. He had been in San Francisco long enough to learn the idiosyncrasies of American landlords. At the same time, he fully understood our predicament that all seven of us had to live in the same place, and that the existence of our five children was an irrevocable fact that, sooner or later, a landlord had to accept.

He knew of a house in the Geneva Terrace District. "It's not what you will want forever," he said, "But you have to start somewhere and then...with five children..." We told him that we had heard this before, and could we just try this house, wherever it was. Ed Nazal, our agent, drove us up Market Street, past Twin Peaks and then down Alemany Boulevard. Compared to Gough and Market, this was paradise, and we couldn't wait to see <u>our</u> house.

Just to be on the safe side, however, we deposited our three younger children at Ed Nazal's office on Mission Street. We didn't want to lie outright by saying we only had two children, and I am much too superstitious to tempt fate with such an untruth. But we felt it was safer to take only the two older girls with us. They were the more mature and well behaved—Pat, almost twelve, and Daniela, eleven years old. They understood what was at stake; it was getting this house or stay in the ugly motel rooms.

The owner of the house on No.67 Seminole Street, an old Irish gentleman, had just lost his wife, and was going to visit his children back East for six months. Perfect. The rental ad said in big letters "No children," but again, we were told, "No problem."

Mr. O'Connor's house was doll-like, small, immaculate and in perfect order.

"Mrs. O'Connor was the perfect housekeeper," he said with a sad smile. "If she ever looks down, I want her to see her house as she left it."

We told him that we would take good care of his home, that, yes, we did have the two girls, but that they would, in turn, help with the housekeeping and that he was our last hope to find a place to live in, and that he would never regret his decision to rent the house to us. We would love it as he loved it. All this was accompanied by our offer to pay him the rent in cash, in advance for six months, an offer which he could never expect from anyone else. He agreed that this was an unusual offer and accepted. We promised that he could visit any time and check on his house, a gesture that made him happy.

We moved into the house a few days later, of course with all five children, after Mr. O'Connor had taken off for the East Coast. Although we felt bad about not having been honest with him, we assuaged our guilty conscience by, first, our utter necessity and desperation of finding a house, and second, by the knowledge that our children had been raised in a European household, where manners and behavior were of utmost importance.

Although I wouldn't go as far as to say our children were angels or better than others, they were certainly aware of the seriousness of the situation. We had explained to each of them, at the level of understanding depending on their age, that we had undertaken this move with their interest in mind. That we hoped it would turn out the way we envisioned it, and that we counted on their help and cooperation.

They did not let us down, and this tremendous change in our lives forged a bond of friendship and trust between the seven of us that exists even today, our children being middle-aged parents themselves.

***

To our surprise, Mr. King, the motel owner, was sorry to see us leave. Watching our children had become a pastime for him and, as he said, "Had broken the monotony of his days, having spent most of them in the sole company of Mrs. King." Besides, he had been able to practice his school Spanish and "was going to miss the little critters."

***

FIRST WEEKS IN SAN FRANCISCO

September/October 1963

M r. O'Connor's house was now ours for six months, a year, perhaps, if we "were good tenants."
Following the advice of our newfound friend, Ed Nazal, the realtor, we rented furniture, limiting ourselves to the minimum, seven beds, a couch, a dinette set with eight chairs, two armchairs for the living room, a radio and, of course, a television. It was definitely not fancy, but it served its purpose. We hated to spend money on kitchen stuff, since I did not plan on developing any cooking skills. We got the bare essentials of kitchen equipment, one small and one large pot, one frying pan and a tea kettle. For our eating habits, this was just enough. We also got plastic spoons, forks, knives and paper plates. We were ready to start our new life

We had shipped a container with all our personal belongings from Santiago to San Francisco, but the vessel that carried what we called "our home" arrived here two weeks later than we did. All our knick-knacks, our nice dishes, photos, books, toys, clothing, sheets and blankets, tablecloths, collectibles, pictures and all the other objects that make a house a home, were still on the water.

In the meantime, we made do with the minimum and laughed about it. "Pass me the silver spoons," I would say, as we threw the plastic "silverware" into the garbage. Or, "Let's use the hand-painted platter," as I took one of the plastic plates.

The next necessity to be addressed was school for the children.

A few blocks from the house was Balboa High School for the two oldest, and San Miguel Grammar School for the two younger ones. They could walk there by themselves.

Andrea, our youngest daughter, was going to be six years old on December 7th, and she was not accepted in kindergarten. Her birthday was just beyond the deadline, which was December 5th. Had we known, we would have gladly lied. But nobody told us.

This presented a serious problem. We had no friends in San Francisco, and Kurt and I had to go out and find work. We looked for a day care center for her. In the meantime, we registered the other children in school, despite their strenuous objections, "We don't speak English. We won't learn anything anyway."

"You will learn—sooner than you think."

"We don't know anybody. Who will we talk to, or play with?"

"You'll meet new kids and make new friends—believe me."

"You will need help keeping the house in order for Mr. O'Connor, in case Mrs. O'Connor looks down."

"She won't."

"I promise to do the dishes instead. Remember we didn't bring Elisa with us." Elisa was our household help in Santiago.

"We will manage, thank you. But your offer is appreciated." This was Kurt, in his quiet way, trying to comfort the children.

The last argument was difficult to fight. "We will die if they make fun of us in school."

To that, I had no answer, and I did feel sorry for them. I remembered my first experience in Chile, when at eleven, I started school right after arriving from Germany. My first weeks in a strange environment, a language that I didn't understand, kids that ridiculed my clothing and hair and manners, were absolute hell. I understood how my children felt. But, as I did, I knew they would get used to the new ways, learn English, make new friends and become part of the American life. The adjustment would make them brighter, more tolerant and give them a better outlook on life and people. I wasn't worried.

The kids marched off to school and within days, we had to make our first major adjustment. Lunch. I had given them, following our European-Latin tradition, sandwiches with liverwurst, sardines or other cold cuts, all on black bread or pumpernickel. They brought the sandwiches back.

"You have to buy something called "peanut butter and jelly" and put it on a white, mushy bread. The kids in school exchange their lunches and nobody wants to share with us. They don't know what liverwurst and pumpernickel is…and we don't get to taste their lunch."

Our first integration process into the American culture was, therefore, to eat peanut butter, jelly and mushy white bread for lunch. The kids did.

Kurt and I continued to eat "civilized food." (I don't think Kurt has ever <u>tried</u> peanut butter.)

We now had to find a place for Andrea, our youngest. Kurt went out to find a day care. He was very clever. On our street, he approached women walking with children about four or five years old, and asked, very politely, where they sent their kids to "school." Kurt, in his unassuming manner, explained to them as well as he could, in English, what our problem was. One of the mothers offered to take him to the day care center that her son attended, and speak for him. Andrea's attendance was successfully arranged due to the kindness of a stranger.

The children learned English very quickly, compelled as they were to communicate with teachers and classmates. In 1963, there were very few Spanish-speaking children in the school, and bilingual education was unheard of. You had to learn English if you wanted to get ahead in school, at work, or socially. You kept your native language as well, and therefore had quite an advantage over "one-language-people." From my own, and my children's experience, I have to this day, very strong feelings against the idea of teaching children in their native language without giving them the benefit of becoming proficient in English.

We experienced many episodes of anguish, laughter and ridicule because of language problems, but that was to be expected and we took it in stride. One day, the two younger children did not come home from school at the usual time. After an hour or so of nervousness, and having called the school to find out if anything special was going on, which was not the case, Kurt and I went to the school to look for them. The classrooms were deserted except for my children, sitting at their benches.

"What is the matter, we asked, "What are you doing here all by ourselves?"

"We can't leave yet," was the answer. "The teacher told us to wait." This didn't sound right.

"It's after four o'clock, why should you wait for her? What exactly did she say? Are you in trouble for something?"

The kids gave me a look that clearly indicated their opinion of my ignorance. "She said, 'See you later' and she hasn't come back yet."

Another time, I caught my daughter Yvonne, then nine years old, studying herself in the mirror. "Do I look like a boy?" she asked.

"A boy? You with your long hair and pretty doll-face? What gives you that idea?"

"One of the boys in school said: You guys want to play? And he was talking to me."

A kind neighbor took the trouble to explain to us certain inconsistencies of the language.

Our son's name was Alejandro David. He wanted to change it to something less Spanish-sounding, and wanted to know, "Which name is shorter to write, Alexander or David?" (!) Based on that, he decided on the name David.

When they asked him in school how he spelled his name, he said, "D-a-v-i-t." The entire class laughed. "You spell David with a "D" at the end."

"No," he insisted, "In Chile, you spell David with a "T". He learned, later on, that "David" was correct, and became officially, "David A." when he became an American citizen.

Our youngest daughter, Andrea, turned out to be a genius. She understood English from the very first day in day care, and announced to us that English was almost as easy as Spanish. She was five years old.

Knowing deep in my Jewish mother's heart that my children were smarter and brighter than the average child, I was nevertheless perplexed at the messages Andrea brought home from school. They made sense!

"The teacher wants me to bring a blanket." Or, "I am supposed to wear my hair in a ponytail. It's neater, the teacher said."

"Does the teacher show you what she wants or tell you?" I insisted.

"She <u>talks</u> to me."

"In what language?"

"English, of course!"

A visit with the day care director solved the mystery. Andrea's teacher was from Mexico, and spoke Spanish to her. But since the Mexican dialect is somewhat different from Chilean Spanish, our little girl thought the teacher was speaking English to her and found it easy to understand.

***

There was no greater adventure than going to the supermarket. All seven of us together. We never left our children alone in the house. We hadn't made contact yet with our neighbors, and had nowhere to leave them.

For us, going shopping became a family outing. Naturally, we had markets and grocery stores in Chile, and every imaginable kind of food. Santiago was even then, one of the most modern, cosmopolitan cities in South America. It has always had a definite European flair, because most of the Chileans have Spanish, Portuguese, Basque and Italian ancestry and have kept the customs, food, ways of life and languages of their forefathers.

In Santiago, I wouldn't even have dared to suggest that Kurt go to a market. The macho mentality in the country did not allow men to go grocery shopping. It wasn't proper. In the circles in which we moved, we all had a maid who did the shopping. Only on very special occasions would the lady of the house go to the market. Even the poor people, who certainly did not have a maid, would never send a man to do the shopping.

There were butcher shops, fish markets, vegetable gardens, bakeries, pastry shops and special shops that only carried cleaning and housekeeping products. We had tobacco shops and stores for paper goods. All very modern, but everything in a different place. Going shopping was a major occupation, time-consuming and cumbersome. You had to go to the Tabaqueria for your smokes, to the candy shop for sweets, to the drug stores for toiletries, and to a place for shoe polish and laces.

It was rather complicated. Prepared or take-out food was just being discussed. Given that most people either had help or did their own cooking, there was no need for it. Everything was made from scratch daily, and the preparation of meals was the pride of every cook.

We had never seen a supermarket where you could buy everything from nail polish and toilet paper to wine and milk, cigarettes and chocolate, from meat to bread to paper napkins. Each visit to the Purity Supermarket on Alemany Boulevard was a new excursion. Our children loved to fill the shopping carts. We bought food that we were familiar with, and others that we had never seen before. We tasted everything, from TV dinners to Jell-O molds, sour cream, soup in cans, minced frozen onions (they impressed me the most,) mashed potatoes in flakes, and some things called "fish sticks."

We ate sardines, (old friends of ours) and were not sure whether halibut steaks were fish or meat—they looked the same, frozen stiff—so we left them alone.

We marveled at the size of the avocados, which we knew from Chile, but not in such giant sizes. And why did they call them EGGPLANT? We bought some and tasted them, but decided that our avocados were much softer and tastier than those overgrown ones!

We also failed to understand the grin on the clerk's face when we asked for <u>RED GARBAGE</u> the day we decided to have sausages and red cabbage for dinner.

One of our neighbors mentioned to me that sweet potatoes were a very healthy meal for the children. Since we could not identify them among all the unknown vegetables on display, I served regular potatoes, which we were familiar with, and sprinkled sugar on them to see what our neighbor meant. They tasted awful, and we decided to stick to the foods we knew until our taste buds became more Americanized.

We burned our stove with apple-turnovers, which per the instructions on the box were to be put on a cookie sheet. Since we didn't own one, we baked them instead on top of the stove.

We used laundry detergent in the dishwasher, figuring that one detergent was as good as the other, never mind what machine it was used in.

My children enjoyed the bubbles of TIDE that overflowed not only the dishwasher and kitchen, but part of the house as well. Needless to say, I didn't find the situation as funny as they did. We got used to reading—and following—the instructions on the packages.

Three weeks after moving into the house, the container with our belongings arrived, and we had an exciting day at Customs, when the official broke the seal on the crate and opened it for inspection. The kids went crazy seeing their books, toys and belongings, and Kurt and I were happy to be reunited with the familiar objects that we cherished. We had fun unpacking and getting organized. The container caused a big commotion among our neighbors, and quite a number of curious "helpers" assisted us in bringing the contents into the house.

Slowly, our life took on a resemblance of normalcy.

***

While we were unpacking the container, something happened that bordered on the supernatural. Although Kurt and I have always been very much down to earth, this experience definitely shook us up.

As we were throwing out the paper, cardboard, and boxes that had been used in packing, a piece of newspaper fell onto my lap. I saw a Jewish Star of David on it, and looked closer. It was the obituary page with my father's death announcement, dated the 4th of January 1962, almost two years earlier.

In Chile, the death announcements in the newspaper were marked with a cross for the Catholics, a Star of David for the Jews, and no identification at all for non-religious people.

I felt my father's presence with us, and took this as a sign of his approval of our decision to come to America. The sensation of his nearness stayed with me for a very long time. Of course, I have kept the torn newspaper page, and look at it in moments of doubt. It always inspires me to keep going.

***

In spite of the difficulties of the first weeks, we tried to have fun. Fun and tears depending on the mood of the day. It was laughter one day, heartache the next. It wasn't easy. Since we had no relatives or friends here, we made a conscious effort to meet people by becoming members in a Synagogue, helping at the Jewish Family Service, joining B'nai B'rith and seeking contacts wherever possible. We missed our friends and family in Chile, and were determined to build new relationships here.

Ironically, forty years ago, Spanish was not as common a language in California as it is now. We had to make every effort to become fluent in English. We knew from experience that you could only become part of a country by mastering the language. We were going to be part of the United States and speak like natives—no matter what. The German/Spanish accent has stayed with us, but we have become fluent in English!

We had quite an experience on our way to becoming Americans.

We learned that a pain in the neck doesn't necessarily require a doctor's visit; that when someone pulled our leg, which happened quite often, we did not end up in a hospital. We also found out that, contrary to our initial belief, our neighbors were not hunters, even when they spoke of "stuffing their turkeys." One of our daughters insisted on visiting a friend who was "having a cow." We couldn't imagine anybody keeping a cow in a small house without a yard and, fortunately, asked around before paying a visit to the animal. We learned that "see you soon" didn't mean anything unless we intended to invite the person, and that "sourpuss" didn't really mean what we thought it meant!

And the money...We found out that ten cents is a dime, twenty-five cents, a quarter and five cents, a nickel. So far, so good. All of a sudden, people talked about "two-bits," "bucks," "big bucks" and a "grand." Was that also American currency?

Life was full of surprises. One of the most remarkable experiences was getting our telephone.

Of course, we had a telephone in Chile. After all, we came from a civilized country where telephones were known and widely used. The problem there was <u>getting one</u>. Once you had it, you could call the entire world, and the cost of the phone calls was not excessive, but to get a telephone installed was a major achievement. Our house in the suburbs was in a beautiful, elegant and modern location, but it took **TEN** years to get a telephone, and then only through connections. Santiago grew so fast that the public services had difficulties keeping up with the increased demands. Water, gas, electricity and mass transportation were never a problem, but a new telephone was considered a miracle achieved only by a privileged few.

Although we didn't know anybody in San Francisco who would ever call us, we knew we needed a telephone. We asked our neighbor how to go about getting one.

"You call the phone company," he said. "Tell them what you want and your address, and they will come and install it. They will ask for a deposit, given that you have no credit references yet."

"Excuse me," Kurt said. "Perhaps I didn't make myself clear. I need to find out how I can get a telephone installed in the house."

"I told you. Call them. Better yet, I will make the call for you."

Nice of him, but what connections could he have with the telephone company? This was a nice, modest neighborhood. If this man was such an important person and could get a telephone for us, why would he be living in this area?

"I don't quite understand it." Kurt rationalized. "But what can we lose?" Our neighbor called the phone company.

"They will come day after tomorrow. Is that O.K. with you?" he asked.

"Day after tomorrow?" Kurt thought he misunderstood.

"The operator says that if that is too late, they could come tomorrow."

Kurt was certain the man was making fun of us. He pleaded, "Don't play with me, please."

"I am not kidding." The neighbor was perplexed. "So what is it—do you want it tomorrow? The operator is waiting."

Kurt looked at me. I could only nod, sure we were victims of a cruel joke. But our neighbor was such a nice man, why would he do this to us?

He saw my face and nodded "it's O.K." He continued his conversation with the operator.

"She wants to know what color do you want?" His next question.

COLOR? Was there anything but black? "Make it black. We are used to black and a color might make us nervous."

"O.K. Black it is. Old-fashioned, but fine if that's what you want. She also wants to know how many children in the family?"

What was this? The government had spies in the phone company? Why did they want to know our family history? Who was our neighbor really calling? Just to be absolutely sure, we lied, "Three children, why does she want to know?"

"She says you will need a children's phone, with that many kids."

A children's phone? Who ever heard of a children's phone?

"No, no, no children's phone. One simple black one will be sufficient."

We got our simple black telephone the next day. We looked at it, loved it, memorized our number.... and cried. The telephone never rang those first few weeks. There was nobody to call us.

***

We learned English. We learned new customs, different habits, new food. We learned to adjust. We adopted the American ways. We no longer walked, but took the car everywhere. We called everybody by their first name, even our bosses and strangers who were introduced to us. We ate sweet Jell-O with our meat, and ordered pizza for dinner. We got a credit card.

It certainly was different from the way of life we had been used to, formal, restrained, and full of "don'ts." We accepted the positive changes and stuck to those customs that made more sense to us. It worked very well.

Our children grew up as Americans, and gave us American grandchildren and great-grandchildren. But they all remember what it feels to be an immigrant, a stranger in a foreign land, and what efforts must be made to become an integral part of the new homeland. Today, forty-three years later, the memories of those first weeks are still fresh, but the pain and uncertainty of the beginning has developed into pride of accomplishment.

We have never regretted our decision to come to live in America.

***

REUBEN & HENRIETTA

(A Gift from Heaven)

1963

I doubt that anybody has ever met a real angel. We are blessed. We found two of them. Their names are Henrietta and Reuben Levetin.

Installed in our rented house on Seminole Avenue, the children in school, and both of us working, our only need is to meet people. We miss our friends and the comfort of sharing experiences, of laughing and crying together, of saying, "Remember when...?"

We decide that the best place to start is the B'nai B'rith. We and all our friends in Chile belong to this Jewish Organization. My grandfather was one of the founders of the Lodge in Berlin, and Kurt and I have been active members for many years in the group in Santiago. We know that a "brother" (or "sister") is always received with open arms.

We visit the office of B'nai B'rith, on Market Street. The District Secretary, Eugene Lerner, offers all the help he can provide. He admires our guts to emigrate with five children. We explain to him that we do not need money or other assistance, we only want to meet people to really start our new life. Gene talks to us for a long time to get a feel of who and what we are.

He suggests that a B'nai B'rith brother contact us, and we take it from there.

He says, "I have this person in mind. Best example of B'nai B'rith brotherhood we have. I will have him call you. In the next few days."

He doesn't mention a name. Perhaps he wants to be careful. This "best example" might not want to take on the burden of a newly-arrived, seven-piece family. Who knows.

We don't have to wait long. The principles of "Benevolence, Harmony and Brotherly love" on which B'nai B'rith is based, are at work. The phone rings two evenings later.

"My name is Reuben Levetin. I'm calling on behalf of B'nai B'rith to see what I can do for you." He speaks loud and clear. "I was told that your English is not perfect. Do you understand me?" I tell him, yes, of course I understand him. I explain to him that all we want is to meet Jewish people. I give him my age, tell him about the five children, try to explain how we came to live on Seminole Street. He promised to call back "with some ideas."

For four weeks, every other evening, Reub Levetin called. He and I develop a pleasant friendship on the telephone. I tell him, as clearly as I can in English, where we come from and who we are. He tells me, making sure I understand all the details, about his wife, his grown children, a married daughter, Judie, and a son, Ron, who lives in Arizona, and that he owns a furniture store on Clement Street.

I mention that we bought some simple furniture for our rented house, things that we will exchange for real furniture once we buy a house. He says, "That's not why I mention it. If I can help, I will be glad to advise you, but please do not feel obligated." He tells me about his activities in Jewish and community circles. I really like him. He is intelligent and seems sincere.

One evening he says, "Now that I think of it, you are supposed to have a husband. I always talk to you. Where is he?" And when I tell him that Kurt is in Real Estate School in the evenings and I am the only one available to take his calls, he complains, "You should have told me that you are an 'evening-widow.' I would have come over instead of calling, and we would be even better friends. You have a very nice personality and you sound cute. Are you?"

I said, "Of course!"

He is joking, but I love to hear it. Compliments, how long has it been that a person of the opposite sex has paid me a compliment, not even an undeserved one. It lifts your spirits!

Reub asks whether we would like to go to a Temple service one Friday night. He wants us to meet his wife, Henrietta. We would love to. He suggests Friday of the next week, unless we have other plans.

I tell him that we have nothing planned—there isn't anybody to plan with. Our calendar stares at us with its blank squares. Nothing! I tell Reub that next Friday is perfect. He offers to pick us up, but I insist on getting directions to Temple Sherith Israel, where he belongs and wants to take us.

I remind him that we have a map of the city, and since we made it from South America to San Francisco, we would be able to make it from Seminole to California Street. I also assure him that he will have no problem recognizing us, because it wasn't easy to overlook two grown-ups with five children hanging on to them.

When we get to the Temple, he apologizes for Henrietta not being there. Their daughter just had her second baby, a son, that morning, October 6, 1963, and she was babysitting her two-year old daughter, Denise.

We can tell that the Levetins are well-known and very well liked in the Synagogue. Reub introduces us to everybody: The Rabbi, Cantor Feldman, the officers of the Temple and his friends. He calls us: his "South American adopted family" and speaks of us as if he has known us for a long time.

Henrietta calls the next day and apologizes for not being there.

(This was our first experience with her love and understanding. Once she made a commitment, she would fulfill it, no matter what.)

She invites us to dinner the next week. We stay until after midnight, just talking and getting to know each other. We realize that we have met the most loving, kind and helpful couple that ever appeared in our lives.

We are invited to dinner every week in another house. Everybody wants to meet us. People cannot believe that we left a comfortable life in Chile to start all over again in the United States. We are a curiosity for most people who were born in San Francisco and lived here all their lives.

"You must have guts," we hear over and over. Or, "How interesting. You need to share your story with us."

We join Sherith Israel and attend services every Friday night, with our children. They attend Sunday School and start making friends. We are invited by the Temple Board to give a talk about our life in Chile and become "famous."

One of Reuben's friends, Mr. Herbert Ginsburg, a prominent member of the Jewish community, and owner of a large industrial company, Western Piping Co., hears that my brother is coming to San Francisco with his family to join us. He immediately offers us a job for Gert, with the comment, "Any friend of Reub Levetin is a friend of mine." (My brother worked for him for over fourteen years.)

The Levetins become family. Henrietta teaches me (or tries to!) cook, and most of the time, she prepares meals and sends them to us "so the children have a nourishing meal" (instead of the hot dogs, sandwiches, or noodles that have become our regular dinner.)

Reub gives us advice for whatever we ask him: Purchase of a house, decent schools for the kids, Real Estate possibilities for Kurt, doctors and health insurance and whatever new decision we need to make.

They love us and we love them. It is not just a friendship, it is the most wonderful relationship, and we keep telling them how lucky we are to know them.

We go on weekend vacations with them; they introduce us to Bourbon & Seven, which I love and could live off of. After I get seriously drunk one evening, Reub watches me prepare the drinks.

"No, no, no." He shakes his head. "You don't fill the glass with Bourbon and put a few drops of Seven-Up in it. It's half and half." Another lesson in American life!

Henrietta explains to me how to make a casserole, but she knows I won't make them, so she prepares them while we visit and send them home with us.

All Jewish holidays are celebrated together with them and their family. We teach them our customs, and they introduce us to theirs.

We share everything with them, there are no secrets.

When people ask Reub where he met us, his answer is:

"<u>Met</u> them? We <u>got</u> them!"

The Levetins care for us in ways that are beyond friendship. A few months after our first meeting, Kurt and I have an opportunity to go to New York on a business possibility for Kurt. We have to decline. How could we leave the children alone? Even with the lady who is taking care of them after school? We have no relatives in this country. My brother is still in Chile.

Reub calls me. "Who is your children's guardian, somebody in Chile?" The answer is yes. It's my brother.

"Do you have a will notarized in this country?"

"No."

He says, "It's settled. Henrietta and I are moving into your house to watch the kids. You give us power of attorney and, G-d forbid, something happens, we will always take care of them. Go to New York." We leave.

They move into our home! Henrietta brings her kitchen knives.

"I can't work with yours. They are not for a real kitchen."

Our kids love her cooking, "unused" as they are to regular meals.

Upon our return, I find that my loving friend prepared several dishes and put them in my freezer, "so that the children get real food for a while."

They stay in our house for a week. The only complaint my children have when we call them from New York is "Reub makes us clean the house **every day**. We tell him that's overdoing it, but he insists. But, otherwise, they are wonderful."

***

When our daughter, Daniela, got married, Henrietta not only made the veil for her, but also <u>all</u> the bridesmaid's dresses. When our first grandchild was born and we had a "Baby-Show-off" party in our house, my friend "Henri" tried to show me how to make "Finger Food," which was unknown to us. Since patience is not one of my virtues, <u>she</u> ended up making hundreds of them and froze them. When I got compliments for them, I pointed at Henrietta—and everybody knew!

A year after living on Seminole, we bought a house. Reub gave us advice on where the best schools were, High School, Junior High and Grade School, since we needed all three. He suggested Westlake, and we found a house big enough for all of us. Naturally, we bought all our furniture from him. We still have it, forty-four years later, and it still looks like new. We think of him every time we set our table. Reub and Henrietta are always in our thoughts.

***

Unfortunately, Henrietta developed Alzheimer's disease, and was not herself for many years. She was in a home, where Reub visited her every day. I went with him many times. Although she did not recognize anybody, Reub did her hair, painted her fingernails and talked to her as if she could understand. It broke my heart to see them.

Reub died after a few years, and Henrietta, who did not understand what happened, passed away two years later. She must have felt that he was no longer with her.

***

Our lives are changed because of the Levetins. Their goodness, trust and kindness can never be repaid. We pay tribute to them by staying in close touch with their daughter, their grandchildren and great-grandchildren.

They were our special ANGELS and we think of them with love and gratitude.

***

LETTER TO MY CHILDREN

(Written after having an argument with them)

October 12, 1966

My dearest children:

Although I am writing this to all five of you, I think that this letter will be, more than anything, for Patty, Daniela and, perhaps, Yvonne. The two little ones probably will not yet understand what I want to tell you.

Today, your father and I have been married for nineteen years, and I want you to remember, later in your lives, what I need to say to you. At your age, there are things that you hear and understand up to a certain point, but later, when you are older, you will realize the true meaning of my thoughts.

You will ask, why do I not _tell_ you what I have to say, and why do I write you a letter, when we see each other every day. If I were to talk to you about my thoughts, you would probably not have the patience to listen, perhaps laugh, or not take it seriously. This way, written on paper, it may look more serious to you and you would, at least, let me finish without interruptions.

What I want to tell you, is rather simple:

Your father and I have been together for nineteen years, and have been very, very happy. We have had our sad moments, as you know, with the loss of both my parents. We have had worries about business, work and, sometimes, also about money. But, more than anything, we have had hours, days and years of great happiness, thank G-d, and we owe this to the five of you. Don't think that you have not given us headaches, school problems, and worries about sicknesses. We have had moments of great anxiety when one of you was sick, or had an accident. But, in all these years, we have had nothing but joy and happiness with you. You are healthy, pretty, intelligent, and, more important, you are very good children. Don't believe that at this moment, I forget how angry you have made us sometimes, with thousand and one little things, but all that matters is the joy and happiness that you have given us over the years.

It is true that we want you to give us even <u>more</u> happiness, with good grades, hairdos that we like, clothes that we approve of, and perfect behavior! But, what I want you to know is that we are perfectly happy the way you are.

You will say, "So why do they complain?" You know the answer to this. It's because it is our duty to educate you and show you the right way, so that one day, when you are on your own, you will know what is right or wrong, what is acceptable and what is not, and be able to distinguish between a correct way of life and an incorrect behavior.

I recognize that the task of teaching is difficult, for you as much as for us, and I am aware that at times we may be guilty of an injustice towards you. But when that happens, you know that we don't do this on purpose. On the other hand, if you are honest, you will recognize that sometimes you make us very angry. So we are even!

What I want you to remember for later in life is the following:

In our nineteen years together, there hasn't been anybody more important to your Papi and myself, than the five of you. All our energies, our thoughts and our efforts have been geared towards you, directly or indirectly. This means that you may not always have <u>seen or noticed</u> what we have done, nor do you need to know. Whatever our decisions have been, we only had your interest and well-being in mind. And you have always responded to us. We are a united family. All the problems we have faced (and there surely will be some in the future), we have solved them together. My only wish is that we continue this way.

As long as we live, you will always have all our love, our support, our understanding, and also our respect. It might seem strange to you that parents should respect their children. If you don't see this now, you will realize when you are a little older, that we will never expect you to be "perfect people." We realize that you are five different people, with different characters, different aspirations and individual reactions to certain situations. We respect this, and will never force you to become anything other than you wish to be. What we try to do, is guide every one of you to become a successful and happy person, satisfied with your life. We all have different aptitudes, desires and limits, and each of you will have her/his own goals and expectations. Our role is to teach you, guide and support you.

I am sure you feel that your father and I are not home enough, that we have a thousand things to do for other people, and that we do not have enough time for you. Please know, that no matter what happens, <u>you always come first</u>.

Your father and I are what we are: good friends, good children, good brother and sister. This means that sometimes, we cannot do exactly what we want, but feel obligated to dedicate time, attention, help, and sometimes even money, to other people. To us, this is part of life. We feel that it is our duty to give back the help, care and favors that have been given to us. That's why people respect us, and love and respect you for being our children.

The selfish people, who only live for their own interests, who do not participate in anything, who do not give of their time or assistance to anybody, certainly have more time to spend with their children. You have seen the results of such attitude, and have learned that in this world, one cannot exist exclusively for oneself. Your father and I believe that one has to become part of a larger "family" and participate, as far as possible, in the life of others, when it is needed.

My only wish is that you stay healthy and that our close relationship remains as intimate as it has been. As you are getting older and more mature, I want you to consider your father and myself as your friends, and if we have our little fights and disagreements, they will only help to get to know each other better, and we can learn from each other.

I confess that we, Papi and I, have a lot to learn. This is our first experience of being the parents of five children, and as you find yourselves with problems to solve, so do we. Believe me, we don't know everything, and this is why we sometimes make mistakes.

I hope you understand what I have been trying to say to you, and remember, that the first priority in our lives are YOU.

With all our love,
Your mother (Mami)

LAND OF MILK AND HONEY OR

LAND OF WORK AND MONEY?

San Francisco, September 6, 1967

Today is our fourth anniversary in this country. I am alone in the house, which does not happen very often. Nobody interrupts my thoughts.

As I do so often, I take out our photo albums. The faces of my friends in Chile, the birthday celebrations, the children's parties, I miss all of it. And then, our last picture on the stairs of the Aereolineas Peruanas airplane that brought us to America. I am not sure how I feel. I miss my friends. I long for the familiarity, the freedom to share joys and sorrows.

I have my doubts. Did we make a mistake in leaving our easy life in Chile? Or was coming here the right decision?

I decide to write a letter to the Silbersteins, the Gruenbergs, the Waldmans and the Brenners, our four closest friends. It won't replace our heart-to-heart conversations, but it may help me search for an answer to my doubts.

Dearest friends:

How we miss you! It seems an eternity since we all sat on the terrace of our house in Santiago and discussed the benefits of "becoming Yankees."

"Del dicho al hecho hay un gran trecho" (There is a great distance between the word and the deed.) How true this has proven to be!

Our lives have changed so drastically in these four years, and the effort of starting over takes all our strength and willpower. We work at our jobs. We work at making new friends. We work at Americanizing our lives, and we work at giving our children the sense of happiness and security that they need. It is a lot of work.

In the meantime, we bought a house in a nice area called "Westlake," twenty minutes away from the center of San Francisco. It is a very nice, modern house, big enough for all of us, and conveniently located near the schools and shopping centers. But it can't compare with our beautiful home in Santiago.

As we told you, Kurt has been in the Real Estate business since we got here, and is doing well, but he dreams of being on his own again. Right now, business isn't very good. The Government has restricted credits to avoid inflation. This will be hard for you to understand. Contrary to our little Chile, where we are used to an inflation rate of twenty and thirty percent a year, in this country, an inflation rate of one, or one-and-a-half percent, is considered a catastrophe. Americans tend to panic easily!

We have therefore, become entrepreneurs once again, and started our own business, 'NOVELTY IMPORTS." We buy imported giftware from an international wholesaler, and sell it to small individual stores, some in San Francisco, but many in outside areas. Kurt is the salesman and is out on the road—he does the real estate business on weekends—and I run the office (in our garage) and handle the shipping, invoices, correspondence, etc., in the evenings. Not easy!

We carry all kinds of "tasteful" gifts: Vases and plates inscribed with meaningful messages, such as "East is East, West is West, at home it's Best," or, "There is no place like home," and other such clichés. We also sell religious statues. A saint with a red coat and a cane. Another one, with a bird in his arm. Since we are unfamiliar with them and don't want to make a mistake, we don't call them by their names. We have a Madonna, which I think is a sacrilege. She has an open hunchback, in which people put tasteless artificial flowers. We also have animals with bobbing heads to place in the back of automobiles, ashtrays in the shape of a body part (which here is called a "butt") and other "refined" gifts. None of these would ever enter our home. But the stuff sells.

However, there is not enough money to be made working as a "jobber," which is what we are. We need to be a direct importer in order to build a profitable business. We therefore, rented a store with a small warehouse in San Francisco, and started to buy Crystal and Porcelain in Germany, Poland and Czechoslovakia. Kurt sells to better gift stores, jewelry stores and flower shops all over California. The leftover samples are sold in our store. We are building this business up, little by little, and will no longer deal in the novelties. Our company is now called K&M MOSTNY, INC.

Since I still have my regular job, it is not easy to build up a business on the side. Fortunately, as you will remember, the Mostnys don't need much sleep. The plan is to quit my job as soon as we feel we can afford it, and we will both then dedicate all our time to K&M.

In the meantime, my job at Balfour Guthrie (International Traders and Shipping Agents) is going well. I have been there for three years now. It is an interesting position with great responsibility. But that is what I like. My boss travels constantly and I run the office by myself. I will be sorry to leave, but it will take the two of us, Kurt and myself, to build up our own company.

Business in this country is very different from what we knew in Chile. There, our European background and desire to work allowed us to achieve success and become independent entrepreneurs. Here, the middle class is as educated and competent as we are, and the competition is much harder, and it is still a man's world. As a woman, selling metal and iron, I have to be constantly on my toes, and prove that I can "keep up with the guys." At least, the job pays a man's salary, so I don't complain. (I can't even use our samples, like the canned fruit from the Silbersteins, the knitwear from Waldmann's, or the shoes from Goldmann's stores. We certainly have no use in our home for large stainless flanges, or iron plates and wire coils.)

I have a secretary working for me and have made an astonishing discovery. Every one of us "Latinos," known for leaving everything for MANANA, can easily compete with the famous American efficiency.

These women are machines. They don't think. They do exactly what they are told, usually with the help of a manual. We didn't depend on reference books. We used our brains and common sense. These girls are trained to work at high efficiency to perform specific and detailed duties, which they do. There is no individual initiative.

I hired a second secretary, who left after a week. She was looking forward to becoming an assistant to my boss, whom she found out was divorced and had money, and declared that, "No way was she going to work for a woman."

Part of my frustration is that I expected so much from the efficient Americans. Our laid-back Chileans are much more loyal and dedicated, and we know what they get paid! Many

Americans women work to buy "things." Extra things. The things that their neighbors have. There doesn't seem to be a commitment on their side. "Paycheck" is the magic word.

You can imagine that my evenings are anything but quiet. A household of five children, grocery shopping, dinner, laundry, sibling arguments, and even a minimum of housecleaning, require a great deal of energy. Kurt is often out of town and, honestly, I cannot compare myself to his Saints and Madonnas!

The children are wonderful and help a lot. The Mostnys haven't been called "**Gypsies**" for nothing! We do the best we can to keep a civilized home without going crazy with our housekeeping duties. We will never become *"bread bakers" or "casserole makers,"* nor will we become efficient users of our freezer (with pre-planned home-cooked meals), but we do our best. Our children enjoy having less supervision than in Chile, without the grandmother and nanny in the house, and enjoy liberties that we would not have allowed there. But we trust them and they take care of each other. They are responsible and becoming aware of what it means to be a "family unit." We are very proud of them. We would not have dared to transplant them to this new world if we had not counted on their resilience, their understanding and their healthy dispositions. They are not spoiled, are intelligent, and they love us and each other.

I am still suffering from my migraines. When I was young, a doctor promised that once I had children, they would stop as soon as I had children. I certainly tried often enough, but, obviously, it didn't help.

***

Next month is our twentieth wedding anniversary, and we are planning to spend a weekend in Las Vegas, with another couple. We need a little break! This will be the first time that we leave our children alone. I hope everything will work out. These are the moments when I miss the carefree life in Chile—with grandmother, maids and friends, and without worries about the kids. Lore and Bert Zanders, old friends of ours, who live a few blocks from us, will keep an eye on our children.

***

However difficult our personal adjustments seem to be, there is a wonderful, irreplaceable side of America, which makes up for some of the disadvantages. To begin with, we live in the most beautiful city of the United States, and we are impressed with the generosity and kindness of the people. They are curious about our different experiences, and are eager to learn. The greatest advantage—the one that makes all the difference to us—is that here in America, one doesn't have to be afraid to say that you are Jewish.

The entire country is aware of our holidays. They wish us a Happy New Year on Rosh Hashana, place banners on the street reading "Happy Chanukah," and know about Passover, Kosher food and Bar Mitzvahs. My Catholic boss would have been shocked if I had worked on Yom Kippur.

Even if we did not encounter any open anti-Semitism in Chile, we felt it was more secure to stay in the background.

You cannot imagine the reaction of the people in my office to the recent war between Israel and the Arabs. The ones who know that I am Jewish—because I volunteer the information—came to me and congratulated me on "our" success. The President of the company came to my office to ask whether I would like to go home to listen to the news in privacy.

The head of the Shipping Department, an Arab who has

been in the USA for only a few years, told me that he wished he were Jewish, so that people would show admiration for him also!

This man has a sister who lives in Cairo. He tells me that he taped a TV concert which Harry Belafonte gave in honor of the Jewish New Year, and sent it to her. At lunch time, he sung for me one of the pieces. It was the Hatikvah (National Anthem of Israel). When I explained to him that this was the Israeli National Anthem, and that his sister would certainly not be celebrated for playing it, he urgently sent her a telegram advising her to close the windows of her house before playing the tape. We laughed about this, and he became a good friend of mine.

During the period of this war, every one of our customers called several times a day to give me the latest bulletins. This was a new, gratifying experience for me. My presence in our office has opened a discourse with my colleagues, who knew very little about the size and influence of the Jewish community in Chile. Suddenly, they are showing a vivid interest in learning more about South American Jews.

Our children are already integrated into this new country and its customs. We, the old ones, will never be entirely assimilated, although we are totally accepted, especially here in California. Accents don't matter. In fact, they are considered "cute." If anything, our customs arouse curiosity and interest. There are so many people of different cultures here, that we are not a rarity. It feels good. It is a freedom that we never had. Certainly not in our years in Germany, nor in Chile, as immigrants.

Nevertheless, there is a negative side to this equality. It means that our children have the freedom to associate, as equals, with Jews and non-Jews. When I think of our four marriageable" daughters, it gives me reason to worry. We have Jewish organizations, Clubs, Community Centers and Youth Groups. But what happens? Because there is no discrimination in this country, these associations are also open to non-Jews. The only exclusive Jewish organizations are the Synagogues. The option of raising our children in an exclusively Jewish environment is almost impossible. Whether this assimilation is good or bad, remains to be seen. We discuss often with our friends the strong possibility of inter-marriage, a concern that we did not have in Chile. Personally, I believe that we will have to accept it. Perhaps by accepting people of other religions to join us, would be one way of keeping our Jewish heritage alive, and perpetuating our traditions.

We have here three different types of synagogues: Orthodox, Conservative and Reform. We belong to a Reform Temple and attend services frequently on Friday nights. The prayers are partly in English. Very few people can read Hebrew, and some of our traditions and mysticism have been lost. It took us some time to get used to the organ and the professional choir, but the atmosphere is festive. Our Cantor Feldman, an opera singer, brings a special joy to the service, and most temple members have embraced us like a family and have given us a sense of belonging.

***

My thoughts jump from one subject to the other, but we have always shared our lives with you and always been honest with each other. Did we make a mistake in coming to America? Was it clever to leave the easier life in Chile? Was this decision good or bad for our children's future? Some days, I am not sure; other times I am sure we did the right thing.

A few more years, and I will know!

We love you and miss you. A big "abrazo" (hug) to all of you. Keep us posted of all the gossip in Santiago.

Your "Yankee" friends,

Marion and Kurt

EPILOGUE

San Mateo, California, May of 2007

Our life has been quite eventful.

In 1968, we became American Citizens. We needed two witnesses, who were, of course, Reub and Henrietta Levetin. However, the judge on duty explained to us that a married couple counted as ONE witness. We needed an additional person. Luckily, we knew a judge at the Immigration Service, Mr. Monty Kroll, also a member of Temple Sherith Israel, and part of the Levetins' and our group of friends. His office was in the same building where the swearing-in ceremony was taking place. We rushed to his office and asked him if he would do us the favor of acting as our second witness. We will never forget his answer: "This is not a favor. I am honored that you asked me. Knowing your family has enriched our lives." He told his secretary that "he was going to leave for a while to fulfill a moral duty."

***

I have just celebrated my eightieth birthday. My husband is eighty-eight years old. We have been in this country for forty-four years, and our lives are happy and stable. Much has happened during this long time.

Our children are married (or divorced.) Our oldest daughter, Patty (Pat) Hejtmanek, is now 56 years old. Pat is a realtor and is doing very well. She is still the "authority" among the five kids. She is smart, hardworking and efficient, and has a wonderful sense of humor. She owns a home in Danville. She has three children: Jenny, who is 28, is an 8th grade mathematics schoolteacher, married to Tom Kriskey, from Nebraska. They have two little girls, Abbie, who is two, and Zoe, four months old. We travel as often as possible to Carmichael, where they live. Pat's son, Steven, is 25, and a graduate of the University of California, Santa Barbara. He is currently working in sales and has turned out to be very successful. Her youngest, Rachel, had her 20th birthday last March. She is a student at the California Academy of Arts in San Francisco and is majoring in Photography.

Dannie (Daniela), married to Jan Van der Steen, from Belgium, is now 55. She met her husband in Ghana, Africa. They live in Boulder Creek, California, in a marvelous house built by her husband. Dannie is an Emergency Room/Trauma nurse in Santa Clara County and loves her job, but she could be a party planner. She organizes the most fantastic parties, cooks and bakes everything herself, and her decorations are the envy of professional caterers. She is the patient one among our children. Dannie and Jan have a son and a daughter. Jeroen, 23, graduated from West Point Military Academy, and is a Second Lieutenant in training for...(hopefully, not Iraq!) As of the time of this writing, he has completed special training and graduated as a Ranger. We are all very proud of him and wish him a happy future. Their daughter, Elke, 21, studies at the University of San Francisco, and is at the present time, at the University of Madrid, Spain, for one semester in order to achieve perfection in the Spanish language.

Yvonne, our number three, is married to Nader Nouri, from Iran, whom she met in Berkeley. She was 53 in February, and worked for the past eight years as a freelance medical transcriber and office manager in the Neurosurgery Division at a hospital in Oakland. She is currently working for the Town of Danville in a very interesting job in the Community Services Department. Besides being very funny, Yvonne is our computer "whiz." Without her help, this book might not have been published. The writing was not the problem, but, without her, I could have never finished the technical part on my computer. Yvonne and Nader own a home in Pleasant Hill, and have three children. Julian, who is 19, studies at Arizona State University and is majoring in Broadcast Journalism. Their daughter, Renee, is 16 years old, a Junior in High School, and plans to continue her education at a university after graduation, and Jordan, the youngest of all the grandchildren, is 11 years old, and has not yet made serious plans for his future.

Our son, David, is now 51 years old. He is divorced and has a 17-year-old daughter, Jacqueline, who is a Senior in High School and plans to continue her studies at one of the Ivy League Universities. David is still the epitome of a salesman. He is charming, clever, hyper, and the life of every party. He is an extremely attentive son. I still work with him, part-time. He keeps me young!

Our number five, Andrea, is not married. She is 49 years old. It seems unbelievable to me that my youngest child is approaching 50! She works as a nurse at the Neo-Natal ICU Department of UCSF in San Francisco, and is the most devoted caretaker for these delicate, feeble babies. Andrea is the most serious one of our children, and enjoys spending time on her own. She is patient and loving, and is always available to entertain her nieces and nephews. Her best time, besides work, is being with her sisters and brother. She loves to hike and travel by herself, and dedicates as much time as she can to us, her parents. Andrea is the proud owner of a home in San Francisco.

Kurt and I are very proud of our children and grandchildren. Our family is as close as a family can be. Our "5" are the most generous, helpful and loving children any parent could wish for. Although they are very different in character, they are close friends, share their thoughts and troubles, and every one of them takes part in the life of the others. They party together, they laugh (a lot) together, they discuss their own dreams and disappointments and most importantly, they are "one for the other." We have family celebrations, get-togethers, enjoy everyone's successes and face the sad moments that are part of living.

Most importantly, all our children and in-law children have instilled in their sons and daughters a deep sense of family and responsibility. Kurt and I have the absolute certainty that, when we are gone, our daughters and son, their spouses and their children, will always be one unit. This is our best reward!

***

For years now, I have begun a tradition of taking one grandchild at a time for a 14-day trip to New York and Washington, in order to spend quality time with each one, share in an educational experience, and get to know each individual grandchild better, hopefully, creating lasting memories that they will keep with them forever.

When we started our own import company, K&M Mostny, Inc., we made our son, David, a partner. We moved from the "store" in San Francisco to a big warehouse and offices in Burlingame. David was born to sell! He placed our crystal and porcelain all over California, Washington, Oregon, Arizona, and wherever there was a customer ready to buy (or not!) He hired additional salesmen and trained them. We attended Gift Shows all over the country and got more compliments on David than on our merchandise! Kurt and I, or Kurt and David, went to East and West Germany, Poland, Italy and Czechoslovakia to purchase product, and David traveled to Egypt, Portugal, and South America to buy merchandise.

Eventually, we opened an office, warehouse and showroom in Moscow, Russia, with personnel, managers and technical support. We kept this up for six years. Unfortunately, the business ethics of the then-called Soviet Union was such that in spite of all our efforts and successes, we decided to leave this "paradise" of unacceptable commercial behavior. After David was attacked, knifed - and almost killed - on the streets of Moscow by a "money seeker," our mind was made up. We closed up and left.

For thirty years, the three of us worked together. We hired a secretary, a computer person, several warehousemen, Kurt did the buying, and I ran the office and kept the books. We loved working together, although quite often, there were disagreements on policies, management style, or money. Kurt was from the "old school," David was the daring one, and I was in the middle, more inclined to agree with our son. Our memories of those years are happy, and we still laugh about some arguments that seemed so serious at the time, but only brought us closer together.

Eventually, David moved the office to an entire floor on Sansome Street, in downtown San Francisco. Four years later, we changed product lines. Crystal and porcelain was being taken over directly by the big retail stores, who bought the merchandise directly from the foreign factories, and the market shrunk for importers/wholesalers like ourselves.

David decided to import Giftwrap (Paper, Ribbons, Gift Bags, etc.) from Indonesia, China and Malaysia, but on direct imports. This meant that we acted as agents, did not keep an inventory, and had the shipments (in container loads only) delivered directly to the large customers. We moved the operation to Pier 23 in San Francisco.

Soon after that, Kurt retired. He dedicates his time to volunteer work and assists David in the business, when needed. I continued working full-time. At the time of this writing, I am still helping David, who meanwhile, bought a beautiful house in Woodside, California and established his office on the lower floor of his house. He is now developing an entire new concept of business, by developing and selling Survival & Safety Technology to the U.S. Government, large industries, the military, etc.

David is a hard worker, full of ideas and very enthusiastic. Whatever he does, I am sure he will be successful.

In 1987, we sold our house in Westlake, and bought a very nice condominium in San Mateo, perfectly located and appropriate for our needs. Although it is definitely not as big as a house, we still have celebrations in our home, Jewish holidays, birthdays and other get-togethers. There is a saying in German "Raum ist in der kleinsten Huete." (There is room in the smallest hut) and we can fill our home with twenty-three people at any time. And we do!

Kurt and I are involved in many organizations, volunteer activities and "jobs" that do not produce any income, but give us much satisfaction, and we have made many good friends. We belong to City of Hope, B'nai B'rith, American ORT; we belong to a Synagogue, donate to the Cancer Society and different hospitals, and volunteer as Spanish translators at the Samaritan House, a free clinic in San Mateo. Kurt also volunteers at the

San Francisco Visitors and Convention Bureau and the San Francisco Airport "Traveler's Aid", using his language skills. Our lives are full and rewarding.

However, we have had our share of great worries. Pat and Dannie both had surgery for breast cancer, and I was diagnosed with ovarian cancer. All three of us went through surgery, chemotherapy treatments, (and loss of hair!) Only the emotional and physical support of the rest of our family allowed us a full recovery, and made the months of pain easier to bear. Not for a moment did we feel alone. The sacrifices made by the other kids were overwhelming. Thank G-d, all three of us are doing well.

Kurt and I have learned that only the big things in life are important. Good health, happy and successful children, good friends, and a close family. We never dramatized the small daily problems that are part of our existence, but kept a positive outlook and our strength for the important decisions.

We enjoy every day, and are grateful for being alive and well.

My brother's and Miryam's daughter and son are an integral part of our family. Jeanette, 43, a smart young woman, is happily married and has three very bright children: Mackenzie, 13, Mason 11, and Paige, 6. They live nearby and we get together very often. Steven, 41, is in the film industry, lives in New York and travels all over the world in his profession. Being a mirror image of my late brother, he brings "Pize" back to me and I have a special feeling for him. We are also in regular contact with him.

I owe a heartfelt "thank you" to my sister-in-law, Miryam, her daughter, Jeanette, her son-in-law, Kerim, and their children, as well as to my nephew, Steven, for their love, friendship and care. Together we have kept alive the memory of my dear brother.

My prayer for my grandchildren and great-grandchildren is:

"May your lives be rewarding and happy.
May you be blessed with good health and success,
and may G-d give you the wisdom to make the
right decisions in moments of doubt."

1358885

Made in the USA